THE EDGE OF THE SWAMP

THE EDGE OF THE SWAMP

A Study in the Literature and Society of the Old South

LOUIS D. RUBIN, JR.

LOUISIANA STATE UNIVERSITY PRESS

Baton Rouge and London

98 97 96 95 94 93 92 91 90 89   5 4 3 2 1

Designer: Laura Roubique Gleason
Typeface: Linotron Trump Mediaeval
Typesetter: G & S Typesetters, Inc.
Printer: Thomson-Shore, Inc.
Binder: John H. Dekker & Sons, Inc.

Library of Congress Cataloging-in-Publication Data
Rubin, Louis Decimus, 1923–
     The edge of the swamp : a study in the literature and society of
the Old South / Louis D. Rubin, Jr.
        p.   cm.
     Includes index.
     ISBN 0-8071-1495-2 (alk. paper)
     1. American literature—Southern States—History and criticism.
     2. American literature—19th century—History and criticism.
     3. Literature and society—Southern States—History—19th century.
     4. Southern States—Civilization—1775–1865. 5. Southern States in
literature.   I. Title.
PS261.R59 1989
810'.9'975—dc19   88-27632
                                                                        CIP

This book is dedicated to
Les and Robbie Phillabaum
and to
Beverly Jarrett and Billy Mills,
who have put up with a great deal
over the years.

CONTENTS

ACKNOWLEDGMENTS

While I was engaged in writing this book, I received two invitations that served to stimulate my efforts and sharpen my thoughts. Among the numerous beneficences of the National Humanities Center is that it brings to the area of the university at which I teach an imposing array of important resident scholars. Three years ago one such was Eugene Genovese, and another was a onetime student and longtime friend of mine, Lucinda Hardwick MacKethan. Between them they set up a conference on conservative thought in the South, for which they invited me to prepare a paper on William Gilmore Simms. Professors MacKethan, George C. Rogers, Jr., and Lewis P. Simpson served as respondents to the paper. From the occasion and the response I profited much. I was also invited to deliver the Eugenia Blount Lamar Lectures for 1985 at Wesleyan College, and especially coming when it did, the necessity for formulating the continuity of the lectures was precisely what I needed. A year's leave of absence from my teaching responsibilities in the Department of English at the University of North Carolina at Chapel Hill greatly facilitated the writing of this book, and I am grateful in particular to the chairman of the department, Joseph M. Flora.

Robert D. Jacobs, James Justus, and Lewis P. Simpson read all or part of the manuscript for me, and offered valuable suggestions. J. Lasley Dameron was kind enough to call my attention to some highly useful material on Poe.

Finally, I could not conceivably cite acknowledgments for help in the preparation of this book without mentioning how much my thoughts on this subject, and just about every other subject having to do with the literature of the South, have benefited from the longtime friendship of C. Hugh Holman. Had Hugh not died seven years ago—though it scarcely seems that long—this would have been a better book, but for whatever merit it may possess I am grateful for having had him to talk with about such things for so many years. Since he left us, it hasn't been the same around here.

THE EDGE OF THE SWAMP

INTRODUCTION
The Old South and Historical Causality .

Recent developments in critical theory have relegated the chronological dimension of literary experience to a position of markedly
less importance in the scheme of things than it had once enjoyed.
For those of us who concern ourselves with the literary imagination of the American South, what we do for a living has supposedly been rendered obsolete. The new dispensation has even
dismissed as largely irrelevant, or at any rate partial and limited,
the assumption on which is based not only the study of Southern
literature but an important way that Southerners both literary
and unliterary have tended to view their world, which is to say,
historically.

The custom of thinking that what something now *is* importantly involves the question of how it got that way has always
been so deeply ingrained in the thought processes of most Southern writers that to identify the region's writings with the "historical sense" is little more than a truism. In that finest and
most profound of all works of the Southern literary imagination,
William Faulkner's *Absalom, Absalom!*, a young Quentin Compson fights a losing battle with his community's history. He would
like to escape its hold, go off to Harvard University, and live un-
encumbered in the Time Present of the early twentieth century,
but he ends up in a dormitory room in Cambridge, lying on his
bed trembling and with his teeth chattering, not from the New
England winter but from the realization that people and events of
a half-century ago and more have irrevocably shaped and marked
his own consciousness.

If *Absalom, Absalom!* exemplifies anything about the South,
both in the way of telling and the story told, it is that the habit of

experiencing the present as if it were importantly and inescapably
the outcome of the past is an attribute of consciousness itself, and
not just a method of accounting for cause and effect chronologi-
cally. Where the usual historical novel—say, Margaret Mitchell's
Gone With the Wind—begins at the chronological beginning and
is recounted in linear fashion, Faulkner's tale opens in the then-
Time Present, with a young man listening to an elderly woman
telling him about events of the past, and simultaneously thinking
about himself *as* doing so. It proceeds to show the impact of what
she and others tell him about the past, and what he thinks and
feels about that past. As he learns more and more and develops
his own conjectures about it, he is presented as becoming ever
more involved emotionally in the accumulating moral revelation
of the events and relationships being reported and deduced. Ultimately he is seen as being both awed and appalled at what he has
learned—and it has been the telling of the story that has both
caused that response and mirrored the process of learning about it.

Both processes are historical; but where the development of
the story of Quentin's enlarging emotional response is presented
in linear fashion, that of his discovery of the events of the long-
ago past is spatial, or what is nowadays called "associative"—that
is, events are being learned in juxtaposition with other events,
existing simultaneously in vertical, or spatial, extension, affect-
ing and being affected by each other. Events are then *arranged* to
emphasize chronological causation, on the assumption that a
proper understanding depends upon a chronological arrangement
to make clear the causality—its moral implications, its underlying meanings, seen in terms of the responsibility for subsequent
events. Such is the nature of historical consciousness.

The student of the Old South and its literature, of my generation at least, finds himself in something of the position of
Quentin Compson in Faulkner's great novel, and, to an extent, in
the position of the author of a book like *Absalom, Absalom!* as
well. For, if one was born in the South and grew up there, one not
only heard and was taught a great deal about antebellum Southern life when one was young, but much of what one afterward
learned over the years has distinctly modified, not just factually
but in terms of underlying interpretative assumptions, the "truth"
of the past. More than that, all of it *mattered* a great deal, indeed

still matters, for knowing it affects one's present attitudes. And if any single thing is certain, it is that one's own experience of Southern history is "spatial" as well as "linear"—which is to say that events learned affect one's thinking not merely in terms of straight logic but also on multiple levels of experience, changing and being changed by one another simultaneously.

Thus in *Absalom, Absalom!* what Quentin learns changes the meaning of what he has known, and because of that changed meaning he is also able to shape the significance of what he is learning as well. Historical knowledge is best seen, perhaps, as a continuum in time and space, in which interpretation—the assertion of causality—is arranged in a linear, chronological pattern in order to be understood. So that we are continually engaged in introducing our knowledge of newly discovered events into an already existing scheme, an activity that both alters the pattern itself and also causes what we believe are the meanings of the events to be modified as well.

Patterns, however—overall interpretations, perceived cause-and-effect relationships, theories of causation—have a life of their own, and they resist such modification. We may believe, for example, that a particular novel by a certain antebellum Southern author exists in a specific relationship to other events in his career, as well as to other events in antebellum history, and that it exemplifies certain patterns of continuity in the history of the community. A newly perceived aspect of that novel, a new way of interpreting the significance of a scene or a characterization in it, may require that we adjust our view of the way that the novel fits into the larger patterning of causality. It may even demand a pronounced reshaping of that patterning. But since the patterning has great significance for the way that we view aspects of our own community identity, it may very well threaten the nature of that identity itself. So we resist its implications—and refuse to adjust the pattern of causality and responsibility to the meaning of the new discovery or interpretation. The interpretation, although seemingly "neutral" in its implications, a matter of purely literary significance, takes on an emotional importance not to be found in any logical, clear-cut, cause-and-effect relationship. We argue about, we dispute, we deny the interpretation at issue, when in actuality not the interpretation as such, but its implica-

tions for attitudes and needs that ostensibly have nothing whatever to do with it, are what may prompt our resistance.

Whatever may be said about the scholarship—by which I mean
critical reading equally with biographical and historical re-
search—that has gone into the interpretation of the literature of
the Old South, no one may claim that it has been written coldly
and dispassionately. Even the antiquarian pedantry—of which
there has always been a goodly supply, and which shows little
tendency toward abatement—customarily arises from the effort to
assert an identification with the traditional social community
through a demonstrated custodial zeal for its history. (I suspect the
same is true for New England antiquarianism.)

The bane of Southern literary scholarship has always been
chauvinism. Because the Old South (and the later South as well,
on up into our own time) was constantly under ideological attack,
primarily because of its racial arrangements, and because in the
nature of the situation the attack has usually been conducted
from a holier-than-thou point of view, it was only to be expected
that many of those Southerners who have written about the
literature of the region have done so in the form of refutation.
Seemingly the obverse of this, but stemming psychologically
from the same impulse, has been a self-consciously iconoclastic
scholarship, written in large part to demonstrate the scholar's
emancipation from simplistic Southern patriotism.

Obviously neither the excesses of patriotic defensiveness nor
those of determined idol-smashing make for good literary scholarship. Yet it ought to be noted that when and if an emotional involvement with one's subject is disciplined and corrected by critical rigor and a zeal for historical accuracy, the result can be the
kind of scholarship written from within the subject, and thus en-
riched by an ability to understand, sympathize, and even to an
extent identify with what would otherwise be an affair of marble
authors writing versions of stony pastorale. And what I think is
the distinguished achievement of some of the scholarly discourse
on pre-twentieth-century Southern literature within recent decades has been due to that balancing of passionate involvement
with notable scholarly rigor. In particular my admiration for the
work of Lewis P. Simpson, about whose writings I shall have

much to say in the pages that follow, is for just that quality: what he writes about the literature of the South means so much to him emotionally, yet the keen intelligence with which he writes will not allow him to overrun his judgment and force his interpretations to conform to his emotional allegiances. The same, in a different way, was usually true for the Southern essays of the late Allen Tate.

If we are ever to understand what the literature of the Old South was and was not, it will be through the kind of imaginative involvement allied with rigorous critical integrity exemplified by the work of these two very different kinds of critical writers. It will not come through trying to elevate, for example, a Southern author of the second magnitude whose work is customarily slighted in comparison with writings by authors of no greater gifts who, however, wrote about and lived in the Northeast, by insisting that the Southern author's work is really of the *first* magnitude, and that only the sheer, blind neglect of critics has prevented its recognition as such. Nor will it come through the kind of patriotic antiquarianism that consists of the uncritical amassing of seemingly endless data in an effort to demonstrate that the vitality of the Old South's cultural life has customarily been downgraded (which, however, it has indeed been), instead of willing to accept the obvious truth that there were crucial factors in the region's social and political life that kept its literary imagination fettered.

William Faulkner, writing of his relationship to his native state of Mississippi, once declared that "you dont love because: you love despite; not for the virtues, but despite the faults."[1] The advice will serve for scholars as well as novelists.

I set out to write this book about literature in the Old South because I found myself, after what are now forty years of consciously and professionally attempting to understand the literature and history of the South and their relationship to the community into which I was born, repeatedly coming up against a problem. As a student not only of Southern literature but of American literature as a whole, I had often to ask myself why it

1. William Faulkner, "Mississippi," *Essays, Speeches and Public Letters,* ed. James B. Meriwether (New York: Random House, 1965), 43.

was that the writers of the antebellum South had played so relatively minor a role in the impressive flowering of the American
literary imagination in the 1830s, 1840s, and 1850s—a period
that has been appropriately called the American Renaissance. (It
ought to be obvious that the fact that this particular question did
present itself to me, and in just this way, had to do with the importance that I automatically placed upon my own regional, community identity. It was not, in other words, merely a matter of
dispassionate scholarly inquiry.)

My original involvement, as a conscious intellectual activity,
with the literature of the South was with what was then contemporary Southern writing. (It was only a few years after World
War II; authors such as William Faulkner, James Branch Cabell,
John Crowe Ransom, Allen Tate, Stark Young, and others were
still very much alive and writing books. Thomas Wolfe had been
dead for barely more than a decade, and Flannery O'Connor,
William Styron, and Walker Percy were as yet unpublished in book
form.) But the historical habit, noted earlier, that was more or less
mine by community inheritance, was not long in impelling me in
the direction of what had come before the moderns—of, that is,
the past. Why was it that the Southern authors of my own day had
been able to produce a literature that was read and admired everywhere, and that was so obviously constructed out of a community
experience that was in key ways similar to my own, while the
writers of the South of a century earlier had manifestly not
been able to use their experience to any such striking literary
advantage?

As authors of American books, Herman Melville, Nathaniel
Hawthorne, Walt Whitman, even to an extent Henry David
Thoreau (not, however, Ralph Waldo Emerson) were able to speak
to me across that gap in time; in their experience I could also
recognize important aspects of my own. Not so the antebellum
Southerners, to anything like the same degree (except for Poe, of
course, but his was a case all its own).

As an incorrigible reader of Southern and American history, I
was convinced that whatever the forces were that divided South
and North in the nineteenth century and at one point set them to
fighting a sectional war, the individual people living in both regions were in most important respects far more alike than differ-

ent. Even the writings, whether in diaries, letters, or memoirs, of the antebellum planter "aristocracy" did not seem to me to reflect any kind of essential human difference in kind between them and their Northern counterparts.

Moreover, the more I learned about it, the less was I able to perceive any kind of profound, absolute difference between the twentieth-century Southerners that I knew, had grown up with, and lived among in my own day, and those of a century earlier who had left the diaries, memoirs, and letters, and about whom political and social historians wrote. I also became increasingly skeptical about the supposed existence of a special order of planter aristocrats who in their ethical and moral values and their commercial attitudes were allegedly different from other Americans during their own time and from their lineal descendants in my day, among whom I had grown up and attended school and college.

More and more it seemed to me that the antagonisms that resulted in the American Civil War, the impact of which was still part of the consciousness of Southerners in my own generation, had brought about an unusual, artificial—though not necessarily unavoidable—war that pitted citizens of a largely homogeneous, largely middle-class nation, without a hereditary, defined aristocracy, in bloody fratricidal combat.

The single and, as it turned out, crucial difference between the antebellum North and South was obviously the existence of slavery in the latter. If as no less a person than Abraham Lincoln had suggested, war was the price that had to be paid to end the owning of human beings as chattel property, then it was worth paying. But, granted that that result was urgently desirable, had a war been indeed necessary to bring it about? And if so, what was the relationship between the impulse to bring about an end to slavery on the one hand, and the subsequent flourishing of such disenthralled, altruistic American patriots and public benefactors as Jay Gould, Jim Fisk, Andrew Carnegie, Commodore Vanderbilt, J. Pierpont Morgan, John D. Rockefeller, Collis P. Huntington, August Belmont, Oakes Ames, Daniel Drew, Jay Cooke, and Henry Clay Frick on the other?

Had I been by profession and inclination primarily a political and social historian instead of a literary scholar, I suspect that my inquiries would have been impelled in that direction (although, I hope, not in an effort to try to show that emancipation *shouldn't* have been accomplished in that way, as was the implication of an entire school of revisionist historians during the 1930s, 1940s, and even the 1950s, for clearly the historian must concern himself with what *was*, and not what should have been but wasn't).

I have come to recognize an odd habit among historians, whether of politics and society or of literature (and I do not exempt myself). It is what I can only describe as a reluctance to use contemporary human nature as a measurement and commonsense corrective for theoretical interpretations of historical behavior. The assumption that people of past centuries and eras were exactly the same, thought and felt exactly the same, as one's contemporaries can of course be highly misleading, just as can the tendency to read into the past the values and attitudes of the present—"the Whig interpretation of history," as scholars of English history have labeled the tendency of Macaulay and other nineteenth-century writers to read the political history of medieval and Renaissance England as if it were a contest between adherents of nineteenth-century parliamentary democracy and the divine right of kings. Yet surely there is a difference between such overbearing ideological imposition and the use of recognizable constants in human nature to help one's understanding of behavior.

To wit. We look back at the citizenry of the Old South, read their diaries and letters and memoirs, and find people who seem in most important respects not very different from our own contemporaries. They laugh at the same jokes we do, become indignant at the same things, use the same metaphors and similes when they speak and write, articulate the same hopes—yet they were capable of believing that an entire race of human beings was so inferior that it could be owned as property. How could that have been possible? For that matter, persons of even my own generation, born in the 1920s, can remember old-timers who when young had, or whose family had, not only believed in slavery but owned slaves and fought to sustain the right to do so.

Yet did not such a willingness to accept African slavery represent a difference only in *degree*, and not in kind, from the capacity to accept and condone the kind of total, massive racial segregation that existed in the South of barely a few decades ago? And if

this is so, just how difficult is it, really, to imagine that the antebellum Southerners of no more than three generations earlier
were as a whole very much like the citizenry of the 1920s and
1930s in their ways of thinking and feeling?

In the same way, the notion that there were deeply fundamental differences between the citizenry of the Old South and those of
the antebellum North and Midwest is difficult to believe. The
only real issue that divided them along strictly sectional lines
was slavery; even the dispute over the protective tariff was based
on that. Certainly it was not race; for it is a fact, sad but true, that
most Northerners were scarcely less racially prejudiced than were
Southerners. It was not abhorrence of chattel slavery, but the
seeming threat that the use of blacks in agriculture posed to free
labor, that made the Midwest view the Dred Scott decision as a
plot among the slaveholding oligarchy to engineer the expansion
of slavery into the free states in the 1850s. Equally it was racism
that prompted the electorate of Ohio, for example, the state
which furnished five American presidents during the six decades
following 1865, to vote twice not to ratify the Fourteenth Amend-
ment to the Constitution because it would enfranchise blacks.
And so on.

The point of all this, as I shall contend in the pages that follow, is
that when one seeks to account for the failure of the Old South to
produce important literature, it will scarcely do to see the region
and its people as being qualitatively different from other American people and places, with a significantly different set of moral
values, or as forming a society more nearly exempt than that of
the North from the moral and social dilemmas that constitute the
subject matter of important literature. And therefore the *only*
place to look for an explanation is in the one characteristic that
did distinguish South from North: the active existence and the
institutionalized acceptance of chattel slavery.

An obvious trouble with such an explanation, however, is that
it immediately triggers the kind of smug moral superiority that
typified facile Northeastern popular moralists during the mid-
nineteenth century such as John Townsend Trowbridge, Josiah
Holland, M.D., Henry Ward Beecher, and the like. (Emerson was
capable of it, too.) The supposed ethical superiority of the saintly,

democratic North to the immoral, slaveholding South was viewed as making possible a true literature of the transcendent Ideal in the former. But this is so only in the sense that the easy, over-weening ideality that characterized the reigning popular theology and literature of the mid-nineteenth century provided the really important Northern writers of the day with a model to react against. The pages of Melville, Hawthorne, and Whitman, and in the postwar period of Dickinson, Clemens, and James, are filled with hostility to and exposures of the bloodless "spirituality" and facile moralizing of the day.

Obviously it was not the inability of the authorship of the Old South to participate in that kind of literary cant that accounts for the failure to participate in the American Renaissance. If the exis-tence of slavery is involved, therefore, it must be for less obvious, more profound reasons, having to do with what its presence in the Southern community either discouraged the Southern author from doing, or else caused him to do, when sitting down to create stories or poems.

It is as an attempt to understand how it did indeed work, and why, that the book that follows has been written. Its chapters are concerned principally with three antebellum Southern authors: William Gilmore Simms, Edgar Allan Poe, and Henry Timrod. As always, I have written to find out what I thought. There was no effort on my part to prepare a rhetorical demonstration of a previ-ously determined conclusion, other than in the most general sense. The argument of each chapter developed as I went along.

In Simms's instance, here was a talented, energetic, prolific au-thor, an influential figure on the national literary scene, gener-ous, with high ideals, of high integrity, and who was also an ar-dent defender of slavery and an active participant in sectional politics. What did the latter involvement mean for him as a writer? What could, or would, this multitalented author *not* do, by virtue of his Southern allegiance, that might have enabled him to create better, more enduring American fiction than he did?

Edgar Poe, by contrast, as the single antebellum Southern au-thor whose work has endured for its own sake, presented a very different problem. For as is well known, Poe did *not* set his work in the region of his rearing, did *not* concern himself with its history or its social arrangements, was never remotely involved in public life, and lived outside of the South for much of his abbreviated adult lifetime. What did slavery have to do with that? What did its presence in the Richmond of his youth mean for that bizarre imagination?

Finally, Timrod: a highly gifted poet whose work, however, attained importance as literature only when secession and war provided him with a theme that allowed him to speak openly *as* a member of his community. Why was this so? What does it have to tell us about the antebellum Southern literary situation?

I might have chosen to make the work of other writers part of my inquiry as well; indeed, at one point I did write the draft of a chapter on John Pendleton Kennedy, only to conclude that it would add nothing to my book that was not developed more clearly elsewhere. For my objective, however imperfectly realized, was not to "cover" the literary scene in the Old South, or even to present a series of case studies of Southern authors. Rather, it was to explore and to try to understand what there was about the situation of the antebellum Southern writer that worked against his participation in the American Renaissance.

It goes almost without saying that I do not pretend to have answered the question for all time. What I do hope is that I have helped to suggest where the answer may lie.

I. THE EDGE OF THE SWAMP

Literature and Society in the Old South

There is an old pleasantry that at the convention in Memphis, Tennessee, in 1850, when the various Southern states met to decide upon a common strategy for the intensifying sectional crisis, resolutions were enacted to the effect that "RESOLVED, that there be created a Southern Literature" and "RESOLVED, that the Hon. William Gilmore Simms, Esq., be asked to write it." Although the story has no basis in fact, it points up a truth, which is that the very idea of a "Southern" literature, as distinct from American literature, had its origins in the slavery controversy. Up until the 1820s and 1830s, residents of the several Southern states mostly thought of themselves as Virginians, North and South Carolinians, Georgians, Tennesseans, and so on, and did not consider literature written in their states as importantly Southern.

As the sectional schism deepened, however, so did the consciousness of being Southern. "We want," wrote John C. Calhoun in 1847, in response to a request to subscribe to a newly planned literary magazine, "above all other things, a Southern literature, from school books up to the works of the highest order."[1] We may assume that the senator from South Carolina had matters other than pure aesthetics in mind in so declaring; an oft-repeated joke in Charleston was that Calhoun was the only man in history ever to have composed a love poem beginning with the word "Whereas."

The thinness of Southern literature during the decades when Cooper, Hawthorne, Melville, Emerson, Thoreau, and Whitman

---

1. Quoted in Curtis Carroll Davis, *That Ambitious Mr. Legaré: The Life of James M. Legaré of South Carolina, Including a Collected Edition of His Verse* (Columbia: University of South Carolina Press, 1971), 45.

were creating the body of literature we call the American Renaissance, and that D. H. Lawrence described as Classic American Literature, was a source of continuing embarrassment to Southern literati during the late nineteenth and early twentieth centuries. Except for Poe, the much-advertised golden days of the plantation South had no counterpart in literature. In a time when cultural nationalism was an important literary force, the South had little that was literary to point to with pride. The embarrassment was rendered the more acute because the overt literary ideality of the genteel tradition made it all too easy to equate the paucity of important writers in the Old South with the fact that the region had countenanced human slavery, and that it had even sought to separate itself from the American Union and fought and lost a war in an attempt to safeguard its right to do so. Did it not then follow that the failure to produce an important literature was proof of moral blight, and that the presence of so evil an institution in the antebellum South was *why* the South's writers had been unable to compose great literary works?

Against all the literary genius north of the Potomac, there was only Poe to counter with; and Poe had actually been born in Boston, had lived in Philadelphia and New York City for most of his adult life, and had almost never written *about* life in the South. Moreover, however widespread Poe's popular appeal, by the standards of literary ideality he was somewhat suspect; his poems and stories were deficient in high morality, which was no more than to be expected of a man known to have been a drinker and not entirely upright in financial matters.

In any event, for generations after the end of the War Between the States the South's literary spokesmen felt impelled to explain why their native region had failed to come forth with important literature during the antebellum years. There were, of course, obvious hindrances to authorship in the region: its rurality, the lack of large centers where literary men might sustain and encourage each other, the absence of a sufficient audience to patronize Southern literary periodicals and thus enable the author to earn a livelihood, and so on. These reasons had been cited at the time. It was only in the years following the end of the Civil War, however, that it became possible to assert publicly that the presence of chattel slavery had been in any way involved in the matter.

The novelist Thomas Nelson Page, whose plantation idyls in dialect during the 1880s and 1890s were aimed consciously in defense of the honor of the Old South, was one who proclaimed that the Peculiar Institution had been the culprit. Now Page was no critic of slavery. He agreed that the South was better off without it, but he would not concede that slavery had been notably evil in practice. But it was slavery, he said, that had exposed the South to the unremitting propaganda attacks of the Abolitionists, so that the South had been forced to suspend any imaginative scrutiny of its own life and to marshal all its intellectual energies in defense of its liberties. In order to keep out dangerously divisive heresies concerning the Peculiar Institution that might weaken sectional resolve, it had erected an ideological wall against new ideas of any kind whatsoever, thus crippling the community's intellectual vigor. Because the obsession with political self-defense left no room for concern with and sympathy for the arts, those ante-bellum Southerners who did seek to write lacked encouragement and readership at home.[2]

The scholar William Peterfield Trent, who identified not with the Old South as Thomas Nelson Page did but with the New South of commerce and industry that Walter Hines Page and other Southern progressives were urging upon a dilapidated turn-of-the-century region, carried the explanation a crucial step further, adding to it overtones that Thomas Nelson Page would never have condoned. Slavery, declared Trent in his controversial biography, *William Gilmore Simms* (1892), fostered a society ridden with privilege, caste, and class, stifled the imagination of the region, enforced conformity, and discouraged intellectual audacity and originality. Simms's career was presented as a pathetic struggle against the undemocratic snobbishness of a smug, intellectually enfeebled ruling class that had no use for the talents of a young author of lowly birth and lively imagination. Slavery corrupted the values of the community, lowered its intellectual horizons, enforced hedonism and provincialism. In Simms's instance a talented parvenu with all the right instincts was led to emulate the planter establishment and to suppress his better qualities in a

2. Page's remarks on the literature of the Old South are contained in his essays "Authorship in the South Before the War" and "The Old South," *The Old South* (New York: Chautauqua Press, 1919).

largely futile attempt to win the admiration of a degenerate, self-satisfied gentry.[3]

In so saying, Trent came remarkably close to the diatribe against the Southern slaveholding leadership delivered by Hinton Rowan Helper in *The Impending Crisis of the South* (1857). Because Trent was describing the slave South of three decades earlier and not the racial and social arrangements of his own day (except perhaps by implication), the reception of his views in the South was not nearly so violent as had been the case when Helper's book had appeared; even so, it was denounced in the Southern press as unpatriotic and a libel upon the memory of the Old South. When a few years later Trent departed from Sewanee and the University of the South and joined the faculty of Columbia University, there were those who were happy to see him depart. By the 1920s, however, his views had become accepted by many scholars in Southern literature.

Trent's assumption, which was shared by most of the New South critics, was that the achievement of the writers of the Northeast during the years before the Civil War was the mark of the relative health of Free State culture, as contrasted with what went on in the slaveowning South. The implied view of the relationship between literature and society, however, was by no means accepted by one of the most incisive critical intellects ever to write about the South and its literature, Allen Tate, who in the 1930s and 1940s published several remarkable essays on the literary situation in the South.

Tate's position was that the arts can achieve true health only when they grow out of a hierarchical, religious social order characterized by a belief in "honor, truth, imagination, human dignity and limited acquisitiveness."[4] Such a society had existed in Europe prior to the Industrial Revolution, but the rise of finance capitalism replaced aristocratic patronage of the arts with the

3. Originally George Washington Cable had been selected to write the Simms biography in Charles Dudley Warner's American Men of Letters series for Houghton, Mifflin and Company, but the Louisiana novelist, by then resident in Massachusetts, decided against doing so. It seems safe to say that had he carried through with the project, the result would have been even more censorious of slavery and the Old South than Trent's book proved to be.

4. Allen Tate, "The New Provincialism," *Essays of Four Decades* (Chicago: The Swallow Press, 1968), 545.

cash nexus, the profession of letters became commercialized, and the writer was caught in a marketplace economy based upon unrestricted acquisitive exploitation.

The writings of the American Renaissance in New England and the Middle Atlantic states, he declared, far from affirming the cultural health and validating the political and social assumptions of the society, constituted an impassioned critique of the nature of that society by authors who were being forced into an abiding alienation from its values. Hawthorne, Melville, and later Emily Dickinson wrote out of the collapse of the grandeur of the fading Puritan imagination as it gave way before the juggernaut of secular materialism in an urbanizing industrial society. Because the Old South by contrast was pre-industrial and feudal, no such alienation occurred.

If the Old South had produced a great literature, Tate declared, it would have been a classical literature along the lines of pre-industrial English and European literature, not a literature of Romantic alienation. No believer in the virtues of industry and progress, Tate saw slavery as an important reason for the Old South's failure to produce important writers other than Poe, but what was wrong was that it was *Negro* slavery. All the great cultures of the Western world, he said, have been rooted in peasantries; "they have been the growth of the soil." But African slavery served to distance rather than unite citizen and land: "the white man got nothing from the Negro, no profound image of himself in terms of the soil."[5] In addition, the inability of Southern Protestantism ("a non-agrarian and trading religion")[6] to instill a proper belief in non-acquisitive, hierarchical values (as Roman Catholicism would presumably have done) and the obvious fact that the defense of slavery placed all the emphasis on politics, with no time for the arts, joined to render the Old South's literature trivial and tedious.

Allen Tate had a distinct taste for playing *épater le bourgeois;* he took considerable satisfaction in flouting the dominant liberal social and critical attitudes of the 1930s and 1940s. It is this, I believe, that accounts for the dubious taste of his remarks about

5. Tate, "The Profession of Letters in the South," *Essays of Four Decades,* 525.
6. Tate, "Religion and the Old South," *Essays of Four Decades,* 570.

slavery; a better way of putting it might have been that the white slaveowner, far from deriving nothing, took almost everything from the Negro *except* a "profound image of himself in terms of the soil." By the 1950s Tate would have phrased the matter differently, for after all, what he was saying was that the presence of African slavery was incompatible with the growth of an important literature in the Old South. But in any event there is considerable validity to his observation that the antebellum Southern literary man was insufficiently distanced from the values and attitudes of his community to produce the kind of imaginative critique that comes with Romantic alienation.

The question is, *why?* Tate's answer was in essence that the Old South was a pre-industrial, feudal society, ruled by an aristocracy. It was a throwback to an earlier time. This formulation has been rejected, however, by the scholar who is by all odds the most perceptive and imaginative student of the cultural life of the Old South, Lewis P. Simpson. It is with Simpson's theory about the antebellum South and the reason for its failure to develop an important literature that the pages that follow will be chiefly concerned.

2.

Lewis Simpson has in recent years published three remarkable books, *The Man of Letters in New England and the South* (1973), *The Dispossessed Garden: Pastoral and History in Southern Literature* (1975), and *The Brazen Face of History: Studies in the Literary Consciousness of America* (1980). In them he has been developing a sustained exploration into the nature of the Southern author's involvement in literature, both in the pre–Civil War period and thereafter. Contrasted with the rigor and consistency of his analysis, the theorizing of most previous commentators seems hardly more than impressionistic dabbling.

Simpson views American and Southern literature not as a unique phenomenon localized in time and space, but as a distinct phase of the cultural and intellectual experience of Western man. The social order of the Western world, he declares, has been one that, unlike that of most other societies, was predicated upon words. Ours has been a verbal culture. In medieval times the social order was united under a belief in the City of God—not merely in words but the Word. With the Renaissance began a gradually accelerating process of secularization. Humanists and *philosophes* knew the term "Republic of Letters," a realm of moral being of which men of letters—the "clerisy," Simpson designates them, using a term borrowed from Samuel Taylor Coleridge—became the conservators. During the eighteenth-century Enlightenment that realm transcended national borders. A balance of power among Church, State, and Letters ratified a social and moral order inherited from the classical, medieval, and humanistic past. Such Southern men of letters as Thomas Jefferson were clearly participants in the clerisy.

Even in the eighteenth century the hegemony of the Republic of Letters had been "threatened by novel historical forces: integral nationalism, equalitarian democracy, scientific specialization of knowledge, industrial and technological specialization of function, and the dynamics of a capitalist market economy." The result was a growing confusion of Church, State, and Letters, making for a loss of order and autonomy, which by the dawn of the nineteenth century was reaching crisis proportions. The lettered clerisy now struggled self-consciously to maintain "the imperatives of the Word" amid and against the ever-intensifying politics of nationalism, democracy, technological narrowness, and finance capitalism.[7] The Romantic artist became pastoral prophet and priest, waging a desperate fight against scientific materialism and mass culture.

The writers of New England and the Northeast, nurtured on the pastoral vision of the redemptive community, the City Upon a Hill, held powerfully onto that myth in the face of the technological materialism of an expanding nineteenth-century America, and long after the religious foundations that underlay such a community had given way to a secular view of man as a creature of history. The result was an alienating self-consciousness and an abiding loneliness. The anguished struggle to assert the humanistic vision, and yet remain loyal to a democratic society characterized by driving secular materialism, produced a litera-

7. Lewis P. Simpson, "The Southern Writer and the Great Literary Secession," *The Man of Letters in New England and the South* (Baton Rouge: Louisiana State University Press, 1973), 233, 234.

ture that dramatized the conflict. That literature was the American Renaissance.

The Southern writer could not participate in the struggle—but not for the reasons proposed by Tate. What was happening culturally in the nineteenth-century South was something that was quite different from the history of the Northeast and the Midwest—something, Simpson says, that was without parallel in Western history. It was not that the plantation economy had brought into being a pre-industrial, feudal community that was a reversion to an older European model, as Tate believed. Instead, the antebellum South, in its role as supplier of cotton to the mills of Europe and New England, had evolved into a community that was *based on chattel slavery*, and was striving toward a social order that "was built securely, permanently, unqualifiedly on the right of men to hold property in other men."[8]

The ideal of the Old South was a hierarchical community of enduring social order, with its goal the achievement of a nation that "would become a salvational world power, bringing global peace and prosperity and redeeming the laborers of all nations from poverty."[9] It was not even a matter of life on the land. Logically such a society need not even be agricultural; it could as appropriately use slave labor to operate factories (as indeed was done successfully at the Tredegar Iron Works in Richmond, Virginia). And, with equal logic, such subordination need not even be restricted to blacks. Although most Southerners were unwilling to confront the consequences of their beliefs, certain thinkers such as George Fitzhugh of Virginia were bold enough to envision a similar chattel role for lower-class whites as well, even though such logic had not yet been faced up to by the planter community.

Sharing in this hierarchical and salvational vision, pressed by the heated politicization of Southern life during the antebellum period, the Southern man of letters had enlisted in the ideological defense of slavery. In so doing, however, he forfeited his membership in the Republic of Letters of the Western world. He could

8. Simpson, "Slavery and Modernism," *The Brazen Face of History: Studies in the Literary Consciousness in America* (Baton Rouge: Louisiana State University Press, 1980), 71.
9. *Ibid.*, 78.

not take part in the inner drama of the humanistic vision in
combat with the technological materialism of the nineteenth
century, for the plantation society with which he identified his
interests was an integral part of the industrial system: "The
Cotton Kingdom was no isolated agrarian world; it was a vital part of the raw-materials supply system of the developing
industrial-technological complex of Western society."[10]

In the Old South, therefore, Simpson contends, "literary pas-
toralism became devoted wholly to the defense of slavery instead
of the defense of poetry." Thus "in the South the literary realm
virtually disappeared"; there was no "crisis of the literary order,"
and the Southern author did not experience the ironic disaffection
or detachment from a secular slaveholding community devoted to
the production of cotton, rice, tobacco, and sugar for the world
market.[11]

With the broader aspects of Lewis Simpson's thesis, having to
do with Western civilization being a verbal culture, with the man
of letters as defender of the Word in medieval Christendom and
thereafter as increasingly beleaguered humanist combatting secular scientific and technological materialism, I have no important
quarrel—other than the lurking suspicion that it is still another
version of the inveterate notion of decline and fall from a past Age
of Gold. Behind all such contentions, however logically expressed,
lies a belief in a millennial Past when human beings were some-
how exempt from having to confront the full implications of their
imperfection. "Oh golden age, when learnyng was sought for farre
and neare: when wyt was exercised, and policie practiced, and
vertue honored," lamented John Florio in the year 1578, long before the invention of the spinning jenny and the steam engine.[12]
This may well be so, although very little that I have read about
medieval times, much less about the centuries that have followed
since, leads me to think that things once seemed notably more
satisfactory to those who had to contend with them. One need
not be a blind worshipper of Progress to remain skeptical about
the assumption that the world has been going to Hell in a basket

10. Simpson, "The Southern Writer and the Great Literary Secession," 238–39.

11. Ibid., 239.

12. Quoted in Harry Levin, The Myth of the Golden Age in the Renaissance
(New York: Oxford University Press, 1969), 167.

ever since the death of Thomas Aquinas. But in any event it does not seem to matter a great deal so far as the nature of nineteenth-century Southern literature and society is concerned. Certain it is that there were problems aplenty to fret Lewis Simpson's clerisy between 1800 and 1865.

With far greater insight into society and the literary imagination, I think, Simpson is developing a thesis that in key respects is like that of Thomas Nelson Page. That is, the failure of the antebellum Southern writer was brought about by the presence of a condition that kept the writer isolated from the chief sources of the vitality that elsewhere characterized nineteenth-century literary and intellectual life. The wish to defend the slaveholding Southern community not only politicized the writers; it shut them off from the larger world of letters.

Simpson concurs with the notion, as Page, Tate, and others including antebellum writers such as Simms have asserted, that there was no adequate audience for sustaining an active literary vocation in the Old South, but he does not accept that of itself as a sufficient reason. *Why* were such conditions crippling for the Southern writer? he asks. For literature to flourish, he asserts, there must be a Republic of Letters in existence, in which the individual participant can be part of the clerisy, the community of men of letters and audience of readers who share an allegiance to language as the realm of ethical and moral truth. Obviously such a clerisy cannot thrive without the presence of sufficient participants to make possible an intellectual situation. It follows that without cities, in which literary centers can flourish as an institutionalized force, the Southern writer had no humanistic constituency to sustain him and to counter the assumptions of the political, economic, and social community. This insight, which points to just why and how cultural communities operate within the larger community, and what their absence meant for the antebellum Southern writer's humanistic views, seems to me perhaps the most useful and important aspect of Lewis Simpson's writings about the Old South and its literary situation.

The recognition that contrary to the mythology of the Old South and the assertion of Allen Tate, the plantation regime hardly constituted any kind of reversion to a feudal, aristocratic society along the European model, seems decisive. However much the Old South might have liked to think so, and however avidly the more literary members of the cavalry of the Army of Northern Virginia thought of themselves as characters in Walter Scott's border romances, the antebellum Cotton Kingdom was a full-fledged participant in the Western world of industrial capitalism, engaged in producing the raw materials for the mills of England, France, and the Northeast.

In so doing, the Old South, in Simpson's formulation, developed an ordered, hierarchical society in which chattel slavery provided the labor that Southerners liked to believe could make possible a community life exempt from the instability, uncertainty, and vicious competition of unrestrained bourgeois capitalism. In that society the acquisitive instinct would be kept in check through paternalistic concern for the labor force, which, because it was owned rather than merely hired when needed, constituted a responsibility going beyond payment of hourly wages. Free from the hunger, misery, chaos, and revolutionary potential that beset Western man under finance capitalism (the same conditions that Karl Marx was observing in the Europe of his day), the South would be a rock of stability and permanence, dedicated to feeding and clothing the world's hungry and needy.

To anchor his assertion in literature, Simpson quotes lines from the poet Henry Timrod's "Ethnogenesis," which he points out was originally titled "Ode on the Occasion of the Meeting of the Southern Congress" and celebrated the establishment of the Confederate States of America, as evidence that the goal and ideal of the Cotton Kingdom, as envisioned by its literary men, was nothing less than the complete redemption of poverty throughout the globe:

> Could we climb
> Some mighty Alp, and view the coming time,
> The rapturous sight would fill
> Our eyes with happy tears!
> Not only for the glories which a hundred years
> Shall bring us; not for lands from sea to sea,
> And wealth, and power, and peace, though these shall be;
> But for the distant peoples we shall bless,
> And the hushed murmurs of a world's distress:
> For, to give labor to the poor,
> The whole sad planet o'er,

> And save from want and crime the humblest door,
>   Is one among the many ends for which
>   God makes us great and rich![13]

Obviously such an ideal is pastoral, and it is also millennial, the accomplishment of a social order that will be exempt from change—in other words, from history. Simpson sees it as a Southern version of Manifest Destiny. By accepting such a vision for his society, he declares, the Southern writer's membership in an alienated clerisy was rendered invalid. In effect he was *alienated* from *alienation*.

Whether sacramental or not (and I must say that I have never quite understood the use of the term in this kind of context, even though Lewis Simpson is comfortable with it), it seems clear that there is little that is pre-industrial, feudal, or medieval about such a vision. For it is founded not on the unity of Christendom, the City of God, or the Kingdom of the Holy Spirit, but on profits from growing cotton, corn, and rice. Benjamin Franklin would have been content with such a formulation, as would John D. Rockefeller. One assumes that the Southern slaveholders were quite happy with it.

One might, however, raise this objection: to what extent does such a vision of national destiny, as enunciated by Henry Timrod, differ importantly from what, say, a manufacturer of textiles in Fall River, Massachusetts, or of bleached flour in Minneapolis, Minnesota, might have contended if asked to justify his role and that of nineteenth-century American society to God and man? Would not such a person claim that he was making it possible for mankind everywhere to be decently fed or adequately clothed against the ravages of wind and weather? Would that manufacturer not view the paternalistic employment of a non-unionized, low-salaried work force as equally an enterprise designed to "give labor to the poor / The whole sad planet o'er" and to prevent crime among the jobless? And would he not—with the calm confidence of a Christian holding four aces, as Mark Twain once said—view such wealth as he managed to accumulate by keeping salaries low and prices high as only the appropriate return extended him by

13. Timrod, "Ethnogenesis," *The Collected Poems of Henry Timrod: A Variorum Edition*, ed. Edd Winfield Parks and Aileen Wells Parks (Athens: University of Georgia Press, 1965), 94–95.

the Almighty for his good deeds, just as Timrod said was true for the antebellum planter?

If, therefore, one were Karl Marx or R. H. Tawney, he might well pose this question: Aren't both the Northern and Southern versions of such an apologia equally and characteristically bourgeois, capitalistic, and materialistic in almost every respect? In what way, then, was the antebellum Southern writer any more disfranchised from participation in an alienated and humanistic clerisy than his counterpart in the Northeast?

The rejoinder made to such questions is that there were indeed significant differences between the antebellum Southern planter ideal and that of the Northern businessman, extending beyond the usual rural/urban division and involving an entirely different relationship between labor and production. There was in the North little or no assumption on the part of its leadership that its members constituted a Master Class, an aristocracy sharing the privileges and obligations of their high calling, and one of whose characteristics was a profound distrust of the naked acquisitive instinct as an inherently desirable attitude toward wealth and property. By contrast, in the Old South that was precisely what *was* being contended: that under slavery, cash money was not the sole connection between the employer and his laboring force. It was an ideal; but as such it significantly modified the behavior and attitudes of the planter leadership.

To buttress this assumption, one can call upon the fascinating and growingly influential body of writings on the nature of the Old South published in recent years by the historian Eugene Genovese. And to understand Lewis Simpson's view of what the antebellum South's ideological rationale for slavery was all about, it is extremely important to take Genovese's work into account. For when Simpson refers to the Southern planter leadership as envisioning "a world in which chattel slavery was established beyond all doubt as the right and proper principle of the social relation, a world in which society was built securely, permanently, unqualifiedly on the right to hold property in other men,"[14] he asserts a view of the ideological rationale of the Old South that Genovese has also been promulgating. Thus, in order to deal with the significance of this way of looking at the Old South and its

14. Simpson, "Slavery and Modernism," 71.

planters, I find it expedient now to take a detour leading away from the literary scene in the antebellum South, and to concern myself with matters having to do with politics and social arrangements, far more than with what the antebellum Richmond editor and savant Thomas Ritchie once termed "the mere beauties of the *belles lettres.*"[15]

3.

The notion that the leadership of the South during antebellum times embraced a social and philosophical way of looking at itself and the world that was radically different from that of the North and the Midwest, I believe, mistakes a temporary and expedient political rhetoric for a far more profound and significant difference of mind and heart than ever existed.

For different reasons, I think, both Lewis Simpson and Eugene Genovese have tended to attribute to that much-written-about entity known as the Mind of the South considerably more consistency and cohesion than I believe existed there. In Simpson's instance the result seems to me to make the Old South into a more evil and culpable affair than I think it was, though I hasten to add that this is certainly not Simpson's intention. If what he says about the intentions of the Old South is true, then whatever may have been the complex motives of the North in going to war in 1861, the people of Simpson's and my native region richly deserved everything inflicted upon them and more, and the sectional conflict was indeed a war between good and transcendent evil, with the Old South amply cast in the latter billing.

As for Eugene Genovese's approach, I happen to believe that with the laudable purpose of showing that the leaders of the Old South and the society for which they served as spokesmen were not the scoundrelly slave-drivers and moral reprobates that self-righteous neo-abolitionist historians have depicted them as being, Genovese has found it necessary to distinguish their motives and their aptitudes from those of the North to a degree that does not square with the actualities of the time. Again, this is not Genovese's intention; but because his assumptions about class and caste make it virtually impossible for him to sympathize with anything that is indubitably bourgeois, in order to accept the

15. Quoted in James Branch Cabell, "Mr. Ritchie's Richmond," *Let Me Lie* (New York: Farrar, Straus and Co., 1947), 123.

human virtues of antebellum Southerners in good conscience he is more or less forced to make the South into an aristocratic stronghold such as would have gladdened the heart of a Metternich or a William Buckley.

Genovese is that rare scholar—rare in the United States, in any event—who can employ the Marxist dialectics of the class struggle without losing sight of the complexity of the human beings who are the historical evidence he is engaged in interpreting. He began his researches at a time when the dominant thrust of historical scholarship was all in the direction of undercutting the plantation mythos. Academic historians as a class tend to be very trendish, and the trend when Genovese was coming along was to demolish the elements of romance, self-satisfaction, and complacency lying behind the traditional view of the plantation as a place of inefficient labor but generally paternalistic racial arrangements—the Thomas Nelson Page/Stark Young thesis, one might call it. In part the trend was set in motion by the civil rights movement, which brought renewed attention to the ugliness of racial injustice in the past as well as the present.

Genovese took a very different approach to the study of the Old South. Looking at the documents, the memoirs, the recorded evidence of what plantation slavery had been like, he declined to accept the Abolitionist stereotype of vicious slaveholder and tormented slave. He saw the Peculiar Institution as a social relationship, in which all the various grades of human behavior might be exhibited, from best to worst. Without losing sight of the fact that it was slavery that was involved, and that therefore the worst excesses were always possible, Genovese saw the slaveholder and slave as caught up in a human relationship that, although it was based on the need to secure and control a labor force, was more than merely economic. It differed significantly from the commercial and industrial labor system of the North and Midwest because, unlike the factory owner, the planter owned his labor, and so the laborer, in addition to being a means of creating value in a commodity, was interposed between that value and the slaveowner himself, thus creating a very different human situation from that commonly existing under industrial capitalism.

Comparing Southern chattel slavery to that in Latin America, Genovese emphasized the striking fact that alone of all slave societies in the New World, that of the Old South proved capable of reproducing itself. The slaves were not imported from Africa and driven and driven until they perished, as was done in the Caribbean in particular. Instead, generation followed generation of slaves; the nineteenth-century Southern slave was a creole, and the slave population steadily multiplied. Because the Southern planter was mostly Protestant and of northern European ancestry, he was racist in a far more absolute way than was the Catholic Latin American slaveholder, and there was an unbridgeable social chasm between white and black. But as an evangelical Christian, he assumed a patriarchal stewardship over the welfare of his slave inferiors—one that went hand in hand with his own economic well-being.

Thus the slaves of the plantation South were for the most part adequately fed, clothed, and housed, and the labor exacted of them, though arduous, was customarily not such as to drive them either into violent rebellion or into an early grave. Moreover, what was economically expedient became what was socially and morally desirable; a paternalistic ethos soon evolved within the slaveowner class, whereby enormous pressures could be exerted upon the owner to treat his slaves decently—as slaves.

Genovese thus clashed head-on with the "concentration camp" interpretation of the Peculiar Institution that has been popular among historians since World War II. Like the leading historian of an earlier generation, Ulrich B. Phillips, he saw the plantation as a social institution, not a detention camp peopled by inmates and jailors. Unlike Phillips, however, he was no apologist for slavery, and his views were not based upon the assumption that the black man was an inferior creature. According to Genovese, Phillips, in his two seminal works, *American Negro Slavery* (1918) and *Life and Labor in the Old South* (1932), "willingly displayed the many-sidedness of plantation life and presented it as a community of white men and black struggling to find a way to live together," even though his racism made him stop short of "where he ought to have begun. Because he did not take the Negroes seriously as men and women he could not believe that in meaningful and even decisive ways they shaped the lives of their masters."[16] Where a scholar such as Kenneth M. Stampp, failing to see that a

16. Eugene D. Genovese, "Foreword: Ulrich Bonnell Phillips and His Critics," in Phillips, *American Negro Slavery* (Baton Rouge: Louisiana State University Press, 1966), xix.

patriarchal relationship was not necessarily one involving kindness, could not accept the fact that the Peculiar Institution was not the sterile one of the concentration camp guard and inmate, Phillips, insisted Genovese, saw it as a human one in which both the slaveowner and the slave were deeply involved. (And what kind of a concentration camp, one might ask, was it, in which the inmates steadily increased in population from one year to the next?)

Prompted in part by Genovese's observations, Lewis Simpson, I believe, has tended to view the political rhetoric of the 1830s, 1840s, and 1850s, the attempt to portray chattel slavery as a Positive Good in response to the mounting denunciations of it as an unmitigated evil, as an authentic expression of the aspirations of the Southern mind. Simpson's premises, however, are very different. Genovese's dialectical approach had caused him to formulate an interpretation of nineteenth-century American bourgeois society as economically anarchic, based upon commercial and industrial exploitation, and devotedly dollar-worshipping. As its Hegelian opposite, the agricultural South of the day is seen as a hierarchical, pre-industrial planter counterforce, which though fatally flawed by slavery had rejected the "cash nexus" in favor of an aristocratic restraint upon mere bourgeois acquisitiveness. Inevitably two such systems must clash and the result would be foreordained: a bourgeois industrial society, because it is in a more advanced stage of the class struggle over control of the means of production, must inevitably triumph over a feudal, pre-industrial agricultural society.

Simpson depicts no such dialectic at work. His basic assumptions are at bottom theological, not economic. For all his sympathy for Genovese's evocation of the planter leadership of the Old South as having developed a view of society in which the cash nexus was not permitted to determine human relationships, Simpson would not accept Genovese's belief that the social and religious ideals of a society are essentially the emotional terms whereby men rationalize control of the means of production. Rather, the Old South's quarrel with the North represents a stage in the decline and fall of the humanistic tradition of Western man, which in turn is a falling away from a timeless society of belief constructed about the medieval Roman Catholic church.

The culprit is materialism, its temptations are those of science and technology, and the result is secular modernism.

In his view of race and slavery, as we have seen, Simpson is too realistic to indulge himself in Allen Tate's effort to dilute the heinousness of slavery in the Old South by viewing it as a reversion to an earlier time when bondage was a customary social condition that went along with feudal society. Nor does he buy Genovese's version of it as pre-industrial. For Simpson, the reliance upon chattel slavery is seen as a conscious and deliberate option adopted by the planter class, just as Genovese says; but it is also a unique attempt to establish a lasting, hierarchical community, one that its men of letters believed would fulfill a spiritual mission of redeeming Western man from secular materialism through solving the problem of a just distribution of the world's goods.

Thus the Old South is seen as an anomaly in nineteenth-century Western society not only through its reliance upon chattel slavery but in the conscious attempt of its poets to reassert a sacramental, hierarchical community anchored on the permanent subordination of—and assumption of responsibility for—the lower class.

4.

What is essential to any such view of what the Old South was up to is the notion of a separate and superior class of slaveholders, adhering to a paternalistic code that had little place within it for unrestrained money-grubbing and the naked acquisitiveness of finance capitalism. In Genovese's view the Old South *was* different; and the difference was one that stood up well in any comparison with the version of an acquisitive society that existed north of the Potomac and Ohio rivers. The Southern planter need make no apology to the Northern factory owner or sharp-trading banker, as far as Genovese is concerned, even though, it must be stressed, Genovese is not a moral apologist for slavery.

The thesis is in its own way a restatement, with considerably more sophistication, of the Cavalier-Yankee opposition that from at least the eighteenth century onward has characterized American sectional mythology. That is, the Northern Yankee stands for self-improvement, making the most of every opportunity, in-

ventiveness, practicality, without subservience to the outdated
social, economic, and political impedimenta of rank and hereditary class, while the Southern Cavalier represents a truce with
nature, gracious living, the stability of an ordered society, and a
high-minded refusal to order one's life by materialistic goals
alone.

In his book *Cavalier and Yankee: The Old South and American National Character* (1961), William R. Taylor has explored
what he considers this largely imaginary division within the
American sensibility, demonstrating how both the Yankee and
the Cavalier stereotypes embodied needs felt by the middle-class
society of expansionist nineteenth-century America, and how the
figure of the Cavalier was used both as a rebuke to the overly
materialistic and disorderly tendencies in American life and as a
scapegoat for the nation's sins. What Taylor shows, in convincing
readings of a group of antebellum literary works, is that in North
and South alike, a middle-class society was engaged in improving
its lot on a new continent where such improvement was genuinely and often rapidly possible. Operating without the restraints
upon such a process that the institutions in older societies imposed, its participants felt a powerful need for the ideal of the
ordered, hierarchical community, as represented by the plantation,
the planter aristocrat, and the society of subordination—a need
arising out of a sense of American society's own inadequacies.

The Cavalier-Yankee opposition also provided a way of drama-
tizing sectional differences. As the crisis intensified, each side
could learn to view the other as something different in kind from,
alien to, and ultimately morally as well as politically antithetical
to itself. All Southerners became slave drivers, privileged enemies
of the American dream of liberty and justice for all (white) men.
All Northerners became soulless moneygrubbers, worshippers of
the Almighty Dollar, a vile race of pious hypocrites who used the
Union as a front to mask their drive to control the agrarian South
for their own economic aggrandizement.

Whatever its justification in actuality, during the War Between
the States the Southern press, and Southern political spellbinders,
accepted the division gratefully. The Confederates were seen as
lineal descendants of the English Cavaliers, the North of the
Roundheads. The Southerners liked to refer to themselves collec-

tively as the Chivalry. The Yankees were dubbed Goths, Vandals, Huns, Levellers, Doodles, and the like. Sometimes the imagery became a little confused—Stonewall Jackson, pious Presbyterian that he was, was called Old Blue Light and Old Noll, and the Army of the Valley the New Model Army—but generally the Cavalier was considered the proper image for what the South was about, with General Lee as its embodiment, *sans peur et sans reproche.*

To what extent, however, *was* the figure of the Cavalier an accurate symbol of the nature of the Old South's leadership? Taylor doesn't think it very accurate at all, as we have seen. But if Eugene Genovese's findings about the Southern planter gentry are to be credited, then there would appear to be considerable validity in the distinction that the Cavalier-Yankee dialectic represents. The Old South is seen as governed by a paternalistic squirearchy holding significantly different social assumptions from those of, say, a Pennsylvania steel-mill proprietor who assumed no responsibility whatever for his labor force's welfare when not able to work, sought to drive wages as low as possible, and judged moral probity by the condition of one's bank balance. In Genovese's words, "At their best, Southern ideals constituted a rejection of the crass, vulgar, inhuman elements of capitalist society. The slaveholders simply could not accept the idea that the cash nexus offered a permissible basis for human relations. Even the vulgar parvenu of the Southwest embraced the plantation myth and refused to make a virtue of necessity by glorifying the competitive side of slavery as civilization's highest achievement."[17] Granting that the actuality did not always conform to the ideal, Genovese would insist that the qualitative distinction between Northern capitalist and Southern planter was genuine. Southern society before the Civil War was governed by a Master Class whose members, transformed by their patriarchal stewardship of property, abjured the cash nexus as their sole link with their work force.

Were there in actual fact any such sectional difference, however, and any such Master Class or gentry? If so, of whom was it composed, and how did it get there? The Old South, Allen Tate

---

17. Genovese, "The Slave South: An Interpretation," *The Political Economy of Slavery* (New York: Vintage Books, 1967), 519.

has said flatly, "once had aristocratic rule."[18] That may be; but it depends on the definition of what constitutes an "aristocracy." Admittedly there was, throughout the states of the Old South, a devotion to the plantation ideal; and undeniably it exercised a hold upon the Southern imagination considerably in excess of the statistical incidence of actual slaveowning planters. Had it not done so, it is highly unlikely that the political representatives of the region in the United States Congress would ever have been so wholeheartedly committed to the cause of slavery expansion into the territories, an issue that had little actual relevance for the non-slaveholding majority of Southern voters. Indeed, without such an ideal to shape the aspirations and ambitions of Southerners it is doubtful that secession would ever have been possible in 1860 and 1861.

Edmund Wilson has noted that William J. Grayson of South Carolina, writing to memorialize his friend and fellow Unionist James Louis Petigru, cited "the approved Carolina custom in closing every kind of career. No matter how one might begin, as lawyer, physician, clergyman, mechanic or merchant, he ended, if prosperous, as proprietor of a rice or cotton plantation. It was the condition that came closest to the shadow of the colonial aristocracy which yet remained."[19] Yet that is not a manifestation of aristocracy, so much as an aspiration to achieve and confirm a self-engineered elevation in economic and social status. In certain respects it does not seem greatly different from the desire of the modern corporation executive to claim a similar symbol of status by purchasing an estate in rural Connecticut, along the Hudson River, in Bucks County, Pennsylvania, or in the horse country to the south of Washington, D.C.

Even contemporary observers perceived that for all the talk of Cavalier heritage, the political leadership of the Old South was, by and large, not furnished by the Old Families. "Of late all of the active-minded men who spring to the front in our government," Mary Boykin Chesnut commented early in the 1860s, "were the immediate descendants of Scotch, or Scotch Irish. Calhoun, McDuffie, Cheves, Petigru, who Huguenotted his name

18. Tate, "The Profession of Letters in the South," 519.
19. Quoted in Edmund Wilson, *Patriotic Gore: Studies in the Literature of the American Civil War* (New York: Oxford University Press, 1962), 337.

[Pettigrew] but could not tie up his Irish. Hammond's father was a Yankee. And Orr—well, he is the Rudolph Hapsburg of his race."[20] It is significant that when the government of the new Confederacy was chosen, the man selected as its president had been born in a log cabin, the vice-president had been raised on an up-country farm of modest circumstance, and only two of its cabinet members were drawn from the old planter families.

What *is* clear is that, given the agricultural economy of the Old South, the plantation ideal did play a notable part in shaping the economic and social aspirations of regional life. The availability of new land to the southwest—Georgia and Tennessee, then Alabama and Mississippi, next Arkansas, northern Louisiana, and East Texas—and the almost certain financial rewards of large-scale cotton culture on that land had the effect of retarding the development of cities and manufactures and of directing the energies of ambitious Southerners toward the acquisition of slaves and acreage. The westward movement also postponed any real confrontation between planter and small farmer, and ultimately wrecked the alliance that had formed between Southern and Midwestern agriculture and Eastern labor and small business during the first four decades of the century, and which had been the basis for the strength of Jacksonian democracy. Once that took place, the coming of secession and civil war was inevitable; the only barrier to the break between South and North was self-restraint, a commodity that by the mid-1850s had all but disappeared from American politics.

5.

An aspiration, however, is not necessarily rooted in an actuality, and I have considerable trouble with the notion that a Master Class actually existed in the Old South with "seigneural" (to use Genovese's term) attitudes toward the ownership of slaves, a disdain for the cash nexus as the ruling factor in human relationships, or imbued with faith in a "hierarchical" order based securely and lastingly on the ownership of slave property. What I should like to know, to repeat, is where the membership of such a

20. *Mary Chesnut's Civil War*, ed. C. Vann Woodward (New Haven and London: Yale University Press, 1981), 366.

Master Class came from, and what actual evidence we have that it ever importantly existed.

One might assume that the old slaveholding families of tidewater and piedmont Virginia, having endured longest as a landed gentry, should have become most nearly emancipated from their bourgeois origins and the cash nexus, and have come closest to embodying the patriarchal responsibilities of a Master Class. How then do we account for the fact that from the early 1800s on up through the 1840s, the largest and most profitable export of the Old Dominion was slaves to the Deep South? Surely such a fact equates very oddly with the enforcement of a paternalistic ethos among the planter class. To break up families and sell their members off for ready cash, whatever one's personal economic needs, seems somewhat inconsistent with a refusal to permit the cash nexus to determine human ties.

To be sure, there is the instance of planters such as Thomas Dabney, who when he found his Gloucester County, Virginia, plantation facing ruin moved his entire establishment out to Mississippi in order not to have to sell off his slave property. Dabney's behavior, however, was so atypical that his daughter wrote a book about it.[21] Other Virginia slaveowners apparently had no such qualms. Surplus slaves were regularly auctioned off. Abolitionists even accused the Virginians of deliberately breeding slaves for the market, which seems unlikely. The result, however, so far as thousands of slave families were concerned, was the same. Postwar writers such as Thomas Nelson Page, in their plantation romances, gave the impression that no true Virginia gentleman would ever sell a slave unless absolutely forced to do so, and then he would see to it that the new owner was a fit custodian. This accords poorly with the plethora of advertisements of slave auctions appearing regularly in all the Virginia newspapers. (Either that, or else the incidence of true Virginia gentlemen was very low, even in Virginia.) So, if the high-minded Virginians could bring themselves to do such a thing, then what of the less firmly established converts to paternalism of the Cotton Kingdom?

21. Susan Dabney Smedes, *A Southern Planter* (London: John Murray, 1889). The American edition, entitled *Memorials of a Southern Planter*, was first published in 1887.

It might be replied, of course, that since the paternalistic code of the Master Class was based upon property and wealth, then debt and the threat of financial collapse rendered the ethos obsolete and inapplicable, transforming the sometime member of the Master Class into a disillusioned bourgeois in search of a new supply of cash nexus. But if so, the paternalistic ethos would appear to have been a fairly shallow affair.

Let me emphasize that Genovese in no way denies that economics and the pursuit of wealth lay behind the acquisition of slave labor. It was the *form* that the acquisitive urge assumed in the Old South, that by placing the slaveowner in a personal stewardship relationship with his labor force created the patriarchal situation and its Master Class ethos, that is important.

Now if the Old South was indeed dominated by a Master Class with significantly different attitudes toward property, ownership, and the like, one would expect that as this class developed, so it began to know its own mind, and to tighten its oligarchal control over government in order to ensure its hegemony in perpetuity, and to safeguard itself from any future leveling efforts by the lower orders of whites. But what are the facts? They are as follows:

1. Throughout the antebellum decades, U.S. Census reports show, there was a growing preponderance of a middle class in every Southern state, and a relative decline in the domination of large estates.

2. The franchise was being progressively extended to all white males throughout the period.

3. Property requirements for voting were being eliminated. By the 1850s not a single Southern state any longer placed restrictions having to do with wealth or landownership on the right to vote. Only South Carolina still limited the holding of public office to owners of property.

4. Throughout the 1840s and 1850s there was a steady increase in expenditures for public schools in the South. It was still inadequate, but it was very much on the rise.

5. When the Master Class, if we are to believe in its existence, succeeded finally in bringing about secession from the Union in order to preserve and augment its hierarchical slave empire, it formed a government and adopted a constitution which, in

William R. Taylor's words, "in no sense meant to set up an aristocracy, and in certain ways . . . provided more assurance of popular government than the federal constitution."[22]

What a strange Master Class was this.

When sectional cleavage ultimately resulted in secession and war, one might expect that if a Master Class dominated the Southern states, its presence would have a significant effect upon the conduct of the war and its aftermath. (That the Confederate regiments actually *elected* their leaders during the early years of the fighting would seem rather odd, especially since the non–Master Class, petit bourgeois Northern regiments did no such thing.) But what is remarkable is the matter of *how* the South lost the war. No important battle, for example, was ever lost for want of munitions and supplies. From beginning to end there was ample manpower available in the South to people its armies. The Union blockade of the seacoasts was never effective enough seriously to cut off a steady flow of needed supplies from abroad, so long as there was uncaptured Confederate coastline to receive the supplies. The leading military commanders had attended the same Military Academy at West Point, learned their trade in the same army, fought their battles with similar tactics, and conducted charges, flanking movements, counterattacks, and withdrawals in the same way.

What finally brought down the Confederacy, as C. Vann Woodward has suggested recently in a masterly review-essay,[23] was the *will* to persevere and win. It did not believe strongly enough, or single-mindedly enough, in the righteousness of its cause. The perpetuation of slavery was an inadequate rationale for separate nationhood, and caused guilt in too many people's minds. When battle casualties began mounting, and prospects for a reasonably quick decision eroded, morale commenced to collapse, desertion became endemic, the war effort disintegrated. For a nation supposedly controlled by a resolute, mature Master Class, this was odd behavior.

22. William R. Taylor, *Cavalier and Yankee: The Old South and American National Character* (New York: George Braziller, 1961), 340.

23. C. Vann Woodward, "Gone with the Wind," review of Richard E. Beringer, Herman Hattaway, Archer Jones, and William N. Still, Jr., *Why the South Lost the Civil War* (Athens: University of Georgia Press, 1986), *New York Review of Books*, July 17, 1986, pp. 3–4, 6.

The collapse was not a matter of a dedicated Master Class of slaveholders proving unable to keep the rank and file properly zealous for the cause. The misgivings, the doubt, suppressed consciously but perceptible obliquely, of the soundness of the Confederate enterprise, the absence of a single-minded, all-devouring passion for the survival of the new nation, are visible throughout the diaries, journals, and letters of the period, almost all of them written by persons of slaveholding status. Even the very work that Lewis Simpson cites to illustrate Henry Timrod's celebration of a sacramental, hierarchical society based upon slavery, the poem "Ethnogenesis," shows this quite clearly. The penultimate stanza, which begins "Nor would we shun the battlefield" and contrasts Northern avarice, deceit, hypocrisy, and materialism with Southern honor, faith, charity, and loftiness of motive, concludes with these lines:

> To doubt the end were want of trust in God,
> Who, if he has decreed
> That we must pass a redder sea
> Than that which rang to Miriam's holy glee,
> Will surely raise at need
> A Moses with his rod!

The closing stanza begins, "But let our fears—if fears we have—be still," then moves into the passage Simpson quotes.[24] Lines such as those just cited, in a poem aimed at the joyous celebration of the birth of Southern nationhood and written in 1861 before military defeat had tarnished hope of an easy separation, reveal the ambivalence lying behind the poet's proud boasts.

In the same year in which "Ethnogenesis" was composed, 1861, Timrod wrote another poem, a sonnet, "I Know Not Why," which is given over wholly to such forebodings. Composed on the eve of the war, when excitement over the new nation's prospects was high throughout the South, the sonnet proceeds to enumerate images of shipwreck, of a "gray / Dull waste" of wintry clouds at sea, "a banner drooping in the rain, / And meadows beaten into bloody clay," and closes with a vision of "faint, warm airs, that rustle in the hush / Like whispers round the body of the dead!"[25]

24. Timrod, "Ethnogenesis," *Collected Poems*, 94–95.
25. Timrod, "Sonnet: I Know Not Why," *Collected Poems*, 100.

It is quite clear that however Timrod as public poet-spokesman for the South sought to express the new nation's optimism and determination, he was in actuality by no means so confident or convinced. Timrod's war poetry is almost the only Southern verse about the Confederacy and its fight for independence that possesses any genuine literary merit; all else is rhetoric in rhymes, dependent upon the reader's ability to bring the emotion to the poem. It is precisely the ambivalence of Timrod's best work that accounts for its superiority as literature.

After the surrender in 1865, what is striking is the alacrity with which almost all Southerners not only accepted the demise of slavery but both publicly and privately expressed their relief at its passing. There are too many fervent expressions of that relief on record, made by persons of unquestioned loyalty to the Confederate cause, to attribute this phenomenon merely to political expediency or a self-serving wish to appease their conquerors. There was almost no sentiment for continuing the struggle by guerrilla warfare in the mountains following the surrender; when the capitulation orders were signed, the South laid down its arms. The number of sufficiently wealthy former slaveowners who, their hopes supposedly disappointed and their chances of establishing a nation based permanently on a hierarchical society of subordination with slavery as its foundation doomed, left the defeated South and set up in Brazil, Mexico, and elsewhere, was extremely small.

All these things, it seems to me, argue strongly against the notion that there was, in the antebellum South, a unique Master Class of slaveholding planters with a patriarchal ethos and an attitude toward society that was profoundly and qualitatively different from other Southerners or from Americans elsewhere. There was *talk* of such things; slavery was earnestly defended as a Positive Good in ingenious tracts; but most of it was only skin-deep in its ideological import. And certainly we know enough about the origins of war by now to realize how little is needed to convert relatively minor tensions and differences into armed conflict that can soon dwarf the supposed causes. There is no need to ascribe the firing on Fort Sumter and the ensuing four years of bloody conflict to any permanent, irreconcilable social and moral cleavage between North and South.

Nothing that I have said in objection to the Master Class theory is meant to suggest that white Southerners, whether slaveholders or not, did not believe in the intellectual and moral inferiority of blacks, or that following the defeat of the Confederacy they did not approve of laws such as the Black Codes that would have severely curtailed the liberties of the recently emancipated slaves. Nor is it to say that the Old South was a hotbed of participatory democracy, or to deny that men of wealth owning slaves and plantations did not exercise considerable power in public affairs, a power that certainly exceeded their voting strength. It is certainly not to deny that the ambition to achieve the Southern community's prime symbol of status, the ownership of slaves and a plantation, failed to play a part in the way that middle-class white Southerners thought, acted, and voted.

The point is, rather, that whatever the ambition or the ideal, the actuality is that the South of the pre-secession period was basically an American community, with some few great planters with inherited social position, and some others with recently acquired requisite wealth and eager for the social rank, but predominantly composed of citizens who were middle class in outlook, attitude, and ambition, engaged like other Americans in attempting to better themselves economically and socially, believing theoretically in equalitarian democracy while at the same time not without assumptions of inequality based on wealth, rank, and race.

The Old South differed from the other American regions principally because it was more abidingly rural in outlook, and because it had in its midst a vast black population, the ownership of which as chattel was accepted both because they could be better controlled and made to work that way and because, since they were black, it was considered no unacceptable abridgement of their humanity for them not to be free.

6.

The basic dialectic that informs Eugene Genovese's approach—that economic relationships must inevitably function in terms of class rivalry—forces him to envision the social and economic structure of the antebellum North and South as one of separate and implicitly hostile classes, possessed of an ideology all their own. It is this that also leads Genovese to place so much emphasis upon the proslavery rhetoric that began to be voiced in the 1830s and 1840s, and which is emblematic of the maturing of the slaveholders into a Master Class, which had achieved the "formation of a world view that authentically represented the position, aspirations, and ethos of the slaveholders as a class."[26] Such "maturation" is in obvious contrast with the views of earlier Southern spokesmen such as Thomas Jefferson, whose ownership of slave labor and dependence upon it did not usually blind him to the monstrous injustice of such ownership and the perils it held in store for American society.

Obviously what was ideologically "mature," in this sense, was politically and socially disastrous. It threw the South into confrontation with the Midwest, ruptured the agrarian alliance of Jacksonian democracy, and made possible the election of a Republican president in 1860.

The question to be asked about the proslavery argument, however, is just how seriously it should be taken as an authentic statement of Southern attitudes and beliefs. It is true that by the 1830s, after the Missouri controversy and the Nullification Crisis had brought about the first important sectional confrontations, and after the Abolitionists had begun their attacks on slavery in the South, public articulation of the Southern stance on slavery began changing. Instead of chattel slavery being depicted as an unfortunate evil with which the South found itself saddled, without much hope for an immediate solution, it now began to be depicted as a Positive Good. The biblical justification of slavery, John C. Calhoun's exposition of a Greek democracy based upon a class of menials to hew wood and draw water, the sociological arguments of George Fitzhugh, and other exercises in rhetorical ingenuity culminated in James Henry Hammond's "Mudsill" speech in the United States Senate, in which the South Carolinian declared that all higher civilization rested upon the availability of a lower class of laborers, and that chattel slavery was superior to wage slavery in virtue, because a chattel slavery society accepted the paternalistic obligation of caring for its workers from cradle to grave.

Yet to take such Positive Good theories about slavery, with

26. Eugene D. Genovese, "The American Slave System in World Perspective," *The World the Slaveholders Made: Two Essays in Interpretation* (New York: Vintage Books, 1969), 99.

their elaborate arguments and strained justification for the superior righteousness of owning Africans as property, as an index to what most Southerners, whether or not slaveholders, were thinking and feeling about slavery goes against both historical common sense and human nature. It is simply not the way that nineteenth-century (or twentieth-century) Southern Americans conceived of who they were and what they wished to be.

The one essential fact always to keep in mind about the Old South is that, massively and inescapably, slavery was a condition of everyday life. The slaves were *there*, four millions of them by 1860. The prosperity of the cotton and rice cash-crop industries seemingly was dependent upon their presence. However much slavery might be disliked by some, by others tolerated and accepted, and by some few favored and extolled, nobody quite knew what to do about it.

To almost all Southern whites, emancipation of the slaves without their removal seemed inconceivable. The colonization societies that had flourished in the late eighteenth and early nineteenth centuries died away in confrontation with the impracticability of sending a rapidly multiplying slave population back to an Africa that the majority of the slaves themselves had never known. Attempts by some few Southerners such as John Randolph of Roanoke to free their own slaves and settle them in the Midwest, the provisions for which Randolph wrote into his will, were usually failures. The free white population of the regions north of the Ohio River wanted nothing whatever to do with blacks as neighbors. And even if they had been willing, few slaveholders could contemplate casually relinquishing such extremely valuable property, without whose capacity for labor the land would be next to worthless and the planter's ability to provide for his children's future welfare severely weakened.

The white Southerners of the 1830s, 1840s, and 1850s had not invented African slavery as an institution; they had inherited it. Accustomed to its presence around them from birth onward, they could hardly be expected to learn to view it, within the matter of a decade or two, no longer as a regrettable necessity but as a searing moral wrong, a crime against God and man that must, at whatever cost in worldly goods and civil order, be stricken from the land.

It is clear that many white Southerners, including numerous

slaveholders, were uneasy with the ethics of owning human beings as property, and also that there was almost universal dislike
of certain features of slavery—as witness the social odium that
attached to slave traders. Yet the evils, financial, social, and political, that Southerners were convinced would accompany abolition were such that emancipation was held to be no realistic alter-
native. Believing as they did—and as almost all other white
Americans did—in the cultural and intellectual inferiority of Africans, they did not view slavery as an intolerable condition for
human beings who were black. That there were abuses, they admitted, but they did not think that by and large, in its everyday
manifestations, Negro slavery as customarily practiced need be
either inhumane or immoral. Mostly they just accepted it, in
much the same way as Europeans in general accepted the existence of grinding poverty and human degradation in the industrial
cities of the eighteenth and nineteenth centuries, or as residents
of New York City today, for example, accept the existence of the
black and Puerto Rican ghettos, or as white Americans of the 1920s
and 1930s accepted segregation.

The massive racism that characterized American life everywhere in the eighteenth century and earlier was what had made
chattel slavery possible in the first place. Most white Southerners
had not seriously questioned it then, or felt any need to be on the
defensive about its existence. Then, almost overnight, with the
controversy over the admission of Missouri into the Union, it
became an active political issue, while at the same time the
development of the cotton gin was making slave labor more re-
munerative, and the opening of the Indian lands in the Old Southwest offered the opportunity to ambitious middle-class white
Americans to become wealthy. During the 1820s, 1830s, 1840s,
and 1850s the Peculiar Institution, as it began to be called eu-
phemistically, came under ever more savage attack, first by ex-
tremists who were considered to be the lunatic fringe, then by
more practical politicians, until finally the expansion of slavery
became the burning political issue of the day.

Placed on the political and moral defensive, faced with the
rapid growth of an antislavery movement, Southerners were as-
sailed as willing participants in evil. Not knowing themselves
what to do about a deeply entrenched, financially profitable in-

stitution of long standing, is it cause for wonder that when they were presented with ingeniously conceived theories that depicted slavery not only as an inescapable economic *fact* but as morally and socially *good*, they welcomed such arguments? And that when attacked for being slaveholders, they sometimes attempted to counter with those arguments?

One has only to recall the attitude of numerous white Southerners to such seemingly "objective" and "scientific" defenses of racial segregation during the 1950s as the Putnam Report to understand the role of such concoctions. Most of the people who passed around copies of the Putnam Report did not believe so much what it "demonstrated" about race and history, as what it represented: "scholarly" rationale for what one thought, or in any event *wanted* to think. In the same way, the various installments and versions of the proslavery argument can best be thought of as filling a like role: intellectual rationalization of a social and economic actuality—in short, sophistry.

To recognize the existence of such material and the uses it served is a very different thing, however, from accepting the contention that the bulk of the citizenry of the antebellum South, as a political and social entity, were so convinced of the positive moral, social, and ethical beneficence of slavery that its members were resolved upon confirming the Peculiar Institution as the keystone of a society "built securely, permanently, unqualifiedly" upon human slavery, as Lewis Simpson describes their ideological goal, or that they joined with poets such as Timrod in solemnly envisioning the extension of such a society as the proper and logical way of ensuring that the laborers "The whole sad planet o'er" would not go hungry.

One might just as properly believe that the tobacco growers of eastern Virginia and North and South Carolina today, faced with increasing scientific evidence that cigarette smoking is dangerous to health, yet dependent upon tobacco sales economically, really believe that cigarette smoking is positively *good* for health. They would, however, happily read and distribute the Tobacco Institute's ingenious "refutations" of reports by the surgeon general, to show that the issue was not completely resolved. What they would really prefer, however, is for someone to come up either with a new crop that would profitably and efficiently replace tobacco cultivation, or else with a method of curing or preparing tobacco that would remove the hazard to health. Until and unless that happens, they will go on growing tobacco until forbidden to do so, and grasp at any comfort they can take against its critics.

Roughly, that was the way it was with the use of slave labor.

It is difficult for me to accept the importance that acute students of the Old South such as Genovese, Simpson, C. Vann Woodward, and David H. Donald have placed on the writings of the proslavery apologist George Fitzhugh, whose two books, *Sociology for the South: or, The Failure of Free Society* (1854), and *Cannibals All! or, Slaves Without Masters* (1857), advanced a theory of society that proposed the enslavement not only of all available blacks but the poor whites of the South as well, as necessary to the establishment of a stable social and economic order.

Simpson describes Fitzhugh as "the most brilliant and ruthlessly logical mind of the Southern clerisy."[27] But if George Fitzhugh was brilliant, it was the brilliance of a gifted crackpot. His arguments can be seen as "logical" only if divorced from all relationship to the actualities of the society he lived in and the human beings who made up the social reality to which his theorizing was intended to apply. It is no wonder that Southern proslavery intellectuals such as William Gilmore Simms were appalled at Fitzhugh's polemics. Not only did what Fitzhugh proposed fly in the face of much Western moral and social thought from at least the Renaissance onward, but it was crudely developed and ahistorical in its premises and conclusions. If one accepts the dialectic of class that underlies Genovese's thinking, it is possible to view the ideological extremity of a Fitzhugh as logical, the articulation of a ruling class's ultimate premises. But only an abiding belief in the primacy of class ideology could thus discount the racial and psychological as well as political absurdity of what Fitzhugh was proposing. The notion that poor whites as well as blacks should be enslaved can be termed logical only if one views all considerations and contexts except that of strict economic determinism as either extraneous or meaningless.

The truth is that, far from being any kind of ultimate spokes-

27. Lewis P. Simpson, *The Dispossessed Garden: Pastoral and History in Southern Literature* (Athens: University of Georgia Press, 1975), 61.

man for the mind of the antebellum South, George Fitzhugh may best be understood as a prime specimen of the village crank. He is to Southern intellectual history what the Marquis de Sade is to French social thought.

7.

I have undertaken so lengthy an excursion into the social and political history of the Old South, without regard to its specific relevance for the understanding of antebellum Southern literature, in order to show the dubiousness of the assumption that there could have existed in the Old South an important paternalistic class of slaveholders whose aspirations, attitudes, and view of human nature were so strikingly different from those of other Americans living in the Northeast and the Midwest at the same time. The fact that the immediate antecedents of those other Americans were the same as theirs, that they had recently cooperated with other Americans to win their independence, establish a nation, frame its laws, and then govern it through political parties that became sectional in allegiance only on the very eve of the Civil War, seems not to matter very much to advocates of the Master Class interpretation. We are asked to believe that overnight, as it were, a vast qualitative social and ideological difference came about. For proof we are given the published proslavery tracts of the period—works offering the controversial, tortured, and twisted logic of polemical apologia. These, we are told, constitute the deepest beliefs of the Master Class; this was the society they were engaged in building. It is as if one were to take the writings of the early church fathers and insist that the attitude toward sexual desire expressed therein was an accurate guide to what most Christians thought about the nature of procreation.

Had the population of the Old South been so stratified that such a separate and unique Master Class of slaveholders *could* actually have existed, it seems to me highly unlikely that Lewis Simpson's perceptive explanation of why the antebellum Southern writer failed to participate importantly in the American Renaissance of the 1840s and 1850s would then apply. The American writer, it will be recalled, is seen by Simpson as a member of the beleaguered clerisy devoted to the pastoral vision in the face of the technological materialism of the nineteenth century, and engaged in a struggle to assert the humanistic ethos while also remaining loyal to a democratic society with a secular and materialistic set of objectives. The inherent contradictions that such a stance involved brought forth the literary classics of the 1840s and 1850s. But because the Southern author shared in his society's slaveholding ideal, and promulgated the vision of a sacramental, hierarchical community of order and stability, based upon permanent social stratification and slavery, and dedicated to feeding and clothing the world's needy, he was in turn alienated *from* the clerisy's abiding alienation, and could not take part in the principal creative dynamics of the nineteenth-century literary imagination.

Why, one wonders, did not this alienation from alienation result, in turn, in a literature such as that of Restoration and Augustan England, satirizing the incongruities, contradictions, and pretensions of so momentous a development in the South's and the nation's intellectual and social life? One would think that the very existence of Genovese's firmly established Master Class, confident of its goals, would have almost guaranteed a literary situation. The writers were in residence; they were publishing an abundance of prose and poetry throughout the period. Surely so cohesive and mature a community, which supposedly knew its mind so well, would have risen to the occasion and produced its own self-scrutinizing critique. If the writer of the Old South was foursquare in his allegiance to the vision of the redemptive society based on slavery, and this in turn alienated him from the alienated Western clerisy, one might expect that separation to produce some genuine expression in the form of stories and poems—if not an *Absalom and Achitophel* or a *Dunciad*, then at least a *Hudibras*. But nothing of the sort exists that is of any literary vitality; that secure, highly literate Master Class, with its seigneural, paternalistic vision of the hierarchical society, apparently had nothing to say to or for itself of a literary nature. The Old South literati's addiction to the form and rhetoric of Augustan England is well known, but not once to my knowledge did an antebellum Southern author ever manage to infuse any real life and vigor into them. The sterile heroic couplets of William J. Grayson's *The Hireling and the Slave* (1856) carry neither passion nor plausibility with them as they limp along.

There is a far more believable explanation of the antebellum Southern literary and social situation, it seems to me. What happened in the Old South from the eighteenth century onward was that the particular features of climate and soil, acting upon the American middle-class drive to pursue its newfound opportunities and better its lot in a new continent, produced not a Master Class ethic with a different world view, but a highly characteristic goal of success, fulfillment, and the good life that took the form of the planter *ideal*—the dream of the plantation. In that direction—and geographically it was generally westward—lay achievement, fulfillment. Its lineaments are first sketched in works such as Simms's *The Yemassee* (1835), Baldwin's *The Flush Times of Alabama and Mississippi* (1853), and Timrod's "The Cotton Boll" (1861), and skillfully dissected a century later in Faulkner's *Absalom, Absalom!* (1936).

That the dream of the great plantation was just that—an aspiration, and not a firmly established characteristic of Southern life solidly and lastingly grounded in generations of aristocratic experience and providing a fixed viewpoint from which to observe the world—is what is at issue. No mere quibble about terms is involved, but a fundamental distinction. For the plantation *ideal*, as a goal powerfully coveted and imagined, is a middle-class affair, representing a normally acquisitive society's hopes. If materialistic in the terms of its fulfillment, it was no more exclusively so than other American aspirations. Place it in the context of twentieth-century American literature and it would fit the situation of Scott Fitzgerald's Jay Gatsby equally as appropriately as of William Faulkner's Thomas Sutpen.

If this is true, then it means that the so-called mind of the Old South can best be understood not as something radically and organically different from American thought and experience, but as an integral manifestation of these. It means, too, that most of the fatuous proslavery rhetoric of the 1840s and 1850s, the strident and even hysterical demands for the expansion of slave territory and the talk of a slave empire that would annex Mexico and the sugar islands, far from constituting any sign of realistic maturity on the part of a Master Class, represented the increasingly frenzied effort to sustain an economy that in the older seaboard South was already in disarray. The Chivalry, as they called themselves, were not paternalistic aristocrats for the most part, so much as middle-class landowners, lawyers, and merchants striving to better themselves and to emulate socially what was left of the tidewater Virginia and low-country South Carolina colonial gentry.

To say as much is not to demean or belittle the society of the Old South. It is not even to suggest that the Old South was notably deficient in the virtues of which human beings can be capable, any more than it would be accurate to suggest that those non-slaveholding middle-class Americans who lived in the North and the Midwest were deficient in human virtues because they chose for their symbol of success the businessman, the railroad builder, the industrialist, the professional men of their time. Certainly the forms that such aspiration took, whether in North or South, were flawed. Sadly, the flaw in the Southern model seems particularly reprehensible to us; but it was history and geography, not greater moral depravity, that bequeathed it.

A former Whig congressman made the point very well indeed in a speech in Peoria, Illinois, in 1854. The Southern people, Abraham Lincoln told his audience,

are just what we would be in their situation. If slavery did not now exist amongst them, they would not introduce it. If it did now exist amongst us, we should not instantly give it up. — This I believe of the masses north and south — Doubtless there are individuals on both sides, who would not hold slaves under any circumstances; and others who would introduce slavery anew if it were out of existence. . . .

When southern people tell us they are no more responsible for the origin of slavery, than we; I acknowledge the fact. When it is said that the institution exists, and that it is very difficult to get rid of it, in any satisfactory way, I can understand and appreciate the saying. I surely will not blame them for not doing what I should not know how to do myself.[28]

It seems to me that anyone who has had much exposure to the ways that twentieth-century Southerners thought and think—and after all, the Southern leadership that persons of Lewis Simpson's and my vintage grew up with during the 1920s and 1930s was only the first generation in which the Confederate veterans no

28. Abraham Lincoln, "The Repeal of the Missouri Compromise and the Propriety of Its Restoration: Speech at Peoria, Illinois, in Reply to Senator Douglas, October 16, 1854," in *Abraham Lincoln: His Speeches and Writings*, ed. Roy P. Basler (Cleveland and New York: World Publishing Co., 1946), 291.

longer played an active role—should be able to understand what William R. Taylor is referring to when he points out the considerable difference between the thinking of the average citizen of the antebellum South and that of an intellectual theoretician such as Beverley Tucker of Virginia: "At no time, I suspect, was the Cavalier ideal as it was defined by Beverley Tucker, for example, widely understood or embraced by Southern planters in general, to say nothing of other people living in the South."[29] And as for Judge Tucker himself, here was no secure aristocrat engaged in formulating and purifying the language of his matured Master Class, but, as anyone familiar with his life knows, a frustrated ideologue hungry for the political power and renown he believed that his rank, intellect, and ancestry warranted, and engaged in attempting to focus attention upon himself through enunciation of a set of extremist views on the merits of the Peculiar Institution.

If we think of the antebellum South as a nineteenth-century middle-class American community, saddled by climate, inheritance, and economics with a cash-crop agriculture dependent on African slavery for the gang labor needed, not knowing what to do about it but without any wish to commit economic hara-kiri, and so constituted that the economic and social unit of the plantation came to be the emblem of Success and the Good Life, then the place of the Southern author within his community becomes understandable. He was indeed, as Lewis Simpson contends, alienated from alienation, because the plantation, after all, provided the obvious scope and subject for the pastoral rebuke that the embattled clerisy would administer to materialistic, disorderly nineteenth-century society. Yet not only was it a *slave* plantation, but its role in the community was a symbol and seal of the very acquisitiveness and social mobility that it is supposed to rebuke! Surely this is a plausible explanation for what brought about that alienation-from-alienation that Simpson so perceptively identifies.

Given the fact that there was in the Old South an insufficient literary audience to make possible the full-fledged development of a Southern branch of the Republic of Letters, made up of a

29. Taylor, *Cavalier and Yankee*, 340.

group of practitioners and readers who might bring about any kind of institutionalized professional literary situation, what was the Southern author to do? He might, like Poe, earn his meager bread as a literary journalist in the Northeast. Or, like John Pendleton Kennedy, he could get so involved in Maryland politics and business that the best he would have time for in the literary line was a confused plantation idyl-satire such as *Swallow Barn* (1832), which reflected his own ambivalence about what the plantation and slavery were and should be. Or, like Simms, he could make his literary vocation and form his professional friendships in the North, while simultaneously pursuing his ardent quest for social and political status and distinction at home in South Carolina, and generally—until the sectional crisis drove him into a frenzy— keeping the two activities separate, with only oblique and sporadic exploration of the contradictions that were involved.

The price that this provincial, ancillary status exacted of the Southern man of letters, it seems to me, included at least one very important limitation. There could not be any kind of intensive imaginative scrutiny of the individual *on the land* as contrasted with the individual *as citizen*. It is not only that the growing sectional political crisis made it unpatriotic to criticize anything having to do with the issue on which that crisis revolved, slavery. Nor is it simply that, as Simpson properly notes, there was an insufficiently large intellectual community. There would have been dissent from the ban on discussion of slavery, and, tiny intellectual community or not, there would still have been *something*. More important than these, I think, was the fact that the dream of the plantation, the imaginative ideal of the society, the symbol of social and material achievement, *itself involved nature, the life on the land, as a central ingredient.*

To see man solitary in nature, on the land, in contrast with and opposed to man *in* society and confronted by its restraints upon freedom, was the most potent, dynamic, imaginatively stimulating insight of the early nineteenth-century American Romantic mind. Whether for purposes of tragedy, comedy, or pastoral rebuke, it is this theme that dominates the literature of the American Renaissance. Such was only to be expected in a nation that was actively, energetically, and often painfully engaged in transforming a virgin continent into a middle-class commercial and industrial republic. But for the Southerners the dream of freedom from social constraint, of life on the land, was inescapably linked *with* human bondage. Nature, the land—these could not be separated imaginatively from slavery. The resulting confusion of image, metaphor, social ideal was more than sufficient to stifle any kind of sustained dialectic within the literary imagination. *For a writer to explore the meaning of individual freedom on the land was inevitably to come up against the existence of slavery as a powerful component of that experience.*

That state of affairs is what Lewis Simpson is describing when he says of the Southern literary clerisy that it was alienated from alienation. It existed, I think, not because of any real Southern commitment to a redemptive, salvific society of order and permanent social gradation. Rather, the very stuff and symbol of individual, spiritual freedom from society, with its constraints, conformities, and compromises, itself involved precisely those elements.

Had the Old South really been a reversion to a pre-industrial, medieval-like social order with an assured aristocracy, on the European model, as Allen Tate claimed, then the demands upon the literary sensibility would have been quite different. A classical or, in any event, neoclassical literary response would have been appropriate, and the presence of African slavery within nature would have constituted no important restriction on the imagination. But the Old South was no such thing, and its authors spoke with the voice and authority bequeathed to them by English and American Romanticism, just as the Southern economy was itself no feudal enclave but an integral part of nineteenth-century industrial society.

" 'Who's over me?' " demands Captain Ahab in Melville's *Moby-Dick*. " 'Truth has no confines.' "[30] And he does not wait for an answer. But how would an antebellum Southern author be able to explore that quintessentially Romantic question? Why would an ambitious young Southerner such as William Gilmore Simms, whose social and cultural goal was to be a plantation owner, even *want* to do so?

---

30. Herman Melville, *Moby-Dick, or The White Whale* (New York and Toronto: New American Library, 1961), 167.

Poor Simms! Hard-toiling Southern man of letters that he was, he wanted his rural seat at Woodlands in South Carolina to be the equivalent of Wordsworth's Lake Country, a place where, like his friend Bryant, he might hold communion with nature in its visible forms and report its various language. But in his best poem, one of the few ever remembered any more, he must portray nature as a swamp, where "A rank growth / Spreads venomously round, with power to taint." In such a place, human history itself can mean little: "Vast skeletons / Of forest, that have perished ages gone, / Moulder, in mighty masses, on the plain." Snakes, alligators conceal themselves to await their opportunities. A butterfly, in search of a place to rest, inadvertently lands atop the head of the all-but-submerged alligator:

> The surly mute
> Straightaway goes down; so suddenly, that he,
> The dandy of the summer flowers and woods,
> Dips his light wings, and soils his golden coat,
> With the rank waters of the turbid lake.

The errant butterfly can discover no "innocent flowers of beauty, no delights / Of sweetness free from taint":

> He nothing sees but sadness—aspects dread,
> That gather frowning, cloud and fiend in one,
> As if in combat, fiercely to defend
> Their empire from the intrusive wing and beam.

Whereupon the butterfly departs the scene, "speeds with free flight, warning us to seek / For a more genial home" than is offered there. "The example of the butterfly be ours," the poet counsels.[31] In other words, when in search of art let us look elsewhere than at what we see here before our eyes. Perhaps without intending to, Simms made his poem into an allegory of the writer in the South.

Thus did it go for that most energetic and devoted of Southern authors, seeking to heed his muse in the Old South in the year

---

31. William Gilmore Simms, "The Edge of the Swamp," in Richard Beale Davis, C. Hugh Holman, and Louis D. Rubin, Jr. (eds.), *Southern Writing, 1585–1920* (New York: Odyssey Press, 1970), 489–91.

1840 as the presidency of Martin Van Buren drew to a close. As was true of Hemingway's fisherman on the Big Two-Hearted River, there was so much that Simms could not afford to look at, standing there where he must, and where his young friend Henry Timrod would find himself standing in the year when the war came, at the edge of the swamp.

II. THE DREAM OF THE PLANTATION
Simms, Hammond, Charleston

It is that mournful, desolating apathy that we deplore—that wretched
listlessness, without discontent as without will, that leaves the mind
and genius of a people in complete abeyance:
> *"Like that fat weed*
> *That hugs itself at ease by Lethe's wharf,"*

That not only knows nothing, but seeks nothing from hope, adventure,
art or enterprise; that sluggishly droops beside its morass, and asks
no higher privilege from fate than the frequent wallow at once in the
sunshine and the bog! . . . This has been the reproach of the South for
a half century.
> —[William Gilmore Simms,] "Literary prospects of the South,"
> *Russell's Magazine,* June, 1858

Charleston, fat weed that roots itself on Lethe wharf . . .
> —Thomas Wolfe, *Look Homeward, Angel* (1929).

The writings of William Gilmore Simms of South Carolina are
little read today. In his heyday as a novelist, however, during the
1830s and 1840s, he was one of the best known and most respected of all American authors, with a literary reputation that
extended across the Atlantic Ocean, and he occupied a leading
place in the literary life not only of South Carolina and the South
but New York City as well. In Joseph V. Ridgely's words, "as the
South's one enduring professional, Simms was for most readers
the ante-bellum author. Certainly he contributed far more to the
Southern literary scene than he received in return."[1]

Simms's father was an Irish immigrant who married into a
family of some substance in Charleston, South Carolina, though
it was not part of the Charleston establishment. When he was two
years old his mother died, and the grief-stricken father left his
child in charge of his mother-in-law and departed for the frontier.
The plan was for the future novelist's grandmother to bring him
west after the elder Simms was established there, but she de-

1. Joseph V. Ridgely, *William Gilmore Simms* (New York: Twayne Publishing
Co., 1962), 33.

clined to do so. A bizarre episode has been described in which, when the young Simms was ten years old, his father sent his brother, Simms's uncle, back to Charleston armed with a power of attorney to fetch his son westward. The grandmother refused to give up the boy, whereupon the uncle attempted to seize the child on the street and carry him away. The young Simms threw himself on the ground and shrieked until neighbors came to his rescue. At a court hearing the judge left the decision up to Simms, who would not leave his grandmother. Several years later the elder Simms, by then well established in Mississippi and a veteran of fighting under Andrew Jackson against the British and the Indians, came back to Charleston on a visit, but apparently did not seek to persuade his son to join him.

When Simms was not yet twenty, in 1824 or 1825, and was preparing to study law, he did make a trip to visit his father in Mississippi, spending some months at the elder Simms's plantation and visiting among the Indian tribes. Urged by his father to stay, he declined, whereupon the elder Simms is quoted by his son as having responded:

"Return to Charleston! Why should you return to Charleston, where you can never succeed in any profession, where you need what you have not,—friends, family, and fortune; and without these your whole life, unless some happy accident should favor you, will be a mere apprenticeship, a hopeless drudging after bread. No! do not think of it. Stay here. Study your profession here, and pursue it with the energy and talent which you possess, and I will guarantee you a future, and in ten years a seat in Congress. Do not think of Charleston. Whatever your talents, they will there be poured out like water on the sands. Charleston! *I know it only as a place of tombs.*"[2]

The youthful Simms, however, was bent on returning home, marrying his sweetheart, and making a career there, not in the law, as it turned out, but in journalism and then in letters. Three decades later, he expressed his regret at not having taken his father's advice.

The question of Simms's relationship to Charleston is an interesting one. A. S. Salley, who wrote the sketch of Simms's life for

2. Quoted in William P. Trent, *William Gilmore Simms* (Boston and New York: Houghton, Mifflin and Co., 1892), 17.

the edition of Simms's letters published in 1952,[3] from which some of the information cited earlier is drawn, insists that the notion that he was of humble birth and lowly circumstance, and that throughout his life he was ignored and looked down upon by the Charleston gentry because of his plebeian Irish origins, has been greatly exaggerated, notably by William Peterfield Trent in his life of the novelist (1892).[4] Trent's thesis was that Simms was a victim of the slaveholding South's undemocratic values and its belief in class distinctions, and that the city of Charleston, which was notorious for its social rigidity, was by all odds the worst offender of all. Trent was thus disposed to accept Simms's outbursts over Charleston's ingratitude at face value. His biography was an early manifestation of the progressivist attitude common among early twentieth-century Southern liberals, and in part a defensive response to indictments of Southern backwardness and racial intolerance by outsiders. Trent obviously felt a need to dissociate himself from the region's historical attitudes. The index to the biography, under the entry of Charleston's "indifference to Simms," contains no less than twenty-eight page citations.

Salley, however, was of an old South Carolina family, and proud of his social credentials; in a "mug book," Who's Who in South Carolina, 1934–1935, he lists as among his attainments that of "Member St. Cecilia Society of Charleston for 40 years,"[5] thus demonstrating his right to belong to that sacrosanct social organization. As an admirer both of Simms and of Charleston, he was obviously eager to find that the novelist had been highly honored and accepted in the city throughout his lifetime, and that Simms's frequent assertions to the contrary were attributable less

3. Alexander S. Salley, "Biographical Sketch," in The Letters of William Gilmore Simms, collected and edited by Mary C. Simms Oliphant, Alfred Taylor Odell, and T. C. Duncan Eaves (Columbia: University of South Carolina Press, 1952–56), I, lix–lxxxix. This five-volume edition, together with a recent Supplement edited by Oliphant and Eaves and published as Vol. VI in 1982, is the indispensable work for anyone writing on the literary history of the antebellum South. It is cited hereafter as Letters.

4. As of the time of this writing (1987), Trent's Simms remains the only biography of the South Carolina novelist, ninety-five years after it was published. Both John C. Guilds and John McCardell, however, are reportedly at work on biographies of Simms.

5. "Salley, Alexander Samuel," in Who's Who in South Carolina, 1934–1935 (Columbia, S.C.: Current Historical Association, 1935), 415–16.

to the city's social exclusiveness than to local discomfort with his sometimes ebullient deportment, and a not-unusual resentment at the failure of ordinary citizenry to appreciate the true worth of literary men. Salley cites numerous instances of Simms having been honored by his native city.

As between the two extremes, I am inclined to go along with Drew Gilpin Faust in *A Sacred Circle: The Dilemma of the Intellectual in the Old South, 1840–1860* (1977) when she makes the point that whatever may or may not have been true of the actualities of Simms's relationship with Charleston society, *he* thought himself insufficiently respected and his achievements insufficiently honored because of his failure to be of the old establishment. At various times he raged against the city's social exclusiveness. I have been told that his failure to be elected to membership in the St. Cecilia Society, the cynosure of social acceptance, vexed him considerably. (The late Jay B. Hubbell, in *The South in American Literature, 1607–1900*, declared that Simms *was* taken into that body, but if so it seems odd that A. S. Salley did not cite the fact as proof of Simms's acceptance in Charleston.)

Simms was recurrently annoyed by what he considered the city's failure to give him his due as a literary man. When the South Carolina Historical Society was formed in Charleston in 1859, he was irate because the elderly James Louis Petigru, a lawyer, was elected president, while he was named only second vice-president, even though he was by all odds the state's leading historian. He declined the post, writing to William James Rivers that "why should men be put into the chief offices who have never identified themselves with History or Literature? Why should men be selected, simply because of their social position, for the rule & dignities of institutions, who can add no lustre or dignity to their authority; who are in fact grossly ignorant. . . . I could have had *patronage* enough, if I had consented. There were fashionable people, and pretentious people, to whose salons I might have had access; but the price was *death!*"[6] (In point of fact Petigru, a longtime friend of Simms, had also made his own way in Charleston, having been born in the Up-country; but he was a college graduate, as Simms was not, and was a distinguished lawyer and writer

6. Simms to William James Rivers, June 13, 1859, in *Letters*, VI, 20–24.

on legal matters, very much respected in the city. Petigru had done his growing up elsewhere, had "Huguenotted" his name, as Mary Boykin Chesnut noted [it had been Pettigrew] before his arrival in the city, and seems to have abundantly possessed the social graces lacking in Simms's deportment. He had long since acquired his own plantation.]⁷

Simms's childhood in Charleston, under his grandmother's care, was certainly not one of luxury. His grandmother was noted for her penuriousness. Instead of being given a classical education, he was apprenticed to a druggist at the age of twelve, and was often to be seen about the city running errands. The intent apparently was to make him into a physician, but by the time he was twenty he had begun reading law at an attorney's office, and was admitted to the bar. His interest in literature, however, had long since manifested itself, and he was constantly writing and publishing verse. He founded a literary magazine, the first of numerous such involvements in editing literary periodicals. By the age of twenty-three he had married and had published his fourth book of verse—dedicated to that selfsame James L. Petigru.

Simms's admiration for Petigru—it was later to abate—was occasioned in part because of their mutual political loyalties. During the Nullification Crisis of the early 1830s, Petigru was a leading Unionist, and Simms in 1830 became editor of the *City Gazette*, a newspaper that strongly and sometimes intemperately championed Andrew Jackson and the Unionist cause. Political passions were at white heat; there were riots and fisticuffs. The Unionists were in the minority, and Simms came under savage personal attack in the Nullification organ, the Charleston *Mercury*. At one point a crowd of Nullifiers threatened to sack the plant of Simms's newspaper. The young editor, who was tall and powerfully built, stood resolutely at the door of the *Gazette* building. Accounts of just what happened vary; apparently there was some scuffling, but no damage was done. The subscription list of Simms's newspaper, however, did not survive the triumph of Nullification sentiment in Charleston, and Simms was forced to sell it.

7. James Louis Petigru is chiefly remembered today for having declined to recognize the secession of South Carolina, and for having lived in wartime Charleston until his death in 1863 without conceding that the city and the South had not gone mad.

It should be emphasized that even at this early point in his career, and although he championed the Unionist cause in the Nullification disputes, Simms was no dissenter from Southern political and racial attitudes. He believed in states' rights, in the need for solidarity in the face of Northern attacks on slavery, and in the virtues of the Peculiar Institution. In taking the Unionist side he was allying himself for the most part with the old Federalist plantation leadership. His first published book was a monody on the death of Charles Cotesworth Pinckney, signer of the Constitution and a dominant figure in the colonial and early national life of the city. It was the old-line Federalists, as Jon Wakelyn points out in *The Politics of a Literary Man*, who represented literature, culture, and the fine arts in Charleston, and who clustered about the Charleston Library Society, the city's cultural center. This gentlemanly group had admitted the talented young Simms into its gatherings and discussions. Its ranks—Judge Thomas S. Grimké, Daniel Huger, Colonel William Drayton, Stephen and William Elliott, Joel Roberts Poinsett, and, foremost of all, the distinguished Hugh Swinton Legaré, the city's leading intellectual and editor of the learned and tedious *Southern Review*—constituted a virtual rollcall of the more intellectually minded gentry of the city's early national flowering. All were Charlestonians; all owned plantations in the Low-country and town houses in the city. Petigru had long since become as one with them. These men had been nationalists and Southerners at a time when the slavery issue had not yet come to dominate politics. When the Nullification Crisis arose, their response was conservative and strongly Unionist.

Yet in allying himself with them, Simms was joining what in effect was the Party of the Past. The battle over Nullification represented a struggle for power between the older establishment and younger, ambitious men from the Up-country as well as Charleston, of whom John C. Calhoun was leader. The newcomers were much better equipped to win and hold power and influence in a state which had, if grudgingly and only partially, opened itself to the perils and opportunities of a less complacent, more democratic political arena, in what had now become the Cotton Kingdom.

If I may make a generalization which has many exceptions, what remained of the old colonial and early national leadership of Charleston probably did come as close to constituting an aristocracy as any Southern state could offer. Their city had been the fourth largest in the nation. Their considerable wealth, drawn from rice plantations, a profitable shipping business with Europe and the Northeast (including, before 1808, the importation of slave labor), and trade with the still-developing interior, provided leisure, education, the opportunities and incentives for culture. Government was firmly in their hands. The lower orders were deferential.

But by the 1810s things were changing for the worse, so far as the old Federalist establishment was concerned. George C. Rogers, Jr., describes what was happening in his excellent *Charleston in the Age of the Pinckneys* (1969). The rise of manufactures in the Northeast meant that Charleston, which had been at the center of the Atlantic world of commerce, was not at the center of the new world of industry. Sailpower gave way to steamships, and New York City became the nation's leading port, because no longer was the voyage from Europe made most rapidly and efficiently by way of the West Indies. Charleston was unable to retain its hold upon the trade of the Southeastern interior through development of an efficient system of rivers and canals and later a railroad network that could funnel the staple crop of the thriving Up-country cotton industry through Charleston rather than through Savannah and the Gulf Coast ports. There was no sustained effort to create a textile milling industry that might make it unnecessary for cotton to be shipped to New England or to France and England for manufacture into cloth. New York City proved far more resourceful, and adaptable, in its ability to use capital to develop trade with the interior.

Moreover, as the Southwest was opened to cotton culture, the basis of wealth and power shifted westward, and the state of South Carolina lagged behind. Politically the South Carolina Up-country was significantly asserting itself. No longer could Charleston expect to dominate state politics by virtue of wealth, class deference, and population.

Thus, as the slavery issue came to the forefront in American politics, first with the Missouri question and then in the form of Nullification and the tariff, and with the example of the Denmark Vesey servile insurrection of the early 1820s to fuel apprehension of a slave revolt, the city of Charleston and the state of South

Carolina became an increasingly volatile political arena. Extreme doctrines, a threatened economy, and inflammatory appeals to a disturbed electorate helped to incite what seems to have become almost a siege mentality. From the mid-1820s up the act of secession in 1860, the politics of the state conform to no national or even sectional party patterns. It was a battle of factions, all of them socially conservative in doctrine but to varying degrees radical in utterance and manifestation. To an incredible degree, life in South Carolina became politicized. Political talk, political considerations dominated everyday discourse; political criteria were the standard for judging almost everything that went on.

What all this meant was that the young William Gilmore Simms, in moving to identify himself with the old Federalist elite in Charleston as the Nullification Crisis developed in the late 1820s and 1830s, found himself on the losing side of a struggle that determined who would control South Carolina in the decades that lay ahead. The result was not only the loss of his newspaper and the acquisition of a burden of debt. It also constituted an abrupt check to his ambition to rise, by virtue of his talents and energies, into a position of leadership in a patrician community that had appeared, until then, to be governed by a cultivated elite of wealth and intellectual distinction.

He had believed that, as in the instance of Petigru before him,[8] careers would be open to young men of talent—and that the kind of talent required could be that in which his own sensibility, enthusiasm, intellect, and cultural distinction were interchangeable with the possession of inherited wealth and influence. What he discovered was that success in South Carolina politics of his day took a coarseness, a toughness in which the kind of intellectual subtlety, emotional sensibility, and cultural concern he had believed useful in achieving public distinction would be no help but a hindrance. The real political power-brokers, the men who carried the day for Nullification, were not the old Federalist gentle-

---

8. What Simms would have thought, having made his newspaper into a Unionist organ, had he known that Petigru was writing to William Elliott in 1831 that he was "in great hope that the *Gazette* will now die a natural death," can only be surmised. Petigru to William Elliott, August 25, 1831, quoted in James Petigru Carson, E.M., *Life, Letters and Speeches of James Louis Petigru: The Union Man of South Carolina* (Washington, D.C.: W. H. Lowdermilk and Co., 1920), 83.

men, but more ruthless, altogether more ardent men who placed little value upon reason and moderation, and for most of whom a concern with culture and the arts was essentially superfluous. The man of the future in South Carolina was not a Hugh Swinton Legaré or even a James Louis Petigru, but someone such as John C. Calhoun.

The young Simms was no conservative, whether in political outlook or personal temperament. His zeal for the Unionist case during the Nullification Crisis had come not from a Federalist devotion to the less democratic, patrician Republic of an earlier day, but from an enthusiasm, amounting to hero worship, for Old Hickory, Andrew Jackson, the strong-willed leader whom his father had followed into victorious battle in the Indian territory and against Pakenham's British invaders in New Orleans.

As a young man Simms was a Democrat and a Unionist living in a politics-ridden community in which the Democrats were mainly the Nullifiers and the Federalists the Unionists. It was an impossible situation. Frequently in his later years he was to express regret at not having taken his father's suggestion and left Charleston and South Carolina for the opportunities that the expanding Southwest offered to a young man of talent and energy. Had he done so, it is quite possible that, possessed as he was of a powerful streak of practicality, he would have prospered and have achieved political distinction. But that he would have been contented is dubious, for he rightly recognized that his strongest affinity was for letters, and along with it an instinct for a solidity of social texture that the far-flung settlements of the Southwest could not satisfy. It was this that so attracted him to Charleston. He wanted very much to attain a position of distinction in his native city's community life, not because it offered prestige and material prosperity as such, so much as because he saw it as constituting a social ideal in which intellect and artistic fulfillment might be combined with a sense of membership in and identification with a complex social and political community.

The shock of political and personal defeat in the Nullification Crisis must have been awesome. It was the first real setback in young Simms's career. Moreover, it was greatly intensified by a series of personal disasters. In 1830 his father died in Mississippi.

At about the same time his grandmother, to whom he remained devoted, also passed away. And on February 19, 1832, the young wife he had married five years earlier died, leaving him for family only an infant daughter. Less than four months later he was forced to sell his newspaper. All that was left to him now, it seemed, was his literary career. So, leaving his daughter with friends, he took his manuscripts and sailed for the North.

2.

That summer of 1832, Simms stayed for a while in Philadelphia, where he met Willis Gaylord Clark, a newspaper editor, humorist, and literary man. In New York City he visited a young playwright and poet, James Lawson, with whom he had already been corresponding. They formed a lifelong personal friendship. He made other friends among the literati of Gotham. He visited New England. He prepared a book-length poem, *Atalantis, a Story of the Sea*, for publication by Harper and Brothers during the coming winter. He wrote a review of Mrs. Frances Trollope's *Domestic Manners of the Americans* for the *American Literary Review*, defending American culture, manners, and religious pluralism, like the enthusiastic Jacksonian Democrat that he was, and also reading her a lecture for her failure to appreciate the institution of slavery in the South. (To a modern audience these may seem contradictory, but anyone who does not understand that in the antebellum South one could be both a vigorous advocate of chattel slavery and an enthusiastic believer in "Locofoco" popular democracy will be unable to understand the antebellum South.)

The friendships and literary associations that Simms formed that summer of 1832 and in subsequent yearly stays in New York City were such as to make him an active participant in the literary life of Gotham, which was in the process of superseding Philadelphia and Boston as the literary marketplace of the new nation. His ties with the poet and newspaper editor William Cullen Bryant, who several times visited him in South Carolina, would endure despite Bryant's antislavery views and, after a break apparently caused not by politics but a difference among their wives, even outlast the Civil War. Among the persons who became his friends were the actor Edwin Forrest, the witty physician-author John Wakefield Francis, the poet Fitz-Greene Halleck, the popular journalist-biographer Joel Tyler Headley, the journalist William Alfred Jones, the historian Benson Lossing, the novelist James Kirke Paulding, the poet-businessman Prosper Wetmore, and numerous others. Somewhat later he formed a strong professional and personal friendship with the editor Evert Duyckinck, who was endeavoring to stimulate an American literature free of European influence. He established publishing relationships with the Brothers Harper and with Carey and Lea, of Philadelphia. For close to three decades, until the war severed all relationships, Simms was a familiar figure on the New York literary scene, and after the Confederacy fell Simms's New York friends did their best to help the now-ruined South Carolina author.

Undoubtedly, during that first gratifying summer and autumn in New York in 1832, he must have thought long and hard about moving there permanently. He had what was absent in Charleston—fellow literary professionals, a market for his literary wares, a society in which success was not ultimately measured by political influence or social ties.

Yet by late October, Simms was back at home in the town of Summerville, in the pine forests north of Charleston, and writing to his friend Lawson "from my own woods. The pines are bending with their monotonous chorus, in concern with the winds all around me. Summer still lingers, and her drapery of flowers and green leaves still carpets the ground and curtains the distance."[9] Often in later years he would threaten, in moments of despondency, to pull up stakes in South Carolina and move to the North, where his literary achievements would be honored and his efforts rewarded. A typical outburst is that to his friend James Henry Hammond in 1847: "I shall determine by the Spring when I go North. Here I am nothing and can be and do nothing. The South don't care a d——n for literature or art. Your best friend & kindred never think to buy books. They will borrow from you & beg, but the same man who will always have his wine, has no idea of a library. You will write for & defend their institutions in vain. They will not bear the expense of printing your essays."[10]

But it was mostly talk, and his friends knew it, sympathized with him over the lack of appreciation, monetary or otherwise, that his native community displayed for his literary labors, but

9. Simms to James Lawson, October 25, [1832], in *Letters*, I, 41–42.
10. Simms to James Henry Hammond, December 24, [1847], in *Letters*, II, 386.

were confident that so long as Simms was alive he would remain a South Carolinian. He was never willing to forgo his membership in the Southern community for the financial and other rewards of a full-time career in literature that would have been possible to him had he set up permanently in New York. And the converse of the matter—Charleston's and South Carolina's preoccupation with politics at the expense of belles-lettres—was also a consideration: if a literary man *were* willing and able to get involved in politics, then there was a ready place for him within the political spectrum, always provided, of course, that the politics were not offensively radical.

Simms's literary affiliations in New York City, as they developed during the late 1830s and the 1840s, were generally with the Democratic editors and publications. He became deeply involved with the Young America group led by Evert Duyckinck, which championed the cause of a distinctively American literature, resisted the dominance of English literary criticism and what its members considered subservience to British taste, and called upon American authors to utilize American themes and subject matter and to be truly American and democratic in viewpoint. They were opposed by a powerful clique of Whig editors and critics who controlled the *Knickerbocker Magazine* and had considerable influence over what was published and praised. Much of Edgar Allan Poe's woe in the 1840s was caused by his heresy on the subject of Longfellow, the favorite poet of the Whig critics, whom Poe labeled an imitator and plagiarist. The young Herman Melville was also a close friend of Duyckinck and an ardent Young American partisan; his well-known review of Nathaniel Hawthorne's *Mosses From an Old Manse* in 1850 was a characteristic Young America document: "But what sort of a belief is this for an American, a man who is bound to carry republican progressiveness into Literature as well as into Life? Believe me, my friends, that men not very much inferior to Shakespeare are this day being born on the banks of the Ohio. And the day will come when you shall say, Who reads a book by an Englishman that is a modern?"[11] The unenthusiastic reception given *Moby-Dick* in 1851 was probably due as much to Melville's literary alle-

11. [Herman Melville], "Hawthorne and His *Mosses*, By a Virginian Spending July in Vermont," originally published in *The Literary World* for August 17 and 24, 1852, and reprinted in Edmund Wilson (ed.), *The Shock of Recognition: The*

giance as to the difficulty its language posed for contemporary reviewers.

Hawthorne himself was a friend of Duyckinck and a sympathizer with the group, though more remotely, for there was a strain of vulgarity and coarseness in the professions and premises of Young America, which Melville could deal with in *sotto voce* fashion and which Simms probably never even so much as suspected was offensive, but which was too much for anyone as fastidious as Hawthorne to accept.

In 1839, answering a request from his friend James Lawson for biographical material, Simms appended the following note: "You may add that I am a Democrat of the Jackson School, a States rights man, opposed to Tariffs, Banks, Internal improvements, American systems, Fancy Rail Roads, Floats, Land Companies, and every Humbug East or West, whether of cant or cunning. I believe in the people and prefer trusting their impulses, than the craft, the cupidity, & the selfishness of trades & Whiggery."[12] The comment illustrates how it was possible for a Southerner who believed in slavery to be at the same time a small-*d* political democrat and an opponent of privilege, in the 1830s and well into the 1840s. For the assorted evils that he opposes were those favored by manufacturing and mercantile interests, and at the same time went against the strict constructionist school of constitutional interpretation that the proslavery adherents favored. But as the American Midwest filled up and the trans-Mississippi was settled, good roads, canals, and railroads that could get farm products to market and American manufactured goods to the interior became important to ordinary middle-class Americans in an increasingly industrialized and urbanizing republic. The interests of the staple-crop Southern planter and the Northern and Midwestern farmer and villager diverged; and slavery became the symbol and the sticking point.

Jon Wakelyn, whose *The Politics of a Literary Man: William Gilmore Simms* (1973) is a detailed reporting of Simms's political career, takes the general approach that Simms was first, last, and

Development of Literature in the United States Recorded by the Men Who Made It, Vol. I, *The Nineteenth Century* (New York: Grosset and Dunlap, 1955), 195.

12. Simms to James Lawson, December 29, [1839], in *Letters*, I, 167.

always a Southern apologist, that his principal political and social concern was always the defense of slavery and the slaveholding South, and that his expressions of nationalism were more or less perfunctory in nature. Wakelyn makes little, therefore, of the Young America allegiance. The name of Evert Duyckinck, with whom Simms corresponded and collaborated for almost two decades, appears only once in Wakelyn's book. Yet however much Simms involved himself in public life—and his involvement was intense, long-lasting, and, from the standpoint of understanding what and who he was, extremely important—there can be little doubt that literature and letters came first for him. Merely to examine the immense quantity of his literary writings is all the evidence needed to show that it is as a literary artist who also involved himself in politics, and not a politician who wrote fiction and poetry, that he must be viewed. Certainly Simms saw himself in that light; the pathetic epitaph he composed for himself—"Here lies one who, after a reasonably long life, distinguished chiefly by unceasing labors, has left all his better works undone"[13]—refers to works of unwritten literature, not to political documents.

I see no reason, therefore, to consider Simms as anything but sincere in his patriotic literary utterances of the Young America years. William Peterfield Trent's summation, it seems to me, is, however oversimplified and one-sided, essentially correct. Simms *was* a Jacksonian Democrat; he *became* an apologist for the plantation system. In that transaction is to be found much of the meaning of antebellum Southern literature.

3.

The decade of the 1830s, when Simms first became a prominent American author, was a good one for the national letters, and not least for the Southern variety. Washington Irving and James Fenimore Cooper were the period's best-known authors, but Emerson, Hawthorne, and Longfellow were beginning to write. Throughout the decade Poe was publishing steadily. In 1835, A. B. Longstreet's *Georgia Scenes*, John Pendleton Kennedy's *Horse-Shoe Robinson*, and Simms's *The Yemassee* and *The Partisan* appeared. *The*

13. Quoted in Trent, *Simms*, 323–24.

Yemassee was Simms's third novel; *Martin Faber* had been published in 1833 and *Guy Rivers* in 1834. His books were well received, went through several editions apiece, and were reprinted in England. His annual lengthy visits to New York extended his literary acquaintance. Importantly, he had begun his use of Southern historical material in fiction. With *The Yemassee*, his first great popular success, he opened his fictional exploration of South Carolina history, choosing for his subject matter an early eighteenth-century Indian war. *The Partisan* marked the commencement of the series of Revolutionary War romances that would constitute his most substantial body of work.

The success of his literary writings elsewhere served to earn Simms increased respect at home. The Charleston newspapers reviewed his books favorably and made much of his national reputation. He discovered, too, that his defenses of slavery against the strictures of English visitors such as Frances Trollope and Harriet Martineau earned him widespread popularity in the South. He was becoming the South's literary spokesman.

In 1836 he remarried. His bride, Chevillette Eliza Roach, was the daughter of a landowner who, though not of the Charleston establishment, was a person of substance and probity. His plantation, Woodlands, located seventy-two miles from Charleston close to the railroad line between Charleston and Hamburg, South Carolina, became Simms's principal residence, although he also maintained a town home in Charleston. During the years to come he would spend the months from October through May at Woodlands, with lengthy and frequent stays in Charleston, and journey to New York in the summer, usually arriving in July and remaining until late September.

Simms had now attained a position of some standing in his native state. He was a member of the plantation gentry, and this, with his literary prestige, gave him considerable status, although Charleston itself was slow in according him the social recognition he desired. It might well be said that at this period in his life—the late 1830s and the early 1840s—he had won his way to the situation he had long coveted. He was a respected figure in the national letters, with influential connections in the Northeast. Moreover, his reputation was as a *Southern* author, writing on Southern history and Southern themes, at a time when the sectional schism had not widened sufficiently to make him less a national writer in so doing. At the same time he was very much a part of the South Carolina scene, residing on a plantation, with a town house in Charleston, writing for the Southern periodicals and editing several of them, becoming involved in state politics, with influential politician friends. The onetime apothecary's apprentice had every right to feel considerable satisfaction.

By no means, however, was Simms content to play a role merely as literary man and planter, or even as the South's literary spokesman in the Northeast. His intense and continuing involvement in literature did not preclude an active role in the everyday life of the community around him. There was always a practical side to his nature that led him to seek an outlet for his abundant energies in assorted non-literary, non-contemplative enterprises, and the intense preoccupation with politics that characterized South Carolina life made inevitable his continuing engagement in the political arena. And as the 1830s became the 1840s and the slavery issue grew ever more central, the Unionism that his Jacksonian affiliation involved gave way to a growing sectionalism in politics.

4.

In 1840 Simms became friends with James Henry Hammond, and in the years that followed, Hammond, who owned an estate near Augusta, Georgia, became his closest confidant. No relationship ever formed by Simms was more important, I think, than this one, both for good and for ill. In recent years Hammond has been the subject of an excellent biography by Drew Gilpin Faust, and a selection of his letters and those of three succeeding generations of his family have been edited by Carol Bleser into a volume, *The Hammonds of Redcliffe* (1981), which is one of the more remarkable documents of Southern history ever to be published.

Carol Bleser aptly describes Hammond as "a tough son of a bitch."[14] Brilliant, gifted, he was ambitious and self-centered, as energetic in his pursuit of wealth and distinction as ever Simms in his own (and far more admirable) way was—and ruthless as

14. Carol Bleser (ed.), *The Hammonds of Redcliffe* (New York and Oxford: Oxford University Press, 1981), 7.

well, as Simms certainly was not. If one can imagine the equivalent of an articulate, intellectually inclined version of William Faulkner's Thomas Sutpen, of *Absalom, Absalom!*, Hammond would come close to filling the specifications.

Like Simms, he was a newcomer in South Carolina society. His father was a New England–born schoolteacher, who managed to get his son into the University of South Carolina. The young Hammond taught school, then successfully practiced law. During the disputes of the early 1830s he was an ardent Nullifier. In 1834 he was elected to the U.S. House of Representatives. Many people considered him the likely successor to John C. Calhoun as the state's political leader.

Like Simms, Hammond "married up"—considerably further up, in fact, and with the quite conscious intention of forcing his way into the Low-country planter establishment. His bride, Catherine FitzSimons, was a rather homely seventeen-year-old Charleston heiress. The family opposed the union, rightly believing Hammond to be a fortune hunter, but he declined to relinquish his suit. His wife-to-be defied her family, and in 1831 they were married. Hammond acquired a dowry consisting of a 7,500-acre plantation and 147 slaves. Studying agriculture, he worked diligently and to good effect at improving the plantation's profitability, declining to use an overseer and personally directing the work of filling in swampland, fertilizing barren soil, and acquiring new acreage. Ultimately he made himself into one of the wealthiest men in the state.

In 1842 he was chosen governor of South Carolina by the legislature, and seemed about to be made United States senator next, when a scandal halted his political ascent. His wife's sister had married Wade Hampton II, a powerful figure in state politics and father of the future Confederate general. Hampton had four teenaged daughters, who spent much time at their aunt's plantation. The girls, ages thirteen to seventeen, became very friendly with their uncle; in Carol Bleser's description of what happened, "the frolics soon went quite beyond the innocent, for Hammond later wrote of all four simultaneously covering him with kisses while he enjoyed with them every intimacy, but the ultimate."[15] Even-

15. *Ibid.*, 9.

tually one of the young ladies became upset at something her uncle did, and reported what was going on to her aunt, whereupon the secret was out. When in 1846 he was being considered for the Senate, Wade Hampton II revealed to members of the legislature something of what had happened. Andrew Pickens Butler was thereupon selected in Hammond's stead, and Hammond retired to his plantation in disgrace and for the next decade stayed out of active politics.

In 1850 Hammond's wife left him, taking the children back to Charleston with her, because he had taken a slave girl as his mistress and would not give her up. Eventually Hammond agreed to have the girl transferred to Charleston as his sister-in-law's maid (!), and after a two-year estrangement his wife and children returned to the plantation. (Within two months the slave girl was back, too, though whether Hammond renewed his intimacy with her is not known.)

Throughout his life Hammond's response to scandal, disgrace, marital estrangement, and a thirteen-year hiatus in his political career consisted neither of remorse nor self-scrutiny, but of imprecation, self-pity, and sustained lamentation at the injustice and ingratitude of state, politicians, family, and fate. Thus:

I will not seek office from the State. She has committed a *great* and *wanton* outrage upon me. I don't even ask reparation for that I can do without. Before I will under these circumstances humble myself and go upon my knees to beg of her either offices or reparation, I will lay my head upon the block. She has given me the example—the first in history—of ostracizing a man for (imputed) want of chastity, but she can offer me no bribe nor inflict upon me any punishment that shall force me to sanction her sentence or succumb to it.[16]

Or, following his wife's departure to Charleston with the children: "I trace it all to the vulgar connection which Satan seduced me into forming with the vulgar Fitzsimons family whose low-Irish deceit and hypocrisy can only be compared with their low-Irish pride, selfishness and utter want of refinement and tone."[17]

In 1857, South Carolina did forgive James Henry Hammond, electing him to the United States Senate. It was there that in 1858

16. Hammond to William Gilmore Simms, August 13, 1857, *ibid.*, 28–29.
17. Quoted *ibid.*, 10–11.

he made his famous "Cotton is King" speech which so shocked Abraham Lincoln and other middle-class Northerners, in which he declared that all high civilizations were dependent upon a class of laborers to do the drudgery, and that the lower orders constituted the "very mud-sill of society and of political government."[18] (During the Lincoln-Douglas debates, Midwestern groups carried signs reading "Mudsills for Lincoln.")

A brilliant, reckless man, Hammond tyrannized over his family, constantly rebuking his sons for their failures, ingratitude, and want of initiative. When one boy wished to marry a girl who was without a sufficient fortune, he broke up the romance, without apparently a moment's reflection upon his own youthful romantic ardor. In Carol Bleser's words, he viewed his family "primarily as extensions of himself. He owned them as he owned his more than three hundred slaves, and as he viewed his black servants, so he viewed his family. He considered them not mature adults but dependents who required constant supervision, material support, and manipulation. At one point he lumped them all together as 'pensioners.'"[19]

When two years after the Mudsill speech the secession of South Carolina, which he had done so much to nurture, grew closer, Hammond drew back—not so much out of fear of the North, his biographer Drew Gilpin Faust says, as from the belief that demagogues would now take over the state and force direct election of judges and senators as well as representatives. Upon Lincoln's election Hammond's fellow U.S. senator, James Chesnut, Jr., resigned his seat, and Hammond decided regretfully that he had to follow suit. "You know the Japanese have an *ancient* custom," he wrote Simms, "which therefore must have its uses, of ripping up their own bowels to revenge an insult." Though loyal to the Confederacy once secession was a fact, he severely criticized its leadership, and when in 1864 the government, facing ruin, began impressing foodstuffs and confiscated some of his corn, he was outraged. It was inconceivable, he declared, "that I should be subjected to such humiliation & degradation at the

18. Hammond, "'Mudsill' Speech" ("Speech on the Admission of Kansas," March 4, 1858), in *Slavery Defended: The Views of the Old South*, ed. Eric L. McKittrick (Englewood Cliffs, N.J.: Prentice-Hall, 1963), 122.

19. Bleser (ed.), *Hammonds of Redcliffe*, 16.

hands of the Southern people."[20] (Vicksburg had fallen, cutting the Confederacy in two; Sherman's army was engaged in enveloping Atlanta; Grant had cornered Lee in Petersburg by then.) Despairing of the future, Hammond died that November. The day before his death, though knowing very well that his faithful retainers had turned disloyal and sullen, he summoned the slave children from the yard to sing to him, preferring, in Drew Faust's words, "to die comforted by the assumptions that had guided him for so long."[21]

Such, then, was the man who in 1840 became the close friend and confidant of William Gilmore Simms. Each man advised the other, and in times of disappointment consoled him. Simms, who possessed a detailed knowledge of South Carolina people and politics, counseled Hammond on tactics and, according to William Peterfield Trent, carefully worked over the drafts of his friend's public speeches. For his part Hammond encouraged Simms's writings, and urged him not to work so rapidly and carelessly, advising him "to penetrate again and again the inmost recesses of your subject, explore every turn & nook until it is as familiar as your daily food, & then to draw it in bold outline adding only *essential* detail, & to paint with strong, broad, harmonious and concentrated colour. There is no other way to produce a great work. And you ought to be put to death if you do not set about producing one."[22] The two men lived close enough to each other's plantations to visit from time to time, and they corresponded steadily.

Neither of them, as we have seen, was born into the gentry; each had made his way on his own, and they shared a mingled contempt for and envy of the old socially distinguished Charleston families. Both felt that their true worth was unappreciated in their communities, and that their intellectual powers merited them positions of leadership that were not forthcoming. Neither seems to have been addicted to excessive self-knowledge. We have

20. Hammond to Simms, November 13, 1860, August 24, 1864, both quoted in Drew Gilpin Faust, *James Henry Hammond and the Old South: A Design for Mastery* (Baton Rouge and London: Louisiana State University Press, 1982), 358, 374.

21. Faust, *James Henry Hammond* 382.

22. Hammond to Simms, May 19, 1845, quoted in *Letters*, III, 61n.

seen how Hammond blamed everyone but himself for his woes. While Simms labored under no such moral opprobrium as did Hammond, his estimate of his own literary performances, especially in poetry, was such that clearly he had little sense of his own limitations: "I flatter myself," he could write to Evert Duyckinck in 1853, "that my poetical works exhibit the highest phase of the Imaginative faculty which this country has yet exhibited, and the most philosophical in connection with it."[23]

Hammond valued the friendship in part because Simms, a certified author and distinguished man of letters, placed a high value on Hammond's intellectual powers, repeatedly urging him to write books and essays, assuring him that his literary style was more than adequate to the task. Although Hammond wrote very little for publication, it was good to know that Simms thought him up to the mark. Simms also assured him that, whatever his present status, the inevitable day would arrive when he would be called upon for leadership, and that meanwhile he was by no means forgotten. Frequently Simms passed on comments by persons in Charleston and elsewhere testifying to the high esteem in which Hammond was held. Moreover, he proved useful to Hammond as a sounding board for Hammond's political strategy, promoting his candidacy in Charleston and elsewhere. Most of all, Simms's friendship offered the moody, restless, dissatisfied Hammond a ready sympathy that could grasp his complexity and respond with intelligence and imagination.

As for what Simms got from Hammond, that seems obvious. He first made Hammond's acquaintance in 1840, while Hammond was one of the powers in state politics. When, in 1842, Hammond was chosen governor, Simms by then was his close confidant. Simms had made his way into the planter establishment; he had secured a national literary fame; but his friendship with Hammond put him, for the first time, in touch with political power. His own political ambitions were by no means inactive; Hammond encouraged him to pursue them. In 1844 he won election to the state legislature. Thereafter he remained deeply involved in the South Carolina political scene. Both he and Hammond resented John C. Calhoun's domination, and were con-

23. Simms to Evert Duyckinck, November 24, 1853, in *Letters*, III, 261–62.

vinced, apparently with some justification, that Calhoun feared Hammond's ascendancy and schemed to block it.

Hammond thus represented for Simms the means whereby, at first actively and thereafter by indirection, he could play a role in the public political arena. Hammond could appreciate the grasp and practicality of Simms's political intelligence; in his view Simms was no literary man dabbling in affairs of state without the realism and expertise needed to deal with the everyday world. Hammond sought his advice, took both it and him seriously. Simms expresses the nature of the relationship very well in a letter in 1846, shortly after the personal scandal that balked Hammond's elevation to the United States Senate:

If, with a cloud upon you,—with many active enemies among the strongest monied men & politicians in the state—in a time of no struggle and no difficulty, this Legislature so much the creation of your opponents,— are yet disposed so strongly to insist upon your claims—what must be the case when the crisis comes,—when the inefficiency of our public men is forced painfully upon the popular sense, and when imbecility, instead of seeking office, skulls timidly from all responsibility. That time seems to me approaching, and you have only to wait for it. A time will come when the South will need its best men, and when it will busily look them up. Whether I should then be pleased to serve with you— under you if you please, or if our people please—at home or abroad, must, I take it, be left to our friends.[24]

Like Simms, Hammond had an imaginative view of politics. For neither of them was it merely a matter of the acquisition of power. However practical their tactics, both men approached politics and political issues conceptually, as an adventure involving ideas, ideals, ideological and emotional fulfillment. As Simms wrote to Hammond in 1857, "We are both of that class of beings who cannot be content merely to Hog and Swill and Sleep; but must wrestle with thought even as we wrestle with a clear passion, which exhausts the strength in its very gratification."[25]

Indeed, for all of Hammond's seemingly calculated approach to such matters as heiress hunting, building a fortune through careful application of scientific agricultural principles to his lands and

24. Simms to Hammond, Christmas Day, [1846], in *Letters*, II, 246–47.
25. Simms to Hammond, January 23, 1857, in *Letters*, III, 491.

crops, and making the most of the political opportunities of his time, and despite his insensitivity toward the feelings of others, no one can read the letters between Simms and himself without realizing that both men were basically Romantics, and that their notions of a public career and the needs of the slaveholding South were at bottom idealistic.

There is a revealing passage in a letter to Simms in 1857, when Hammond was on the verge of being summoned from exile. Like others of their time, both of them were much interested in spiritualism, and Simms had written to tell of his consultation with a medium in the North. Hammond responded as follows:

I thought like you that I should be dreadfully shocked by communicating with the Dead. The only time I ever did it—if I did it then—I had no such feeling whatever. I think all this is pre-arranged and that the Power that permits the communication pre-arranges every thing according to our needs. I wish I could have constant communications. I am sure they would do me good. But they are not for me. I never even dream. The night my mill burnt I slept like a top. I never had a pre-monition, but from my wide-awake intellect. I am out of the pale. Isolated. Left to do my worst or best without sign or help and bound to all the Consequences. I know that with you the battle of life had been a fierce one and that all you are you are to your own powers. As to me, except those grand creatures in human form, who towered above humanity so high that human aid, or sympathy could never reach them, nor human intellect comprehend— such as Alexander and Napoleon, it seems to me that no man ever lived less comprehended, sympathized with or helped than myself.[26]

Obviously he saw himself, like Napoleon, as having a star, a destiny that was beyond everyday considerations. By such a standard of attainment did he measure himself. For both Hammond and Simms the rise from obscurity to fame and fortune was a matter of deepest imaginative aspiration; their ambitions were directed toward considerably more than material success for its own sake. They perceived themselves as destined for great achievement, and they believed themselves to be extraordinary souls who, forced to exist among others incapable of their perceptions and given to mere getting and spending, were heroically

---

26. Hammond to Simms, January 31, 1857, in Bleser (ed.), *Hammonds of Redcliffe*, 24–25.

lonely. As Drew Faust remarks of Hammond in particular, both were "nurtured on Byron and Shelley, on romantic notions of spiritual exile as well as visions of friendships that 'link *soul* to *soul.*'" Hammond, she says, "craved that intensity of feeling and intimacy of human relationship that his outward coldness and his judgmental defensiveness made all but impossible to achieve." Unlike Hammond's, Simms's own personality would seem to have been more suitable for forming close friendships, despite the assertive manner that he apparently exhibited in company. Like Samuel Johnson, he drew friends to him, and the younger literary men cherished him. Yet he was quite sincere in declaring to Hammond in 1845 that "I have never known that cordial sympathy, in any of my pursuits among men. I have been an exile from my birth, and have never learned nothing but to drudge with little hope, and to think and feel and act for myself."[27]

5.

It has been contended that had Simms lived almost anywhere except the South, and in particular South Carolina, he would have spent much less time and energy on politics, and his literary achievement would correspondingly have been greater. Whether or not this was true—in some ways I think it quite likely—it is undeniable that, living where and as he did, it would have been extremely difficult for anyone of his gifts and temperament to stay out of politics. But this is not merely because South Carolina was politically under attack during the decades before secession. It is more complicated than that.

As we have seen, from time to time Simms would grow discouraged, and either threaten to remove himself to the North or else bemoan his failure to have done so while there was yet time. Still, he never came close to doing so, and this even though it certainly would have been possible had he made the attempt. He was, after all, in effect a part of the literary scene in New York during the 1830s and 1840s; as Perry Miller demonstrates in *The Raven and the Whale* (1956), he was deeply engaged in the Young America controversy and other intra-Gotham rivalries. By the

---

27. Faust, *James Henry Hammond,* 225; Simms to Hammond, May 20, [1845], in *Letters,* II, 65.

1840s and 1850s, to be sure, his involvement in South Carolina affairs was so extensive, and in so many realms of activity, that it would have been difficult to extricate himself. But earlier on this had not been so; in 1832, following his first visit to the North, there was little in the way of commitments and obligations that bound him to South Carolina had he wished to leave. Even after his second marriage the move could have been made without any massive rearrangement of his affairs. His literary career would have prospered in New York or Philadelphia; he had friends, position, influence.

Why, then—to repeat a question posed earlier—did he not do so? Or as he himself put it, in a personal memorandum about his decision of years earlier to remain in Charleston after his father had urged him to come west, "Great God! what is the sort of slavery that brings me hither!"[28]

If one wished to play word games, one might point to the very noun that Simms chose to image his plight as the key to what it was that kept him in South Carolina: slavery. By this I mean not the Peculiar Institution as such, but the social and cultural ideal represented in the plantation—which was based on chattel slavery. Hammond's Mudsill argument is another way of expressing the same relationship; a society based upon leisure and comfort and gentility, which did not attempt to minimize its addiction to the kind of life connoted in the clichéd expression "Gracious Living," and which depended upon the availability of menials to make its blessings possible. The plantation was its emblem; the dream of the plantation was the dream of success, fulfillment, the good life. The political implication of such a dream, of course, was expansion of slavery into the territories, for only there might continuing middle-class ambition be translated into opportunity.

Early on, Simms had formed a taste for the role of gentleman-author; he wanted to be a writer, and to live the life of a respected man of letters. For Simms that kind of life involved a position of stature and status within a clearly defined and textured social community. It involved participation in the concerns of that community, and playing a part commensurate with the role of distinguished and honored citizen. His youthful models had been the

28. "Personal memorandum," October 30, 1858, quoted in Trent, *Simms*, 239.

old-line Charleston Federalists, who contributed their erudite essays to the *Southern Review*—that journal, in Jay B. Hubbell's description, of "review-articles of the quarterly type, long, substantial, learned and—for the modern reader—heavy and often tedious."[29] (Trent says they were equally as tedious for readers in their own day.) For four years, 1828 to 1832, under Hugh Swinton Legaré and the Elliotts, the *Southern Review* was published in Charleston. The young William Gilmore Simms, so far as is known, was never invited to contribute to its pages.

Simms was no amateur of letters, one of those dilettantes whom Henry Timrod described as "gentlemen who know Pope and Horace by heart, but who have never read a word of Wordsworth and Tennyson."[30] He was a professional author, proud of it, and jealous for recognition as such. But as we have seen, what he wanted very much was to enjoy an active and prominent public role, *as* a professional man of letters, *within* such a community as Charleston.

We have seen how he became angry when the newly formed South Carolina Historical Society chose Petigru for its first president, relegating him to the second vice-presidency, which he declined. Petigru was an amateur, a dilettante. Yet Charleston preferred the cultivated attorney who dabbled in legal history to the professional historian. If we examine Simms's complaints about Charleston and the South, we will notice how they tend to focus on the role, or lack of it, of a professional man of letters within the community. As early as 1830 he wrote to his friend Lawson in New York that "you can have no idea of the general dearth of letters prevailing among us, and indeed, it is not a strong epithet to say as I have said before, with us & in our city, a man betraying the most remote penchant for poetry is regarded as little less than a nuisance."[31] In a letter published in a Georgia magazine in 1849 he declared that "there is no greater stimulus to literary effort, than to feel that your neighbors appreciate your toils, and are proud of them—a stimulus which has been but too commonly

29. Jay B. Hubbell, *The South in American Literature, 1607–1900* (Durham: Duke University Press, 1954), 270.

30. Henry Timrod, "Literature in the South," *The Essays of Henry Timrod*, ed. Edd Winfield Parks (Athens: University of Georgia Press, 1942), 86.

31. Simms to James Lawson, November 1, 1830, in *Letters*, I, 8.

denied to the native of the South, where the popular mind has been too frequently taught to despise all intellectual exercise which is not political."[32] To Hammond he wrote in 1853 saying that "I have never known public honors, or rewards; and encouragements of every kind, saving the sweet solicitude of a few friends, who in one way or another succour my wants & encourage my self-esteem have always been denied me."[33]

Certainly Simms exaggerated his situation, for he was by no means without esteem and recognition in South Carolina. One can only assume, however, that in South Carolina's civic and social life, particularly in Charleston itself, Simms continued to be considered—or thought he was considered—something of an upstart, a pariah, and so on, and that on various accounts he felt slighted.

In April of 1850, for example, after the death of John C. Calhoun, that statesman's body was escorted to Charleston by railroad, and placed in a catafalque at the City Hall, where it lay in state under charge of a guard of honor composed of two hundred eminent Charleston citizens. The event is described in the *Yearbook of the City of Charleston* for 1883, as part of an elaborate historical appendix prepared by Mayor William A. Courtenay. There were nine watches, and I have been told by the late C. Hugh Holman, whose scholarly writings on Simms are among the most distinguished work on the novelist, that considerable significance was placed upon who was assigned to each watch. According to Holman, Simms's relegation to the third watch was believed to be something of a symbolic affront, indicating as it did that at least forty local citizens were thus considered more important than he for such a position of honor.

It would require someone with more knowledge than I possess of the intricacies of antebellum Charleston political and social life to determine just what the priorities were among the various persons involved. The point, however, would seem to be that in the eyes of the managers of the event, the fact that Simms was a nationally and even internationally distinguished author, the acknowledged leader in Southern literature, did not merit him any

---

32. Simms to Charles L. Wheeler, [May 8, 1849], in *Letters*, II, 521.
33. Simms to Hammond, October 4, 1853, in *Letters*, III, 255.

particular preeminence in Charleston public life. One is reminded of the well-known incident that W. P. Trent described in his biography of Simms, in which George William Frederick Howard, Lord Morpeth, seventh Earl of Carlisle, was visiting Charleston, and asked for the whereabouts of Simms. His hosts replied that they did not know, intimating that Simms was not considered such a great man in Charleston. "Simms not a great man!" replied the astonished visitor. "Then for God's sake, who is your great man?"[34]

There are enough such stories, and enough gossip and innuendo, both during Simms's lifetime and afterwards, and sufficient protestations and explanations of their misrepresentation, as well as Simms's own frequent venting of his frustration in correspondence, to make one believe that, the statements of A. S. Salley and others to the contrary notwithstanding, Simms did indeed labor under sufficient social disapproval in his native city to feel uncomfortable throughout his lifetime. His friend the poet Paul Hamilton Hayne, whose own social credentials were impeccable, wrote that Simms had a manner about him, a way of behaving in public and in conversation, that was highly assertive and even dominating, which Hayne attributed to the circumstances of Simms's humble origins. It was a protective shield, he suggested, that Simms had developed as a way of compensating for being made to feel inconsequential in early cultural life in Charleston. Simms's friend Hammond, too, several times lectured him about his social combativeness; how can you, he asked Simms, expect others to seek you out and enjoy your company when you habitually attempt to overpower their arguments and dominate them?

Questions of personality aside, however, just what kind of recognition did Simms expect to get in Charleston and South Carolina that *would* have satisfied his requirements? The answer would seem to be that he wanted the same degree of deference and acclaim that the leading New England authors of the mid-century enjoyed in Boston and thereabouts, and which Henry Nash Smith has aptly described as quasi-religious veneration. In New England the intellectual leadership, which in earlier times had been exercised by Calvinist and then Congregationalist and Unitarian min-

34. Trent, *Simms*, 129.

isters of the gospel, a heritage of the Puritan theocracy, had descended to the men of letters, whose literature was strongly infused with idealism and even ideality. The "Good Grey Poets" of New England—Emerson, Holmes, Longfellow, Whittier—filled a public role. But no such role, and no such intellectual tradition, existed in the South. It is no mere coincidence that where many of the New England literati had studied for the ministry, most of the Southern writers had studied law. The law was the approved route of advancement for an ambitious but unconnected and impecunious young man of talent. From the practice of law to the practice of politics was a natural next step: a *legislator* was a *lawmaker*. The kind of public recognition that was forthcoming in the South was thus inevitably political.

Nowhere in the South—or, for that matter, in the prewar United States—was there the kind of upper-middle-class reading public that by the middle of the eighteenth century, from the day of Richardson and Johnson onward, had made it possible for the leading men of letters in Great Britain to enjoy careers of reasonable financial independence and public distinction, and that in Simms's time made Wordsworth, Dickens, Thackeray, Tennyson, and Arnold into public figures. Nor was there a tradition of patronage; there was no Civil List, no system of reward for cultural distinction through the public exchequer. The best that might be hoped was appointment to a foreign consulate, and only in New England was literary merit occasionally perceived and rewarded in such fashion. Simms himself had aspirations of this sort at one point, but nothing was forthcoming, for his politics, as was inevitable in South Carolina by the 1840s, were too factional in affiliation. There was no Southern intellectual community functioning apart from the political community. In New England, the public role of man of letters might carry with it a distinction and station that could mean something within a significant reading public; but not in Simms's South Carolina.

It was public recognition that Simms wanted, and in the South politics alone could provide it. His single term in the state legislature was scarcely a sufficient measure of it to satisfy him. In his letters to his South Carolina friends, from the 1830s until the outbreak of the war, the note of his ongoing wish for high public office, whether elected or appointed, is continually sounded. He

professed unconcern, attempting to pass off his political disappointments as not mattering, but it is obvious that he yearned
for his fellow citizens to reward his literary achievements with
public office.

Nor is this surprising, because in antebellum South Carolina
nothing—the law, religion, even the military—took precedence
over political distinction. As Allen Tate wrote, the Old South was
"hag-ridden with politics,"[35] and nowhere more so than in South
Carolina. In this respect Simms was very much a South Carolinian. His letters to his Northern literary friends make almost no
mention of politics until the years just prior to secession; those to
his South Carolina correspondents often mention little else. He
wanted, in short, the kind of public role that the leading New
England authors enjoyed; and being a South Carolinian, he wanted
it not as quasi-theologian but *in political terms.*

As the sectional crisis intensified, the defense of slavery became the focus of political endeavor and the test of political orthodoxy, and not surprisingly, Simms grew ever more assertive of
the virtues of the Peculiar Institution. As Drew Faust succinctly
puts it, "By publicly defending slavery, a Southerner of the forties
or fifties was certain to gain attention and earn the acclaim of his
compatriots."[36] Just as following the close of World War II the
passionate assertion of anticommunism proved an Open Sesame
for numerous ambitious young Republican politicians, so the ingenuity with which a bright young Southron might present the
case for slavery and express its political slogans was a ready avenue to public distinction in a region that was under unremitting
political attack.

Simms's friend Hammond had learned the lesson very early.
Where the Nullification Crisis had wrecked the young Simms as
a newspaper editor, it made the fortune of Hammond, who had
happily stumbled into an opportunity to edit a pro-Nullification
newspaper in Columbia in 1830. His ringing assertions of South
Carolina's duty to declare null and void any despotic acts of a

35. Allen Tate, "The Profession of Letters in the South," *Essays of Four Decades* (Chicago: The Swallow Press, 1968), 523.
36. Drew Gilpin Faust, *A Sacred Circle: The Dilemma of the Intellectual
in the Old South, 1840–1860* (Baltimore and London: The Johns Hopkins Press,
1977), 116–17.

national government that might threaten the perpetuation of slavery (and Hammond did not flinch from making the direct connection between slavery and the Tariff of Abominations) brought him the admiring attention of his elders. It was not long before John C. Calhoun himself was taking the young editor aside to consult with him on future strategy.

Hammond had been on the winning side; Simms, in casting his lot with the old-time Federalists of Charleston, had been on the losing side. By the late 1830s, however, Simms had made his peace with the dominant faction. His defense of the Peculiar Institution against the criticism of Mrs. Trollope and Harriet Martineau offered satisfactory proof of his soundness.

The point has been made about antebellum Southern politics that the leadership of the proslavery ranks tended to be provided by the new men. This was as true in South Carolina as anywhere else. The avenue of distinction was via the law and politics; political renown led to a place among the gentry and, whether through marriage or by purchase, the ownership of a plantation and slaves.

The social and cultural ideal—the plantation—by definition involved soundness on the slavery issue. The numerous instances of lowly born young men winning their way to leadership demonstrate that the planter establishment, such as it was, was by no means a closed society. There may have been, in Charleston during the 1800s, something that might be said realistically to approach the condition of an aristocracy, for in Simms's native city there had been considerable wealth in some families for generations that went back well into the colonial period. But even in Charleston its walls were frequently breached. Elsewhere in the Old South, careers were abundantly open to talent. Even in South Carolina the plantation swiftly became a symbol of middle-class aspiration and attainment.

I doubt that anyone can properly grasp the nature of the society of the Old South, including that in South Carolina, without properly understanding just how important the fact of that accessibility was. Had it not been so, the tension in South Carolina between Charleston and the Up-country would have been radically and even explosively divisive. The state could never have maintained the system of government codified in the 1790 state consti-

tution whereby political power remained in control of the legislature, which chose almost all state and many county officials,
including presidential electors, United States senators, and the
governor, and even county tax collectors. Since election to the
state legislature was easily enforceable by the local landowners,
political power was an arrangement made between gentlemen,
and it was the elasticity of the requirements for entering that group
that made men such as Calhoun, Petigru, Hammond, McDuffie,
and even Simms eager participants within the community rather
than thwarted rebels against the status quo. (Simms, however,
remained a Jacksonian to the extent of continuing to advocate the
popular election of state officials, in contradistinction to the
views of Hammond, who, though like Simms a man of the people,
greatly feared popular exercise of the franchise.)

New men of imagination and energy such as Hammond and, in a
different way, Simms thus had, like William Faulkner's Thomas
Sutpen, what in effect was a Design. It involved wealth, prestige,
political power, yet it was something more than these. There was
almost an abstract quality to it; it could be image, dream, and
role. The plantation symbolized its meaning. Even more so than
Simms, Hammond was captive to the dream of plantation glory.
At one point, irked by his sons' seeming impracticality and their
apparent lack of enthusiasm for remaining at home and helping
him direct the plantation (they wanted to pursue careers of their
own), he complained to his brother that "you think it hard for
them to be buried here and compelled to oversee. Well, I have
done it for 27 years *alone* while they are three of them and the
rest of us right here. I have worked like ten overseers and made
every sacrifice to make my sons well educated and well bred *independent* So. Carolina *Country Gentlemen* the nearest to noblemen of any possible in America." Such was his dynastic ambition.
We have seen how, even as Hammond lay dying, he could close
his mind to the South's imminent defeat and the certain end of
the Peculiar Institution, ignore the inescapable evidence of the
passive rebelliousness of his slaves as their liberation from bondage grew near, and assuage his dream of the gentleman-slaveowner
and his faithful black retainers by summoning the slave children
outside his window to sing to him. "Hammond," concludes Drew

Faust, "identified himself and his life with the myths of the Old South, even as they crumbled around him."[37]

If somewhat less crudely, Simms shared that dream. His near-lifelong allegiance to the cause of Southern literature, not only with his own writings but in his editorship of magazine after magazine devoted to its promulgation, constituted a fervent effort on his part to make the reality of the always threadbare Southern intellectual scene come closer to the cultural ideal he envisioned: the community of shared passion and warmth, leisure and manners, receptive to the arts and appreciative of its men of letters. His recurrent rage over South Carolina's disinclination to cherish its writers—"The South don't care a d——n for literature or art"—never caused him to desist from trying to provide that literature. To close friends such as Hammond or Paul Hayne he might lament the region's neglect of the arts; but let an outsider venture to criticize his home and his people, and he would counter-attack vigorously, taking no prisoners. By the 1850s, even to close Northern friends such as James Lawson or Evert Duyckinck, he had largely ceased to admit to any serious Southern cultural shortcomings. Hammond's remarks about the Southern landed gentleman as American nobleman are scarcely more expansive or adulatory than Simms's scornful post-1865 retort to the Northern journalist and abolitionist John Townsend Trowbridge: "'Charleston, sir, was the finest city in the world; not a large city, but the finest. South Carolina, sir, was the flower of modern civilization. Our people were the most hospitable, the most accomplished, having the highest degree of culture and the highest sense of honor, I will not say of America, sir, but of any country on the globe. And they are so still, even in their temporary destitution.'"[38]

6.

Years earlier, in 1845, under the aegis of Simms (though his name is nowhere mentioned), there was published an annual, *The Charleston Book: A Miscellany in Prose and Verse.* Pleased with the idea of displaying in the pages of a single volume the numer-

37. Hammond to Marcellus C. M. Hammond, August 25, 1858, in Bleser (ed.), *Hammonds of Redcliffe,* 49; Faust, *James Henry Hammond,* 382.
38. Quoted in John Townsend Trowbridge, *My Own Story* (Boston and New York: Houghton, Mifflin and Co., 1903), 310–11.

ous writings of his fellow Charlestonians, Simms had scurried about seeking subscriptions to help pay the cost of having Samuel Hart of Charleston print and bind the volume. The "Advertisement" preceding the table of contents noted that enough material had been collected to fill several volumes, and that if the present edition met with success, a second would be published for the next holiday season. Apparently it did not, for a sequel never appeared.

Simms was concerned to point out that none of the contributors whose work appeared in *The Charleston Book* was a professional author. The names of a few of them are still remembered by students of nineteenth-century Southern culture. There was Washington Allston, the Charleston-born painter and poet who had studied painting abroad and then settled in Massachusetts, where he published verse and worked for years on a never-to-be-completed painting entitled "Belshazzar's Feast." There was Hugh Swinton Legaré, lawyer, antiquarian scholar, editor of the *Southern Review* for several years and former attorney general and acting secretary of state in President Tyler's cabinet. There were the playwrights John Blake White and Isaac Harby. There was Joel Roberts Poinsett, stalwart Jacksonian during the Nullification Crisis of the previous decade, former ambassador to Mexico and secretary of war, best known today for having a Christmas flower named after him. There were the Gilmans, Samuel and Caroline, transplanted New England Unitarians; he is remembered principally for having written the words to "Fair Harvard," and she for her several books and editorship of *The Southern Rose*. There was J. D. B. De Bow, soon to leave for New Orleans and the editorship of the proslavery *De Bow's Review*. There were Penina Moise, the blind Jewish poetess, and William Crafts, poet and socialite of the early decades of the century, whose dilettantism H. S. Legaré had savaged so masterfully in the *Southern Review*. (Crafts's contributions to *The Charleston Book* include a paean to the Pilgrim Fathers and the pride they would feel if they could see the New England that they founded in its present glory; it would not be long before no Southern publication would want to praise anything having to do with *that*.) There were John Bachman the naturalist, Stephen Elliott the botanist, Charles Fraser the miniaturist, and William Henry Timrod, father of the poet Henry Timrod. (Two of the elder Timrod's poems are the best by far in the collection.) There was the poet James Mathewes Legaré—and so on.

The table of contents is not exactly a roster of literary or intellectual greatness, but *The Charleston Book* was a very respectable showing for a small Southern city whose reading public all told was probably no more than a few thousand persons. If none of the contents of the annual seems worth reading today, that is because literary and journalistic fashions have changed so utterly since the 1830s. Surely the average was about as good as any American community the size of Charleston could have produced at the time.

In pointing out that all the contributors were amateur authors, Simms, no amateur himself but a thoroughgoing professional, noted:

What is done among us, in a literary point of view, is the work of the amateur, a labor of stealth or recreation, employed as a relief from other tasks and duties. From this fact the reader will be able to account for that air of didactic gravity, that absence of variety, and of the study of artistic attributes, which would not strike him so obviously had the sources of the collection been found in the more various fields of a national literature. He will discover, however, that in most of the pieces which follow, there is a liveliness of fancy, a fluency of expression, and a general readiness of resource, indicating such a presence of the imaginative faculty, as leaves no doubt of the capacity of the community, from which the work is drawn, to engage with great success in the active pursuits of literature. Should this little miscellany contribute in any degree, to bring about a result so very desirable the reward of the publisher will be ample.[39]

One might wonder why an author such as Simms, busy with his professional commitments, involved in South Carolina politics, and with an enormous correspondence to take care of, would expend so much time and labor on a project such as this, which could neither benefit his literary reputation nor be translated into political gain. However, if one knows very much about Simms and his relationship to the city of Charleston, there can be little doubt of what was involved.

39. [Simms], "Advertisement," *The Charleston Book: A Miscellany in Prose and Verse* (Charleston, S.C.: Samuel Hart, Sen., 1845), 3–4.

What Simms craved most of all was to be recognized and honored as an outstanding man of letters, a distinguished literary personage, *in* a city-state (as was often said) in which literature, culture, learning were strongly allied with wealth and civic position. By the early 1800s the city had already developed the peculiar combination of civic pride, hedonism, gentility, and self-satisfaction that has since characterized it. The powerful lure of community membership and status that it offered its citizenry went along with a complacent self-congratulation that permeated a fairly active, if usually superficial, cultural life.

What galled Simms was that his own fame as a nationally distinguished author, surpassing by far that of any other author in the South, seemed to mean little more in Charleston than that of any locally prominent poetaster. In the final reckoning, political and social distinction counted for more than artistic renown. No matter how imposing his reputation might be elsewhere, in Charleston there was a sense in which Simms was and would always be the talented but rough-edged youth who had once delivered drugs about the city, and whose subsequent attainment might mitigate but never completely cancel out that fact.

Indeed, in some ways his national success as an author seemed to be resented by local citizens; in addition to the Lord Morpeth episode, we have the incontrovertible testimony of both Hayne and Timrod to that effect. It was almost as if the fact that he had shown himself unwilling to content himself with local renown, and had advanced far beyond the limited literary horizons of amateur status, was actively resented. (One thinks of Poe in Richmond.)

The opportunity to preside, as editor, over the publication of such a project as *The Charleston Book*, in which dozens of locally prominent litterateurs were participants, thus gave him considerable satisfaction. No one knew better than he the limitations of almost all of the work being anthologized, or the obvious fact that the Charlestonians not only could not distinguish between such work and writings of genuine distinction but did not care. He recognized all too well the self-congratulatory nature of such civic cultural enterprises; that Charleston's intellectual life was in the nature of a mutual admiration society was quite evident to him.

For all that, he still liked to be part of it. Moreover, the very self-sufficiency and self-satisfaction were attributes of the community's solidarity, emblematic of the powerful sense of community identity that had so attracted him as a young man struggling to be accepted. In a very real sense he had never put it aside; it had shaped his life, made him into the kind of writer that he was. The old-time Charleston Federalist aristocracy of wealth and social distinction, with their plantations and town houses, their pleasant if amateur concern for literature and culture, became and remained his ideal—which, however, he pursued with an ardency of spirit and a professional skill and boldness that in themselves served to prevent his ever fully being part of the circles he so admired.

The "Advertisement" to *The Charleston Book* embodies the ambivalence of his emotions. If only there could be, within and as part of the Charleston community, a professional literary situation, one that would be free of the dilettantism and complacency of the community identity! What he could not see was that the two goals were self-contradictory. The professional literary situation he craved could have been achieved only at the cost of setting aside the intellectual and artistic limitations that enabled the literary activity to conform to the standards and expectations of the social community.

Yet in the early 1850s it did begin to look as if Simms's wish was coming true, and that a genuine professional literary community might be forming in Charleston. Two young poets, Henry Timrod and Paul Hayne, were now active, and both made it very clear that they had no intention of settling for a genteel amateur standing. Other promising young men began gathering about them. It was Simms's pleasure, as distinguished elder, to play host to Hayne, Timrod, and certain of the mostly young Charlestonians of intellect and promise, at his home in the city. It was there that the idea to publish a literary magazine of their own was hatched. Simms had been in on the birth and death throes of not a few previous such ventures, but he was always game for another try.

Realizing that the venture would require for its success considerably more in the way of both literary and financial resources than were available to them, they joined with a larger, older, and generally more influential group of citizenry, the lawyers, physicians, clergymen, and others who convened regularly in the "sanctum," the back room of John Russell's bookstore, to discuss matters of cultural and civic import. "Lord" John Russell (so-called because he was so very pleased at his fancied resemblance to the English statesman) agreed to finance the enterprise until it reached self-sufficiency.

Russell's Magazine published its first issue in 1857 and its last in early 1859.[40] For most of the period Hayne served as editor, which soon turned out to be, in his estimation, a thankless task, for few of the gentlemen amateurs of the group proved ready to produce the material that had been counted on to fill its pages. Hayne, Timrod, and Simms, however, wrote regularly for it. *Russell's* might have succeeded, had it not been for the intensifying sectional crisis which not only meant that the magazine failed to win the interest of an increasingly distracted public but also obviously diverted the attention of the contributors, including Simms, who by this time was so caught up in the political conflict over slavery that he was giving less and less heed to matters of literature. During its brief existence, however, the magazine did become the occasion for several of Henry Timrod's essays on poetry. It seems clear that Timrod was the most genuinely gifted member of the group, one who in other circumstances might have developed into an important poet.

But it is also evident, if one reads Timrod's essays on poetry carefully, that what the *Russell's* writers suffered most from was a political atmosphere that prevented them from doing what similar literary groups customarily do—ground their literary interests in a cultural and social position that placed them in a judgmental relationship with the larger community. Timrod's exchange with William J. Grayson on the nature of poetry, in which he championed the modern poetry of Tennyson and Wordsworth against the eighteenth-century neoclassical writers, was implicitly political. The younger man was attacking an attitude toward poetry which held it to be the considered utterance, in rhymed metric feet, of general community wisdom, asserting a settled truth that was past argument. In his several *Russell's* es-

40. Richard J. Calhoun's essay, "The Ante-Bellum Twilight: *Russell's Magazine,*" *Southern Literary Journal,* III (Fall, 1970), 89–110, handily places the magazine in the context of pre-secession Charleston.

says, Timrod wrote in glowing terms of the Romantic movement as a much-needed revolution in sensibility; and he raged at Southern patriotism for its insistence upon viewing all literary utterance in terms of sectionalism. It is true that he suggested that one value of good literature, as opposed to mediocre work, would lie in its ability to report to the world the "truths underlying the relations of master and slave,"[41] but in context the statement seems in the nature of an afterthought, as if it were expected of him to make clear that his claims for literature posed no threat to the community's political and social arrangements.

What seems obvious in almost everything that Timrod wrote for *Russell's* is his general dissatisfaction with the attitudes and tastes of the community. But if so, it does not carry over into a criticism of the social and political arrangements in Charleston and the South. One can only speculate on the extent to which, in a politically less volatile and militant atmosphere, the young professional writers of *Russell's* might have been emboldened, through mutual encouragement, to undertake a radical critique of Southern institutions that, in the situation in which they found themselves, they showed little evidence of wanting to make. In any event, the coming of secession and civil war ended not only the magazine but the very existence of the group.

7.

The historical fiction that Simms himself wrote, and which is by all odds his best work, has been interpreted, by Jon Wakelyn and others, in terms of its relevance to contemporary political issues. Thus Wakelyn remarks that in the Revolutionary War fiction the author's themes "were shaped less by class conflict or by his view of status in South Carolina society than by his interpretation of the need for unity in the state after the Revolutionary War. To build its power inside or outside the Union, South Carolina had to demonstrate that the Revolution had unified the state. Simms felt that it was particularly important for the average citizen to accept the leadership of the conservative and privileged elite in tumultuous times." And he notes that the Charleston newspapers were quick to recognize that message.[42]

41. Timrod, "Literature in the South," *Essays*, 91.
42. Jon Wakelyn, *The Politics of a Literary Man: William Gilmore Simms* (Westport, Conn.: Greenwood Press, 1973), 170–71.

Certainly when Simms wrote about the South, whether in fiction or nonfiction, he was aware of contemporary political needs. But Wakelyn's approach—fiction as political persuasion, shaped by the author's political views, written out of a conscious intention to promulgate political doctrine—entails some serious handicaps. He is unable to take account of the ways in which artistic necessity can modify, distort, and even contradict conscious political purpose. He does not see that Simms the literary artist is at least as important a storytelling presence within the fiction as is Simms the political propagandist, and that it is the storytelling artist who confers importance upon the political commentator, not the other way around. Wakelyn's approach cannot distinguish between the fiction of Simms and that of someone such as his friend Nathaniel Beverley Tucker, whose fiction not only *was* shaped purely as political statement but possesses almost no artistic dimensions whatever.

Specifically, the approach overlooks or neglects one of the most important ties between the author and his work: the personal, emotional needs out of which its composition arose. It has room for no curiosity about any dimension other than conscious political intention. Yet Simms's extraordinary zeal for Southern and particularly for South Carolina history grows in intense ways out of his wish to identify himself with his community's past. It is an act of possession, a way of asserting his claims, as a Charlestonian and a South Carolinian, to full-fledged membership in the community. His father was a latecomer on the scene, but his mother's family, specifically his great-grandfather, did play a role in Charleston's life during the Revolutionary War era. Simms not only described an incident involving his ancestor in his novel *Katharine Walton* but he gave the family name, Singleton, to the well-born hero of his first Revolutionary War fiction, *The Partisan* (1835). In *The Yemassee*, his first venture into South Carolina history, published that same year, there is an episode in which an Irish settler bravely defies the torture of the Indians; it is obviously a tribute to his father.

In becoming an expert on his community's past, Simms was enabled to instruct the Charlestonians on their own history—and be it remembered that it was in part because his own family ties to that past were oblique that he was not himself a member of the Charleston gentry. To say this is not to portray Simms as a sycophant or a social climber; in no important way was he either, which is one of the reasons why he had failed, as someone such as James Louis Petigru had succeeded, in securing full social acceptance. But the impassioned fascination with his community's past is testimony to the hold that Charleston had on Simms's affections, and the force that the ideal of membership in the community exerted upon his imagination throughout his life. It helps us to understand, for example, why he became so enraged when Petigru and not he was chosen president of the South Carolina Historical Society.

When one examines the zeal which men such as Simms and his friend Hammond displayed in the defense of slavery during the period of rising sectional tensions, it is important to bear in mind the allure which that ideal of the aristocratic gentleman-planter held for them. For someone like Hammond it was intricately involved with dreams of wealth and power. In Simms's instance the wealth and power would seem to have been less important than the public acclaim. But in both cases the enormous amount of imaginative abstraction involved in the transaction must be recognized.

It is a mistake, I think, to approach the views that these men, and others like them, expressed about the Peculiar Institution principally as ideology, in the sense that any logical and coherent exposition of ideas is what is at issue. Visionary theorizing, the reification of emotional longing even, is a better way to look at their utterances. That they believed, like most antebellum Americans, in the congenital inferiority of black people is undeniable; that both Hammond and Simms thought that the condition of chattel slavery constituted no unwarranted hardship for the chattels is likewise beyond question. But when one gets into the extravagant theorizing about Mudsills and slave empires, it seems obvious that what is involved is not calculating, realistic political and social thinking, as some would have it, but passionate hyperbole, rhapsodic conceptualizing of abstractions, a sometimes giddy and often self-contradicting mingling and extending of thought and fancy. Like Thomas Browne, both men loved to pursue "reason to an *O altitudo.*"

Consider, for example, Simms writing to Hammond in 1847

about proper Southern political strategy. The time is that of the dispute over whether the territories of the far Southwest were to be admitted into the Union as slave states:

At all events, the slave interest must be held intact without reference to the soil upon which it happens to labor now. Remember that! It is one inevitable necessity with slavery that it must accommodate its habitation to its profits—in other words that slave labor will only be continued where it yields an adequate profit. Slavery will be the medium & great agent for rescuing and recovering to freedom and civilization all the vast tracts of Texas, Mexico, &c., and our sons ought to be fitted out as fast as they are ready to take the field, with an adequate provision in slaves, and find their way in the yet unopened regions. The interest is one which must be maintained without reference to places.[43]

Did Simms really believe all this? Only in the sense of a political abstraction. In actuality it goes against everything that most characterizes his life and work. He wanted most of all to be a South Carolina landed gentleman, if not in the area adjoining Charleston then in the Barnwell district, and to enjoy a position and public renown in his native state. Twice he had turned down attractive invitations to move southwestward in search of greater opportunities. Imaginatively and zealously he sought to establish his antecedents and sink his art deeply in his community's past. To belong, to be part of a stable, rooted, social community steeped in history and memory, was his consuming passion.

What, therefore, could *his* life and work possibly have to do with an economic interest "without reference to" place? Or Hammond's, for whom a "well educated and well bred *independent* So. Carolina *Country*" gentleman represented a status "the nearest to noblemen of any possible in America"—and who summoned the slave children to sing outside the window of his deathbed?

Clearly the cause of expansion of the slaveholding South was being made into a shibboleth that bore little or no real relationship to the deepest personal concerns and objectives of either man's life and career. Yet so thoroughly had Simms and Hammond identified themselves and their dreams of status with the political rhetoric of their community, and so histrionic was Simms's response to

43. Simms to Hammond, July 15, 1847, in *Letters*, II, 332.

the growing criticism of the South during the dispute over the annexation of Texas and the Wilmot Proviso, that he sounds like a fire-eater such as William Lowndes Yancey at his most hyperbolic. He and his friend Hammond obviously derived much satisfaction from demonstrating rhetorically to each other just how intransigent and uncompromising a Southron each was, and they did so with a zeal that only two self-made men, not born into the planter squirearchy, could muster. One is reminded of Samuel Johnson displaying his Toryism. The passage, with its mixture of Manifest Destiny, sectional bellicosity, and dogmatic generalization, is as truly and as extravagantly Romantic as anything to be found in Emerson, Victor Hugo, or Thomas Wolfe.

It should be noted that this seemingly "pragmatic" and "practical" approach to the practice of slavery as a labor and social system devoid of attachment to a time and place is in almost ludicrous contrast to the practice of the Peculiar Institution as observable on Simms's own plantation. Simms's inability and unwillingness to make his slaves work at a reasonable rate kept the annual agricultural yield so low that he was in constant debt. Hammond, who was considerably more realistic about the function of slavery as a system of forced labor, chided him for the lamentable inefficiency at Woodlands. Visitors there recorded their astonishment at the exorbitant prices that Simms paid for the produce that his slaves grew in their own gardens. Some of the slaves at Woodlands were even permitted to own firearms! The novelist blamed his father-in-law for the failure of Woodlands to produce profitable crops, but there is little evidence that the situation improved after he took personal charge. The incompetence of Simms's slave labor force was apparently a source of amusement among his friends. It was Simms's literary earnings that kept the plantation going. When William Cullen Bryant came to visit Simms, he did not change his opposition to slavery, but he pronounced it about as innocuous there as it could ever be.

To say all this is not to excuse slavery in the Old South, either on Simms's plantation or anywhere else. Rather, it is to indicate that Simms's insensitivity toward its evils, one that he shared with his neighbors, was not hypocritical. The fervor with which he defended it against hostile criticism, the ferocity with which he spun out his theories for its perpetuation and expansion, can be viewed most usefully neither as defensive rationalization nor as abiding philosophical conviction, though certainly both were involved. Rather, such all-out enthusiasm might best be understood as the product of his lifelong effort to demonstrate his orthodoxy as a Charlestonian and a South Carolinian, a way of gaining the respect he coveted within a community that, as he constantly complained, was less than passionately committed to the fine arts, and that was also under relentless ideological and political attack, even while its economic and political power within the Union was steadily ebbing.

Simms and Hammond each provided what the other needed: a companion in ambition and sensibility who could understand the intensity of the other's desire to achieve status and distinction within the South Carolina establishment, and who could recognize, too, that there was so much more to that ambition than materialistic advancement. Like almost every other important figure in the political and cultural life of the antebellum South, both were outsiders, not to the establishment born, and the status which both had managed to secure had come in spite of, and not because of, the early attitude of the dominant community leadership toward them. Unlike Simms, Hammond had achieved a college education, at South Carolina College—and one can imagine that checks and rebuffs had not been unknown to a youth whose father was in charge of provisioning the school's dining hall and the proprietor of an open-air market in Columbia. If so, a onetime apothecary's apprentice and delivery boy could be trusted to understand. Simms had the finer sensibility of the two, and seems so much more attractive a figure, less self-centered, gentler, and certainly far less ruthless in pursuit of his ambition, but even so their common possession of high intelligence, depth of emotional hunger, powerful ambition, great energy, and self-made status were sufficient to bind them closely together.

It is Simms's friendship with Hammond that makes one realize what the absence of any real literary community, or clerisy as Lewis Simpson calls it, in the South of Simms's upbringing meant for him. Had there been companions who could share and understand his literary ambitions and imaginative gifts when he was a youth, it is quite possible that his efforts would have been directed more firmly and more exclusively toward literature in its own right, rather than toward its fulfillment within and on behalf of the political and social community. Had there been anyone to be for the young Simms what a generation later the youthful Hayne and Timrod were for each other, or for that matter what the older Simms himself was for both of them, the achievement of William Gilmore Simms might have been a different and, from a literary standpoint, more enduring affair than it turned out to be. All such speculation, of course, is moot; but with Simms's drive, talent, and ambition, there is no telling what might have resulted. In any event, it was not to be.

8.

Paul Hamilton Hayne, in a memoir written after the novelist's death, has described the first time he saw Simms. It was during the period of the Mexican War, and Hayne was attending a meeting in a Charleston theater. There were a series of speeches, and then, as some in the audience began to leave, "there was a cry, at first somewhat faint, but rapidly taken up, until it was earnest, even vociferous, for Simms, Gilmore Simms!" As a fledgling poet, Hayne had long wished to see the great man. "He now came forward with a slow, stately step, under the full blaze of the chandeliers, a man in the prime of life, tall, vigorous, and symmetrically formed."

He began his speech, Hayne says, with a "bold startling paradox," thereby gaining the full attention of his audience.

An extraordinary speaker, certainly. For some time his manner was measured and deliberate; but once plunged *in medias res* he became passionately eager. His gesticulation was frequent, unrestrained, now and then almost grotesquely emphatic. . . .

His peroration I vividly recall. It was a scathing rebuke of the selfish, time-serving politicians who sacrificed to personal and party ends the interests of their people and the dignity of their country.[44]

The occasion Hayne describes, which took place at about the same time that Simms wrote the letter to Hammond about the need for slavery to "accommodate its habitation to its profits," was probably a Democratic party rally attendant to the forthcom-

44. Paul Hamilton Hayne, "Ante-Bellum Charleston: Second Paper," *Southern Bivouac*, n.s., I (October, 1885), 257–58.

ing political campaign of 1848, and it is likely that the call, "at first somewhat faint, but rapidly taken up," for "Simms, Gilmore Simms!" was a deliberately planned maneuver of the Young Charleston group, with whom Simms was at the time busily engaged in promoting the candidacy of Zachary Taylor and the return of Hammond to office. Taylor was a Whig, and the dominant Democratic organization and newspapers in Charleston were reluctant to join in a move in which open sectionalism—Taylor was a slaveowner and a Southerner, while the Democratic candidate, Lewis Cass, was neither—would for the first time take precedence over national party allegiance.

What the Young Charleston faction was doing was attempting to take over control of the local party, and late that summer a convention of Charleston Whigs, independents, and Democrats did formally endorse Taylor's candidacy. Thus one may assume that what the seventeen-year-old Paul Hayne may have thought was a spontaneous outcry and an impromptu oration had been carefully arranged in advance of the meeting.

What is important, however, is that it was through political activity, not literary achievement, that Simms could experience exhilarating moments like that, with enthusiasts shouting for "Simms, Gilmore Simms!" and partisan audiences listening eagerly as he denounced time-serving politicos and called for the conquest of Mexico and the annexation of new territories for slavery. Such a condition was hardly peculiar to the state of South Carolina, of course. But the inescapable fact is that it was because William Gilmore Simms was a South Carolinian, and because as the son of an Irish-born father he craved the status and recognition that in antebellum Charleston could never be his as a result of cultural distinction alone, that he sought the limelight and rewards that public politics could afford him.

Nathaniel Hawthorne of Massachusetts was also involved in Democratic politics. It was his party affiliation that secured for him the consulate at Liverpool. Herman Melville of New York was likewise a Democrat; his brother was President James Knox Polk's selection for secretary of the American legation in London. Can anyone, however, imagine either Hawthorne or Melville engaged in active politics, in the way that Simms was, or delivering a stump speech such as that described by Paul Hayne?

One may readily concede that Simms was no Hawthorne and no Melville. Yet to say that is to beg the issue, for we do not know the form or the range that Simms's talents might have assumed had he grown up in New England or the Northeast under circumstances different from those he knew in Charleston.

What we do know is that through the sheer force and persistence of his character and will, Simms had all but *created* a professional literary situation in Charleston in the early 1850s. He had assembled and encouraged a group of gifted young men, who were learning to view the writing of literature as something other than a pleasant amateur diversion. In particular his two young poet friends Henry Timrod and Paul Hamilton Hayne were showing themselves ready for truly whole-souled engagement with literature. The founding of *Russell's Magazine* beginning in 1857 not only gave Simms's circle an organ but touched off critical discourse that resulted in Timrod writing several important documents about the nature and role of literature.

From the standpoint of nineteenth-century Southern letters, the situation with the *Russell's* group is a fascinating might-have-been. If what Lewis Simpson has pointed out is true concerning the role of a clerisy, the group of writers, intellectuals, and informed readers who make up a genuine artistic and cultural constituency to which the writer can belong in contradistinction to the social and economic community in which it exists, one can only say that this is what *seemed* to be developing in Charleston in the 1840s and 1850s. If so, the war destroyed it utterly. There are few more melancholy documents in American literary history than the sketches that Paul Hamilton Hayne wrote for the *Southern Bivouac* in 1885, describing what had been and now was gone for good. Not until the early twentieth century would another such literary situation begin to exist anywhere in the South again.

If we read the frantic, sometimes inchoate correspondence that Simms was scribbling at exorbitant length to his friends during the late 1850s and early 1860s, given over almost wholly as it is to politics, secession, and the coming of the war, we see the collapse of his literary vocation taking place right in front of our eyes. Repeatedly he quotes to his New York friends the Latin tag,

Quem Deus vult perdere, prius dementat, "Whom the Gods would destroy, they first make mad."[45] He meant it to apply to Northern political opinion, but he was really writing about himself. Simms, wrote one such puzzled friend to another, seems to have gone quite mad. He was witnessing the utter collapse of the equilibrium that he had managed, however unevenly, to maintain between his literary interests and ambitions and his involvement in the political and social life of his community. It was no longer possible to be a professional man of letters in the South; henceforth he must put aside his artistic vocation and sink his entire hopes into his identification with the secular, political Southern community.

Not given overmuch to introspection as he was, it is impossible to say whether he realized what he had done to himself, by virtue of his involvement in his politically obsessed community. Yet it had not really been a matter of choice on his part. Being the man he was and in his time and place, he could not have done otherwise. For the gifted young parvenu in Charleston the dream of the statesman-author-planter had proved irresistible. Who had there been, in the South Carolina he so loved, to help him resist it? Surely not his friend Hammond.

The public goal had become irretrievably entangled with the artistic vocation. He had sought earnestly and bravely to weave them into the single harmonious entity: to be a *Southern* writer, to create *Southern* literature. But in the antebellum South of slavery and the plantation, that was more than any man could bring off—not even one with his energy, his willpower, and his integrity. He was too close to his subject matter to be able to discipline his Romantic passion for it through a detachment that would make possible seeing himself and his experience with the irony that could have converted argument into dialectic. For all his fascination with the past of South Carolina and the nation, he could not view history as something that was happening to *him*.

When it was over, his once-imposing plantation gutted and his library burned, his slaves freed, his wife dead, and his and his community's cause blasted beyond imagining, he sought to re-

---

45. Simms gives it as "Quos" rather than "Quem" in a letter to James Lawson, November 13, [1860], *Letters,* IV, 265.

sume his literary vocation. It was all he had left. The plantation dream of the Old South had vanished into smoke. In late 1865 he prepared to go to New York in a forlorn attempt to restore his professional ties. To his friend Evert Duyckinck, his onetime ally in the exciting literary wars of Young America, he wrote as follows: "After four, nearly five, dreadful years, it will give me the greatest pleasure to meet with you again. But say as little as possible to me about the war, and my miserable Country."[46]

46. Simms to Evert Duyckinck, October 1, 1865, in *Letters*, IV, 523.

III. THE ROMANCE OF THE FRONTIER

Simms, Cooper, and the Wilderness

I have sought to show how William Gilmore Simms's life and career were very much a middle-class American affair, and how his ardent pursuit of the status of respected and honored man of letters within the politically obsessed planter community of antebellum South Carolina impelled him toward the defense of slavery almost as if it were an abstract Romantic ideal. I have also suggested that the lack of an indigenous literary community within the South of his day does much to account for the ferocity with which he pursued the plantation ideal. What I want to do now is to turn to Simms's fiction, and specifically to one novel, *The Yemassee* (1835), to try to show what the presence of that ideal meant for his artistic imagination, through a comparison of that work with another novel of Indian warfare, written not by a Southerner but by a resident of the state of New York, James Fenimore Cooper.

Simms and Cooper were the American authors who first made important literary use of the frontier, the wilderness, and the Indians as shaping forces in the national history. Seventeen years older than his Southern compatriot, Cooper got there first with *The Pioneers* (1823). It was, however, the second of the five Leatherstocking Tales, *The Last of the Mohicans* (1825), that obviously had most to do with encouraging Simms to write his own tale of early frontier war. Like Cooper's novel, *The Yemassee* was set in the forest of the New World, involved warfare with the Indians, and reenacted the death of a once-mighty Indian nation. And just as *The Last of the Mohicans* was the most popular of Cooper's novels, so *The Yemassee*, of all Simms's numerous books, has lasted best. It went through three printings in its first year, appeared in new editions throughout the nineteenth century, and since then has been resurrected from time to time for classroom use.

As C. Hugh Holman has pointed out, Simms later learned how to handle narratives in more skillful fashion, develop characters of greater complexity, and pay more heed to realistic detail, but "never after *The Yemassee* was he to find again a group of characters, a situation, an action, and a poetic vision of experience that would speak with as much directness and force to as large a segment of the American public."[1] *The Yemassee* may not be Simms's best-crafted work of fiction; it may be written in slipshod, careless fashion at times; but beyond question Simms's third novel remains his most compelling.

Almost nobody today reads either Cooper or Simms without being instructed to do so. The New York novelist, however, wrote a series of books that enjoy a considerably higher reputation among scholars, not so much because he was a better technician of the art of fiction or even a more felicitous writer of prose, as because he was able to tap a vein of myth and meaning that has been of more profound significance to the Western imagination than ever Simms managed. From that moment in *The Pioneers* when, having set out to create a novel of manners, he introduced a dilapidated old frontiersman, Natty Bumppo, and his aged Indian companion Chingachgook ("pronounced Chicago, I think," according to Mark Twain), Cooper's imagination moved swiftly and decisively into the high romance of civilized man's arrival in the virgin forests of the New World. The Leatherstocking Tales are the saga of our bittersweet conquest of nature, a transaction that offered not only the excitement of the clash of white versus red man but the pathos inherent in the fall of timeless innocence in nature before human complicity in history.

However awkwardly handled—and as Mark Twain pointed out, it can get pretty awkward[2]—the characterization of Natty

---

1. C. Hugh Holman, Introduction to *The Yemassee*, by William Gilmore Simms (Boston: Houghton Mifflin, 1961), viii–ix.

2. Clemens' demolition of Cooper, "Fenimore Cooper's Literary Offenses," has been frequently reprinted, in various editions. I have used *Selected Shorter Writings of Mark Twain*, ed. Walter Blair (Boston: Houghton Mifflin, 1962), 226–38.

Bumppo, alias Deerslayer, Hawkeye, Leatherstocking, La Longue Carabine, etc., functions at a level of elementary magnificence worthy of the theme being reenacted. The white hunter who puts Western civilization behind him to live in the woods, and in whose personality are joined the natural freedom of the wilderness and the moral conscience of civilization, embodies in his thought and actions the stirring possibility of human nature being reborn into purity through willed innocence, and the inevitable realization that the effort at regeneration must fail. The price of his personal survival is the doom of the circumstance that made the attempt possible: as mediator between wilderness and society, he is the unwilling agent of the community from which he flees in its relentless encroachment upon the forest in which he seeks refuge.

So great a drama is not only a central fact of our nation's early history; it is also a symbolic representation of the commencement of that history. When in *The Last of the Mohicans* the chief of the Mohicans, Chingachgook, articulates his loneliness after the death of his son Uncas, the last warrior of a once-mighty tribe, Leatherstocking's pledge that he remains as the Indian's friend and companion will not alter the outcome of what has happened. The North American continent is now open to conquest, and whether as friend or foe the Indian must relinquish the forest to the civilization of the white race whose reluctant pathfinder Leatherstocking is.

Like *The Last of the Mohicans*, Simms's *The Yemassee* is set on the frontier and involves Indian warfare. It too recounts the death of a once-mighty Indian tribe, and like Cooper's saga it deals, in C. Hugh Holman's words, "with one of the great matters of American tragic romance, the conflict of Indian and white cultures, the pain and injustice with which civilization hacks its path into the American wilderness, the suffering and the tragic grandeur of being one of a fated folk overwhelmed by the onrushing wave of history."[3] Much of the power of Simms's narrative comes from the starkness and finality with which he portrays the Yemassee Indians' desperate effort to drive the early white colonizers of coastal South Carolina back into the sea.

3. Holman, Introduction to *Yemassee*, ix.

Set during a period early in the history of the Carolina colony, Simms's novel is based on an Indian uprising in the year 1715, when, after a period of steady white encroachment on their lands and probably with the encouragement of the Spanish in Florida, the Yemassee Indians banded together with a number of other tribes to fall upon the English settlers, massacring hundreds before they were halted and defeated. The subsequent fighting went on for almost two years, until the last hostile Indian tribe was subdued. The victory cleared the way for English settlers to move from the lands immediately adjacent to the coast into the Carolina backcountry and westward into what is now the state of Georgia.

It has often been pointed out that Simms actually knew considerably more about Indians than Cooper did. Not only had he observed them as a small boy growing up in Charleston, but when a young man, visiting his father in the Southwest, he had spent time among them. Neither for Simms nor for Cooper, however, did the presence of Indians ever constitute a threat to the communities they lived in. They were writing in a time when the Indians had been thoroughly and effectively eliminated as a menace to the Eastern Seaboard and were being removed to areas west of the Mississippi River. In their presentation of the Indian side of the clash of cultures, therefore, both novelists could write with detachment, and were able to recognize the genuine pathos involved.

Undoubtedly much of the appeal of *The Yemassee* to its readers lay in the detail with which Simms depicted his Indians, as well as in the exciting if melodramatic plot. In the former instance he improves on Cooper by showing a great deal more about tribal organization, customs, and little details of Indian life, and by making the story of their defeat dramatically as well as symbolically central to the action of his story. The melodrama of the expulsion of the now-dissolute young Yemassee warrior Occonestoga from his tribe because he has been corrupted by the white man's gifts—in particular, whiskey—and the dramatic act of love on the part of his mother, Matiwan, in braining him with a hatchet before he can be disgraced for eternity by the removal of the sign of his tribal totem, the Yemassee arrow, from his shoulders, made for heady reading for novel-readers of the 1830s.

Cooper set *The Last of the Mohicans* in the time of the French and Indian War. The good Indians—mainly Chingachgook, Uncas, and the friendly Delawares—take part on the side of the English, while the wicked Magua and his Hurons aid the French. The obligatory love story accompanying the historical action, with romantic hero and heroine, involves a Virginia-born British officer attempting to escort several young Englishwomen through the forest to the safety of a fort. Cooper hints at a little race mixing by setting up a secondary romance between Uncas and one of the English girls—who, however, turns out to be part Negro, so that no affront to the sensibilities of Cooper's audience is offered. Moreover, both are killed off before any permanent genetic damage can be done, and only the pureblood officer and his equally pureblood sweetheart survive to plight their troth.

Simms's love plot, which is even less relevant to the historical situation than Cooper's, carries no hint of miscegenation. Lord Craven, operating under the alias of Captain Harrison, is in love with the virtuous Bess Matthews, daughter of a frontier dissenting minister. Craven/Harrison easily wins his suit, at the expense of a local swain, Hugh Grayson. There is also a dastardly pirate, Henry Chorley, who improbably is from the same town as the Matthewses in England, and is now on the scene with his ship to deliver Spanish arms to the Yemassees. Chorley attempts to make off with Bess Matthews, but Craven/Harrison, every bit as redoubtable a marksman as Natty Bumppo though considerably less talkative about it, dispatches the pirate with one well-aimed rifle shot.

No one except Craven/Harrison's faithful black slave Hector and one or two others is supposed to know that the masterful Captain Harrison, so skilled in Indian fighting that the Yemassees term him the "Coosaw-killer," is in reality the Lord Palatine and Governor of the Carolina colony. The reader, alas, is scarcely deceived; as Holman says, it is one of the most poorly maintained secrets in the history of the novel in America.[4]

The historicity of Simms's novel does not extend to the love story; there was indeed a Governor Craven whose energetic

4. *Ibid.*, xi. Holman's writings about Simms are usually the best criticism available on his fellow South Carolinian. See the essays in Holman, *The Roots of Southern Writing: Essays on the Literature of the American South* (Athens: University of Georgia Press, 1972).

leadership defeated the Yemassee attack in 1715, but he certainly had nothing in mind in the way of matrimony with any colonial lass known to historians. Simms's theory of the historical novel readily permitted such tampering with known historical fact—as did Cooper's on occasion, though usually not so flagrantly.

The South Carolinian's performance in this respect is not unlike that of certain contemporary writers such as E. L. Doctorow, but for very different reasons and to considerably different effect. Doctorow and others are deliberately toying with historical authenticity for purposes of undercutting the traditional authority of "objective reality," historical and otherwise, whereas Simms believes so strongly in the firmness of naked historical fact that he sees no danger whatever in taking pleasing artistic liberties and extensions in order to make it more interesting.[5]

2.

What is largely absent from Simms's version of the white man and the Indian in the forest, as distinguished from Cooper's, is the vital dimension that makes the Leatherstocking Tales, for all their clumsiness, so deeply engaging a reenactment of the conquest of the New World wilderness: the tension between nature and society, the possibility of moral regeneration within nature, the inevitability of failure in the attempt. It is this that in the Cooper fiction gives philosophical depth to what is otherwise a social confrontation between two competing races. And it is important to try to understand *why* the theme is missing in Simms but present in Cooper.

That Simms saw the matter almost exclusively in terms of a social, historical confrontation is made clear in several quite specific passages in *The Yemassee*. Early in the novel the Indian chieftain Sanutee sets out for the forest, and Simms deposes as follows:

5. Occasionally Simms sounds like a deconstructionist a century and a half before his time, as when, after discoursing upon how the novelist's imagination can make history come alive, he declares that "each man becomes his own historian. Thought, taking the form of conjecture, ascends by natural degrees into the obscure and the infinite. Reasoning of what should have been from what is before us, we gather the true from the probable" (William Gilmore Simms, "History for the Purposes of Art," *Views and Reviews in American Literature, History and Fiction*, ed. C. Hugh Holman [Cambridge: The John Harvard Library, Harvard University Press, 1962], 35). But his premises, to repeat, are quite different.

He was one of those persons, fortunately for the species, to be found in every country, who are always in advance of the masses clustering around them. He was a philosopher not less than a patriot, and saw, while he deplored, the destiny which awaited his people. He well knew that the superior must necessarily be the ruin of the race which is inferior—that the one must either sink its existence in with that of the other, or it must perish. *He was wise enough to see, that, in every case of a leading difference betwixt classes of men, either in colour or organization, such difference must only and necessarily eventuate in the formation of castes; and the one conscious [sic] of any inferiority, whether of capacity or of attraction, so long as they remain in propinquity with the other, will tacitly become subjects if not bondsmen.*[6]

The comment is worded carelessly enough; surely Simms meant that it was the inferiority itself, and not the consciousness of it, that would doom the group. But what the passage indicates is that Simms was thinking of the Indian-white relationship of the early 1700s in terms of the slavery controversy that was beginning in the 1830s to attain such momentous proportions in American political life. The same motif is sounded in his handling of the relationship between Craven and his faithful slave Hector, who toward the close of the novel saves his master's life, after which Craven informs Hector that henceforth he is a free man. This produces one of the earliest examples of what in years to come would become almost a standard scene in Southern historical fiction, in which a slave, upon being told he is free, indignantly declines to accept his new status. In thus refusing his master's offer, Hector is made by Simms to propose a frequently used proslavery argument against emancipation: "'Ha! you make Hector free, he turn wuss more nor poor buckrah [*i.e.,* lower-class white]—he tief out of de shop—he get drunk and lie in de ditch—den, if sick come, he roll, he toss in de wet grass of de stable. You come in de morning, Hector dead—and, who know, he take no physic, he no hab parson—who know, I say, maussa, but de debble fine em 'fore anybody else?'" (355–56). Left to his own devices in a society dominated by his racial superiors, that is, he will be unable to fend for himself. For a black man, freedom is thus no blessing; he is much better off under the philanthropic care of his

---

6. Simms, *The Yemassee*, ed. C. Hugh Holman (Boston: Houghton Mifflin, 1961), 20, italics added. Subsequent page references will occur parenthetically in the text.

master. If given his freedom he will do just what the young Indian chieftain Occonestoga has done: become a prisoner to his baser instincts, and lie about drunkenly in the streets.

Now Fenimore Cooper's views on the competence of Africans were much the same as Simms's, as any reader of *The Pioneers* knows. If anything they come across to a twentieth-century audience even more offensively, because, not being on the defensive about the Peculiar Institution, he therefore feels no need to present it in a favorable light. In the first of the Leatherstocking novels, for example, he shows a slave terrified of his master's lash, and clearly considers it highly amusing. But that was in New York State in the eighteenth century, and by Cooper's own day African slavery had all but disappeared north of the Mason-Dixon Line.

Cooper's views on racial superiority and inferiority, as expressed in *The Last of the Mohicans*, are about on a par with Simms's. At one juncture in that novel the wicked Huron chief Magua delivers an oration on race and skin color that, obviously with Cooper's approval, makes the point that the Great Spirit created black-skinned people to be slaves, white-skinned people to be clever owners of slaves, and red-skinned people to be brave, free children of the forest. But while both novelists could portray the Indian-white confrontation as pathetic, and the extinction of the red man's hunting society by the more technologically advanced Europeans as tragically inevitable—the Indian was equally gone from Cooperstown as from Charleston—Cooper could identify the Indians *with* the forest, and their disappearance with the disappearance of primitive naturalness. There did not exist for him, in the countryside of rural New York State, another supposedly "inferior" race which not only had no ties whatever with the receding American wilderness but also played a role in the regional economy that made their preservation, as a subordinate race, of great economic importance to the community he lived in. And of course there is the obvious difference that in Simms's South Carolina of the 1820s and 1830s much of the wilderness had by no means been replaced yet by farms and homes.

There is more to the matter than merely a question of physical propinquity, and later on we will return to such considerations. But for now I want to compare Simms's protagonist in *The*

Yemassee, Lord Craven/Captain Harrison, to Cooper's great hero, Natty Bumppo. We have seen how Simms combines his love story with his adventure plot, in that the hero who directs the defense of the Carolina colony against the onslaught of the Yemassees is also the romantic lead, engaged in winning the hand of the beautiful Bess Matthews. Cooper by contrast builds his love story around a high-minded young Virginia major, Duncan Heyward, and an English girl who is the daughter of a colonel in command of Fort William Henry.

Although courageous and noble-spirited, the Major is of little use in fighting off hostile Indians; it is the dauntless Leatherstocking (usually referred to as Hawkeye in this particular story) who takes the lead in forest warfare. But Simms's English-born Lord Craven, in his guise as Captain Harrison, is as adept as Leatherstocking at combating hostile red men on their own terms, in the wilderness. Although not given to the kind of ingenious use of woodlore that Cooper's hero employs, such as turning streams out of their beds to discover footprints or determining the direction of a fort from the impact of cannon balls on the grass, Craven has long since earned the respect of friend and foe as a frontier fighter. He is an effective frontiersman because he pays attention to signs that others ignore, identifies and analyzes evidence carefully and dispassionately, and generally combines physical dexterity and strength with sharp reasoning and calculated audacity.

Craven/Harrison's gift for leadership is as fully developed as his fighting skills. A stranger among the settlers in the backcountry, he inspires trust and resolution through his demonstrated good judgment and bravery. Thus when, the battle won, he reveals to the borderers he has led to victory that he is the governor of the Carolina colony, the Lord Palatine, Charles Craven himself, he only confirms a status that he has *already earned*, through his accomplishments as a frontiersman. A century later, and instead of an English lord he might have been Andrew Jackson.

Though as skilled a fighting man as Craven/Harrison, Cooper's Leatherstocking himself customarily functions not as a commander of men, so much as an expert on woodcraft and Indian behavior whose advice is very good to have when there is danger about. In *The Last of the Mohicans* he is able, from his long experience in the forest, to match the Hurons' cunning with similar cunning and to function in their milieu equally as effectively as they can, while also bringing to that milieu the superior knowledge, mental powers, and skill with firearms of white civilization. No Indian can hope to equal his exploits with his rifle, named Killdeer; well do the red men call him "La Longue Carabine." But Leatherstocking/Natty/Hawkeye would not think of presuming to the leadership of a beleaguered colony, or of acting in any other than his capacity as a scout. And in any kind of complexity of social situation involving the workings of white society he is out of his element, for he is a humble backwoodsman, scarcely educated, with no claims or pretensions whatever to rank or position.

The difference, then, between Simms's and Cooper's protagonists is, in part, one of class. The English-born aristocrat Charles Craven *disguises* himself as Gabriel Harrison, a man without public social status, in order to lead the borderers in the defense of the Carolina frontier; whereas Natty Bumppo *is* a member of what in pre-1776 rural New York State is incipiently a middle-class yeomanry, even though it has thus far not had opportunity to do much more than begin clearing the edges of the forest. In his strength of character and purity of morality, Leatherstocking might be said to be "nature's nobleman," but insofar as any relationship to the social community around him is concerned, his position is lowly. He cannot seriously think, for example, of forming a romantic attachment to Colonel Munro's daughter Alice.

It is interesting that Simms gives his protagonist a double identity. Whatever his dramatic reasons for so doing—one thinks of the Saxon-born Wilfred of Ivanhoe and his alter ego the Disinherited Knight in Simms's favorite Walter Scott novel—the social implications of the division are instructive. It was as if Simms could conceive of an aristocratic young governor, the Lord Palatine of the recently established colony, being associated with the ugly, catch-as-catch-can warfare of the frontier, but not *in* his role as aristocratic young governor. What might have been feasible in a Scott novel set in England or Scotland was not appropriate to the Carolina backcountry. (Had there been an organized military situation involving professionally trained armies, it might have been different.) To lead the settlers in forest fighting, to command the respect and trust of men who lived on the frontier and knew its ways, Craven's status as English-born aristocrat would not do; he must masquerade as Captain Harrison. When there is Indian fighting to be done, the attitudes and assumptions of a sophisticated, well-born gentleman are inappropriate qualifications, just as they are for Cooper's Major Duncan Heyward in *The Last of the Mohicans*. Yet where Cooper cannot so much as conceive of the two separate sets of qualifications existing within a single characterization, Simms can imagine it happening—provided an alias is used.

We might note certain differences in the backgrounds of Cooper and Simms. The older novelist was the son of a distinguished judge, and was on both his mother's and father's side descended from colonial gentry. As is well known, his attitude toward democracy and the political role of the common man was ambivalent; a Jacksonian Democrat, he nevertheless believed strongly in social subordination, and his stance was always that of the assured patrician. In his social fiction he repeatedly rebuked his fellow countrymen for their vulgarity and their lack of respect for manners and tradition. Simms, by contrast, was self-made, without antecedents among the gentry, and as a young man enjoyed neither wealth nor social status. As a Jacksonian Democrat, he associated Old Hickory with his Irish-born father, who served under him in the Indian wars. Like Jackson himself, though on a lesser scale, Simms more or less forced his way into the gentry, through his literary distinction and his keen intelligence. When his first wife died and he later remarried, it was to the daughter of a plantation owner.

Now in respect to plot and to fictional plausibility, it would have been simple enough for Simms to have chosen to write his novel about the Yemassee War with a member of the plain folk as the hero of his action plot, without undue violation of historical credibility. (Indeed, from that standpoint one could wish that he had not decided to give Lord Craven a fictional frontier bride.) His decision to make the aristocratic Craven his protagonist has been ascribed to his attachment, as a Southerner, to the Cavalier ideal of the highborn leader.

We might, however, look at the matter the other way around. If, as we have noted, Simms could envision an aristocratic English lord as also an effective frontiersman and Indian fighter, albeit in disguise, then does it not also follow that he could envision a frontier figure *as Lord Craven*—as an aristocrat? As he saw things, in other words, it was possible for a man who was an effective leader of middle-class settlers, a vigorous fighter, intelligent, able to outthink his savage foes, and thus a person of proven practical virtues, to *be* the Lord Palatine, and thus fulfill within a single characterization the social assumptions of the romantic love story as well as those of the action plot.

Simms knew, of course, that historically the leader of the defense of the Carolina colony against the Yemassees in 1715 was Lord Craven, that he was not of the plain folk and did not come from the backwoods milieu. To portray Craven as a backwoods resident would have been to stretch creative embellishment of historical truth too far, even for Simms. In early eighteenth-century South Carolina, colonial governors and lords palatine were simply not drawn from the ranks of the plain folk. But in the nineteenth century, after the American Revolution had brought an end to British hegemony, similar careers *would* be open to talent. A citizen of humble circumstance, if his mettle were sufficient and his abilities superior, could aspire to lofty status and could gain it by virtue of his own merits—as witness Andrew Jackson, Sam Houston, and numerous others.

With a writer such as Simms it will not do to place too much significance upon what he does with a character for purposes of plot; not only was the convention of historical romance of his day, by Cooper out of Scott, an extremely loose affair, with what a modern audience might consider realistic probability subordinated to melodramatic possibility, but as a writer of fiction Simms was, especially at this early point in his career, more loose and more inventive than most. What *can* be legitimately and intensively scrutinized, I think, is why a particular characterization or plot development gets into a story in the first place. What does its presence represent, about and for Simms's imagination?

Consider the characterization of Craven/Harrison. Joseph V. Ridgely, in an excellent study of Simms, has noted how Simms's hero's views on religion correspond closely to those of Simms himself.[7] The hero of *The Yemassee* also possesses Simms's keen

7. Joseph V. Ridgely, *William Gilmore Simms* (New York: Twayne Publishing Co., 1962), 56.

sense of humor, which sometimes gets him into trouble with the overly pious, just as it did for Simms. Moreover, the qualities of leadership and practicality that enable Craven/Harrison to gain his ascendancy over the Carolina backwoodsmen and mobilize them for defense against the Indians are those of the "natural aristocrat," the born leader, rather than the titled nobleman who assumes command by virtue of birthright and decreed position. At no point does Craven/Harrison draw upon his privileged social status to gain his ends; he leads, he cajoles, he persuades the settlers to do what he wishes, and they follow his direction not because he possesses royal warrant but because he can perform better than they can in the woods, against the Indians. He reveals his noble status only after he has achieved all that he sets out to do, including the winning of the fair Bess Matthews' hand.

What I am getting at is that in *The Yemassee*, Simms took the historical figure of an English-born royal governor and converted him into what is essentially a *middle-class American*, a frontier hero, who shares a great many of the attitudes and opinions of Simms himself. Charles Craven *pretends* to be Gabriel Harrison; surely the only reason for his doing so is in order to gain the confidence of the backwoods settlers. It is as if Simms felt that, whether in 1715 or in his own time, what was required to make middle-class American frontiersmen accept someone's right to lead them was not hereditary status but true leadership qualities, which meant demonstrated mastery of the frontier situation. To be Lord Craven was not sufficient; it was necessary to be Gabriel Harrison. Only after proving his right to command by virtue of his ability may Craven then assert his right to do so by virtue of his noble status.

3.

There are numerous indications that in writing his first historical romance of Carolina, Simms brought into play powerful emotional involvements having to do with his own situation. There is in the novel a minor character, an Irishman named Teddy McNamara. Almost his sole plot function in the story is to be shown as taken prisoner by the Indians, subjected to torture, defying it, and in his flight involuntarily revealing the hiding place of Craven/Harrison, so that the governor is himself captured. Why, however, an Irishman? It seems clear that he constitutes, in his

defiance of his torturers and his willingness to fight back, a tribute to Simms's own Irish-born father out in Mississippi, who had
died not long before the novel was written.

As noted earlier, when Simms had visited his father there in
the mid-1820s he had spent much time among the Indians, while
his father had earlier served under Andrew Jackson in the Indian
campaigns. The elder Simms had urged his son to leave Charleston
and live permanently in the West, where he could practice law
and enter politics. In the newly settled territories Simms's lack of
highborn social status would be no barrier to his advancement,
his father had impressed upon him, while if he remained in
Charleston he would never be able to overcome his lowly origins.
Thereafter Simms recurrently expressed regret at not having followed his father's advice.

The characterization of the gallant Teddy McNamara, and his
presence there on the frontier in the novel, obviously bears a symbolic relationship, in the mind of the novelist, to the whole
matter of leadership, authority, and the frontier. The very nature
of his sudden appearance, arbitrarily and with no foreshadowing,
and the strong emphasis on his Irishness, increases the sense that,
given Simms's carelessness with plot and plausibility, there is
something significant involved in the episode for him over and
beyond its convenience as plot.

If this is so for Teddy McNamara, it is even more true with
another character in the story, Hugh Grayson. He is one of two
brothers, the older of whom, Wat, is one of Craven/Harrison's
most loyal and resolute aides among the frontiersmen. Hugh,
however, potentially the more able of the pair, is rebellious, jealous of Harrison's ascendancy over Bess Matthews, and at one
point almost does in the captain by foul murder, until his better
instincts prevail. The characterization of Hugh Grayson is one of
the *sturm und drang* figures, popularized by Klinger, Goethe, and
the German preromantics and coming into English literature by
way of William Godwin, that Simms and other American writers
liked to introduce into their fiction and drama from time to time.
Such Hamlet-like characters, "sicklied o'er with the pale cast of
thought," are given to dark passions and conflicting emotions,
customarily expressed in soliloquy form. They serve the burgeon-
ing need of the romanticism of the day, through providing a
means to portray the man of ambition, sensibility, and introspec-

tion doomed to live among mundane, ordinary folk who know not the divine discontent, and fated to loneliness and frustration because of his inability to discover an outlet for his talents. Depending upon his nature and the particular circumstance involved, he may opt for good or for evil.

We first encounter young Hugh Grayson with his brother, who taxes him for his jealousy of so admirable a figure as Captain Harrison. Hugh replies, "I cannot like that man for many reasons, and not the least of these is, that I cannot so readily as yourself acknowledge his superiority, while, perhaps, not less than yourself, I cannot help but feel it. My pride is to feel my independence—it is for you to desire control, were it only for the connexion and the sympathy which it brings to you. You are one of the millions who make tyrants. Go—worship him yourself, but do not call upon me to do likewise'" (45). Nothing, of course, about the fact that the Captain has captured the affections of the girl that Hugh loves, Bess Matthews, is said. Later in *The Yemassee*, Hugh's mother also recognizes his discontent, and takes him to task for his unreasonable dislike for the Captain, merely because he seems to be a gentleman. Hugh agrees: "'Aye, that is the word, mother—he is a gentleman—who knows, a lord in disguise—and is therefore superior to the poor peasant who is forced to dig his roots for life in the unproductive sands. Wherefore should his hands be unblistered, and mine asore? Wherefore should he come, and with a smile and silly speech win his way into people's hearts, when I, with a toiling affection of years, and a love that almost grows into a worship of its object, may not gather a single regard from any? Has nature given me life for this?'" (209).

Now the truth is that Grayson has no basis whatever to suspect that Harrison is a nobleman in disguise, nor has the Captain refused to get his hands blistered in the dirty work of preparing for frontier defense. At this point in the proceedings Hugh Grayson seems to be all set for villainy, motivated principally by jealousy of Craven/Harrison's way with Bess Matthews. But there is more to Hugh Grayson than this: "'Mother, I am a slave—a dog—an accursed thing, and in the worst of bondage—I am nothing,'" he declares. And (the speech is long, but worth quoting):

"I would be, and I am not. They keep me down—they refuse to hear— they do not heed me, and with a thought of command and a will of power in me, they yet pass me by, and I must give way to a bright wand and a gilded chain. Even here in these woods, with a poor neighborhood, and surrounded by those who are unknown and unhonoured in society, they—the slaves that they are!—they seek for artificial forms, and bind themselves with constraints that can only have a sanction in the degradation of the many. They yield up the noble and true attributes of a generous nature, and make themselves subservient to a name and a mark—thus it is that fathers enslave their children; and but for this, our lord proprietors, whom God in his mercy take to himself, have dared to say, even in this wild land not yet their own to people who have battled its dangers—ye shall worship after our fashions, or your voices are unheard. Who is the tyrant in this?—not the ruler—not the ruler—but those base spirits who let him rule,—those weak and unworthy, who, taking care to show their weaknesses, have invited the oppression which otherwise could have no head.'" (210)

The widow Grayson is alarmed at such talk, and understandably so. Why cannot her boy be content? she asks. Hugh responds that content is for the sluggard and the idle: "'Discontent is the life of enterprise, of achievement, of glory—aye, even of affection.'" When his mother asks why he must think all these strange thoughts, he tells her that it is because "'I have thought for myself, mother—in the woods, by the waters—and have not had my mind compressed into the old time mould with which the pedant shapes the skulls of the imitative apes that courtesy considers human'" (210). And so on. His mother urges him not to cherish such hate for the Captain and contempt for his brother, to try to live at peace with himself, and above all not to go around being so unhappy all the time. Hugh is not very optimistic about the prospects for being able to do so, but he promises to do his best, and the scene ends.

Ultimately he repents, and thereafter uses his energies and talents for good causes, for as Simms tells us, "Hugh Grayson, with all his faults, and they were many, was in reality a *noble fellow*. Full of a *high* ambition—a craving for the unknown and the vast, which spread itself vaguely and perhaps *unattainably* before his imagination—his disappointments naturally vexed him somewhat beyond prudence, and now and then beyond the restraint of right reason" (304; italics added). Fortunately Craven/Harrison, despite almost being murdered during one of those moments of vexation beyond prudence, recognizes Hugh's latent leadership abilities, puts him in charge of a troop of defenders, and when the Yemassees are driven off and after Hugh has shown his true mettle, invests him with full military command of the county of Granville, as his deputy and spokesman. It is in so doing that he finally reveals his identity as the Lord Palatine, whereupon Bess Matthews falls into his arms, and everybody present shouts for joy. Even Grayson is reconciled: "'I take your commission, my lord,' replied Grayson, with a degree of firm manliness, superseding his gloomy expression and clearing it away—'I take it, sir, and will proceed at once to the execution of its duties. Your present suggestions, sir, will be of value'" (357).

Joseph V. Ridgely describes the characterization of Hugh Grayson as displaying a Southern "fieriness" that Simms saw both as a virtue and potential menace.[8] But Grayson is not an aristocratic young Southern hothead such as Ralph Colleton in Simms's previous novel, Guy Rivers. It is far more likely that Grayson's function, so far as Simms's imagination goes, is to embody an issue that, especially for the youthful Simms of the early 1830s, was of much emotional importance. For when he wrote The Yemassee, Simms had not yet married Chevillette Roach and become a gentleman-planter by marriage. He was still nursing the wounds of his losing battle against the Nullifiers as editor of the Charleston City Gazette; he bitterly resented the class system of Charleston, and what he considered his rejection by that city's elite. Throughout his life he felt himself unappreciated by a politically obsessed squirearchy, even though he ended up adopting many of its tenets.

There can be little doubt that Hugh Grayson is expressing views about democracy and the common man that the young Simms also held, and that made him describe himself to a Northern friend a few years later as "a Democrat of the Jackson School" and insist that "I believe in the people and prefer trusting their impulses, than the craft, the cupidity, the selfishness of trades & Whiggery."[9] Hugh Grayson is, in a real sense, a portrait of the

8. Ridgely, William Gilmore Simms, 55.

9. Simms to James Lawson, December 29, [1939], in The Letters of William Gilmore Simms, collected and edited by Mary C. Simms Oliphant, Alfred Taylor Odell, and T. C. Duncan Eaves (6 vols.; Columbia: University of South Carolina Press, 1952–56, 1982), I, 167.

youthful Simms, lonely and without status in class-conscious Charleston and its mercantile-planter gentry, denied a college education, apprenticed to an apothecary, given to wandering by himself in the woods and thinking his own thoughts.

For as noted, there is little reason for Grayson to attribute to Gabriel Harrison the smug lordliness that he identifies him as exhibiting; in his behavior among the settlers the Lord Palatine in mufti has not acted at all as if deference and obeisance were due him by right. It is as if, for a brief moment, Simms the storyteller has become so caught up in what Hugh Grayson represents that he transfers his narrative persona from Craven/Harrison to the unhappy young frontiersman, in order to express his resentment of the highborn authority and inherited privilege, which as Grayson declares is, even in the early days of the Carolina colony, already imposing hierarchy and subordination upon free men in the forests of the New World. The passion with which Grayson denounces such subservience seems considerably in excess of what is necessary for the *sturm und drang* set-piece; indeed, so genuine does it come across that it causes the reader, for the moment, to view Grayson and his attitude toward imposed authority quite sympathetically.

But if this is so—and it appears quite obvious—then clearly there is a basic social tension present in Simms's thinking that manifests itself in the relationships exhibited in *The Yemassee*. For whatever the believability of his Jacksonian social views, Hugh Grayson is *not* the hero of the novel, and except for his brief set-piece, it is Charles Craven, alias Gabriel Harrison, upon whom the author centers his attention.

We have already seen how the sectional politics of the 1830s intrudes into the novel in terms of the need to defend slavery. The incipient North-South schism also makes itself felt in other ways, as in the characterization of the dissenting minister who is Bess Matthews' father. Pastor Matthews, dour, self-righteous, convinced of his own rectitude, and unwilling to tolerate differences of opinion and belief, has little historical legitimacy for being on the Carolina frontier in the year 1715; what he really is, beyond question, is a New England Calvinist, who but for the time and place would be an Abolitionist. Simms rings the changes on his smug holier-than-thou attitude, the naïveté which enables him to believe that the hostile Yemassees are his friends. It is almost as if not an Indian uprising but a slave revolt were in the offing!

When Simms declares of Matthews that "he was a bigot himself, and, with the power, would doubtless have tyrannized after a similar fashion," the Parson's antebellum political role is unmistakable: "The world within him was what he could take in with his eye, or control within the sound of his voice. He could not be brought to understand that climates and conditions should be various, and that the popular good, in a strict reference to the mind of man, demanded that people should everywhere differ in manner and opinion" (51).

Matthews is depicted as a Puritan, and Craven/Harrison is set in direct opposition to him as a Cavalier. When the humorless Parson chides the Captain for his seeming levity, Harrison replies that he will undertake to reform his ways

"when you shall satisfy me that to laugh and sing, and seek and afford amusement, are inconsistent with my duties either to the Creator or the creature. . . . It is you, sir, and your sect, that are the true criminals. Denying, as you do, to the young, all those natural forms of enjoyment and amusement which the Deity, speaking through their own nature, designed for their wholesome nature, you cast a shadow over all things around you. In this way, sir, you force them upon the necessity for seeking for less obvious and more artificial enjoyments, which are not often innocent, and which are frequently ruinous and destructive. As for the irreverence to religion, and sacred things, with which you charge me, you will suffer me respectfully to deny." (56)

It is not merely the English civil war of the previous century that Simms is importing into the Carolina frontier in 1715. The laughing Cavalier–dour Puritan dichotomy he is using was a staple of the rhetoric of the sectional division during Simms's own time. As we have seen, it was customary for Southern pamphleteers to depict the North, and especially New England abolitionism, as made up of Roundheads and Levellers, and the South as the home of the Cavalier, the Chivalry. According to the rhetoric that came to dominate the schism, "the Yankee was a direct descendant of the Puritan Roundhead," as William R. Taylor writes, "and the Southern gentleman of the English Cavalier. . . . Under the stimulus of this divided heritage the North had developed a leveling, go-getting society and the South had developed a society based on the value of the English country gentry."[10]

If we look closely at Simms's language, it becomes clear that his idea of democracy was not one that focused principally on the notion that all men were equal and that therefore human distinctions were without a basis in nature. What he has Hugh Grayson denounce is *hereditary* rank and caste, class distinctions that are institutionalized into a caste system, and that prevent or hinder true merit from rising. Hugh Grayson, we have seen, was a "noble fellow"; and what he objected to was a system that kept his innate nobility—his powers of imagination and leadership—from being properly recognized.

The enormous popularity of Andrew Jackson in the United States of the 1820s, 1830s, and 1840s was in part a corroboration of the notion of "nature's aristocrat," the remarkable man who, living in a country in which the hereditary institutions of the Old World no longer acted to stifle individual merit among all but the aristocracy, was able to rise by virtue of his own genius to heights previously reserved for kings and members of the nobility. Melville's great Invocation to the Muses in *Moby-Dick*, his apologia for daring to make a Nantucket whaling captain into a tragic hero, is a memorable statement of the theme. Like Simms an enthusiastic member of the Young America literary movement, Melville makes the specific analogy with Jackson: "Bear me out in it, thou great democratic God! who didst not refuse to the swart convict, Bunyan, the pale, poetic pearl; Thou who didst clothe with doubly hammered leaves of finest gold, the stumped and paupered arm of old Cervantes; Thou who didst pick up Andrew Jackson from the pebbles; who didst hurl him upon a war-horse; who didst thunder him higher than a throne! Thou who in all Thy mighty, earthly marchings, ever cullest Thy selected champions from the kingly commons; bear me out in it, O God!"[11] Melville was writing in a Western society which had only recently been rocked by the French Revolution and the rise of Napoleon Bonaparte from obscurity into a position of power and

10. William R. Taylor, *Cavalier and Yankee: The Old South and American National Character* (New York: George Braziller, 1961), 15.

11. Herman Melville, *Moby-Dick, or The White Whale* (New York and Toronto: New American Library, 1961), 124.

might that had sent long-established kingships toppling, and whose armies, staffed with marshals who had found careers open to talent, had won victory after victory. The belief that the individual who possessed the requisite genius and followed his star was fated to achieve fame and glory was nowhere more popular than in a new nation founded on the stated belief that all men were created equal. The career of Jackson seemed to exemplify the principle.

If we think of this ideology in terms of the young, ambitious, obviously talented William Gilmore Simms, self-educated, without assured social credentials, growing up in a city in which caste and class were considered highly important, it is hardly surprising that the fame and success he coveted would be strongly infused with the notion of lofty position, and that the shape it would assume would be that of the gentleman-planter, the possessor of a landed estate. Just as Andrew Jackson rose from obscure beginnings in the Waxhaws of Simms's native state to military glory, political supremacy, and the occupancy of the Hermitage near Nashville, Tennessee, so Simms aspired to literary fame, political influence, and a country seat of his own.

His exemplar of achieved status, Charles Craven, in the Carolina colony of 1715, and the young frontiersman who so resents his own humble status, Hugh Grayson, can be seen as separate halves of what, a century later, Simms believed need no longer be separate and discrete individuals, but one and the same person. Republican virtue, intense ambition, lofty status, and noble bearing could and should coexist in the same person. The New World was indeed the Land of Opportunity, the frontier was the place for democratic aspiration, the plantation would soon be the sign and seal of virtue and success, and the gentleman-planter, the Cavalier who replicated the landed aristocrat of Old England, the symbol of successful achievement.

So thought Simms, and in *The Yemassee* he showed what would make it possible. In this novel of his early literary maturity there was much that grew out of his deepest emotional needs and fondest hopes.

Yet, as we have noted, when we compare it with James Fenimore Cooper and his Leatherstocking Tales, what is largely missing in the South Carolina author's novel is the conflict between individual freedom in the wilderness and the needs and commitments of society. Simms's frontier folk may go out into the woods, may even do so, as Hugh Grayson tells his mother, to "'walk—out of sight—in the air—I must have fresh air, for I choke strangely'" (211). The wilderness may have things to teach the free man who frequents them and who may, like Grayson, learn to think for himself "'in the woods, by the waters,'" and thus avoid the rote learning of pedantry and custom. But there is nothing in *The Yemassee* of that self-identification *with* the forest, the deliberate choosing of the wilderness as a way of escaping from the complexity of civilized society, with its falseness and hypocrisy, such as sends Cooper's Natty Bumppo beyond the settlements.

Leatherstocking, as we have seen, as mediator between the forest and the town, can achieve for himself that access of freedom possible to a life in which, to quote from his own words, he is able to "eat when hungry, and drink when adry; and ye keep stated hours and rules: nay, nay, you even overfeed the dogs, lads, from pure kindness; and hounds should be gaunty to run well. The meanest of God's creaters be made for some use, and I'm formed for the wilderness; if ye love me, let me go where my soul craves to be ag'in!"[12] Thus the veteran frontiersman of *The Pioneers* reaffirms his purpose to stay clear of society. But he pays a price for that freedom: he remains celibate, alone. There can be no marriage, no children, no inheritors, for these are the product of social existence, and require for their survival and their flourishing the institutions of the social compact. And in paying that price, Leatherstocking is but the first of a long line of American literary figures who discover the cost of living away from society, in the wilderness and therefore outside of history; I think of such diverse fictional characters as Huckleberry Finn, Isaac McCaslin, and the hunter Wilson in Ernest Hemingway's "The Short Happy Life of Francis Macomber."

With characteristic understatement D. H. Lawrence has enunciated a truth concerning James Fenimore Cooper: that novelist "loved the genteel continent of Europe, and waited gasping for the newspapers to praise his WORK." His "actual desire was to be

---

12. James Fenimore Cooper, *The Pioneers, or The Sources of the Susquehanna: A Descriptive Tale* (New York: New American Library, 1964), 434.

Monsieur Fenimore Cooper, le grand ecrivain americain," but his
"innermost wish was to be: Natty Bumppo." Lawrence very properly emphasizes the extent to which the dream of Leatherstocking
represented escape for this author—flight from all that society
was and what the concerns of being an author and a property-
owning gentleman demanded of him. The Natty-Chingachgook
myth, he keeps repeating, "is a wish-fulfillment, an evasion of
reality."[13]

Simms's dream, then, turns out to be diametrically opposed
to that of Cooper. It is a dream not of solitude but of society, and
the attainment of a position of comfort and dignity within it.
Simms's frontiersmen live at the edge of the forest, which, however, they are busy converting into farmland. The freedom that
Hugh Grayson declares ought to be the proper condition of the
settlers, and which is being negated by their willingness to accept
European notions of subordination and class, is one not of escape
from society into a classless (and childless) state of nature, but of
the right to pursue one's objectives and to make the most of one's
abilities within society. Nor is that ideal merely one of the small
farmer, Thomas Jefferson's virtuous husbandman who tills his
own acres and owes not any man. It involves the dream of status,
of recognized accomplishment among one's fellow men: the right,
one might say, to be a Thomas Jefferson—or an Andrew Jackson.

Life in nature is not romanticized in The Yemassee or elsewhere in Simms's border novels. The forest is the place of out-
lawry and violence, with few ennobling qualities for those whites
who put the territories behind them. The summit of civilized attainment for Simms is, to repeat, the great plantation, and like
most of his fellow white Southerners of the time he did not see
the use of the slave labor that made it possible as importantly
marring its perfection. In the inability to recognize the hide-
ousness of such a blemish and so helping to doom any promise of
lasting fulfillment, he only shared in the common failure of his
time and place. As we have seen, fortunately for James Fenimore
Cooper no such crucial moral awareness was required of him.

13. D. H. Lawrence, Studies in Classic American Literature (New York:
Thomas Seltzer, 1923), in Edmund Wilson (ed.), The Shock of Recognition: The
Development of Literature in the United States Recorded by the Men Who Made
It, Vol. II, The Twentieth Century (New York: Grosset and Dunlap, n.d.), 951, 954.

When that well-born New York novelist set out to compose a historical romance involving Indian fighting and woodcraft, he could not envision his practical, lowborn frontiersman, skilled in coping with life in the primitive forestland and its Indian inhabitants, as also possessing the sensibility and cultural sophistication needed for the hero's role in a love plot. For the plebeian Simms no such division of labor was necessary; a cultivated English aristocrat could also be a hard-fighting, intensely practical border captain, and vice versa. At the close, when the Lord Palatine weds the Parson's daughter, not only will Bess Matthews henceforth be a great lady, but the marriage will symbolize what Simms envisions as the culmination of the New World social experience: the union of the innate refinement and virtue of the nontitled American with the assured status and implicit dignity of the titled aristocracy of the Old World.

If the transaction makes possible the nature-schooled dignity of an Andrew Jackson and the imposing grandeur of the plantation house, however, it deprives the antebellum Southern imagination of the dream of natural freedom in the wilderness, the mythic escape from history and society into the pathless forest that a Leatherstocking may choose. For Simms's dream is of fulfillment *in* society and history—just as a century following the publication of *The Yemassee* a parvenu named Thomas Sutpen would make his way into the Mississippi forest to clear the land, build his great house, and seek to establish his dynasty. But in Faulkner's magnificent novel the price to be exacted for such fulfillment on the terms sought, which Simms and his contemporaries could overlook, is all too clear. At the close of *Absalom, Absalom!* the weeds and thickets of the once-virgin Southern forest reassert their timeless dominion over the fire-gutted ruins of Sutpen's Hundred.

IV. THE INWARD IMAGINATION
Poe

Of my country and of my family I have little to say.
—Poe, "MS. Found in a Bottle"

In the January, 1836, issue of the *Southern Literary Messenger* there was published a review of William Gilmore Simms's novel *The Partisan*, the first of the novelist's historical romances of the American Revolution. Simms had dedicated the book to a Charleston friend, Richard Yeadon, Jr., as follows:

DEAR SIR,

My earliest, and, perhaps, most pleasant rambles in the field of literature, were taken in your company—permit me to remind you of that period by inscribing the present volume with your name.

THE AUTHOR[1]

For reasons puzzling but perhaps not beyond all conjecture, the dedication seems to have infuriated the reviewer, Edgar Allan Poe, who was also assistant editor of the *Messenger*. Poe tore into Simms. He paraphrased and acted out the supposed presentation of the dedication to Yeadon in order to make it appear servile and fawning. He spent several pages belaboring Simms's style for its awkwardness and grammatical faults. The future author of "Murders in the Rue Morgue" and "The Facts in the Case of M. Valdemar" censured Simms for depicting the ugly and repulsive. He scolded the use of profanity—"d——m," "d——d," etc.—in the speech of Lieutenant Porgy: "Such attempts to render profanity less despicable by rendering it amusing, should be frowned down indignantly by the public." Porgy he branded "a

---

1. [William Gilmore Simms,] *The Partisan: A Tale of the Revolution*, "by the Author of 'The Yemassee' and 'Guy Rivers'" (New York: Harper and Brothers, 1835), v.

most insufferable bore."[2] He cited numerous examples of what he labeled Simms's "villainously bad taste," only to follow this personal and literary onslaught with the statement that "'The Partisan' is no ordinary work. Its historical details are replete with interest. The concluding scenes are well drawn. Some passages of swamp imagery are exquisite. Mr. Simms has evidently the eye of a painter." That said, he ended by undercutting it: "Perhaps, in sober truth, he would succeed better in sketching a landscape than he has done in writing a novel."[3]

Poe had been studying the notorious slashing reviews in the British journals, and was now out to build a reputation for himself by adapting their methodology to the American literary scene, where book reviewing had tended to be bland and in most instances laudatory. Such tomahawking did indeed attract attention to the *Messenger*, and also helped to get its assistant editor fired by the proprietor, who believed that the tactics his difficult, temperamental young assistant was using were offensive, ungentlemanly, and embarrassing. The jobless Poe thereupon departed for Philadelphia and New York City, where he engaged in whatever editorial work he could find, wrote most of his best poetry and fiction, and got himself embroiled in the vicious literary wars of Gotham that Perry Miller has chronicled in *The Raven and the Whale* (1956), thereby acquiring some enemies who after his death besmirched his none-too-stainless literary reputation by making him out to have been a full-time toady, hypocrite, and scoundrel.

Simms was considerably vexed by the *Messenger's* review of his novel. Poe was "no friend of mine," he wrote to Evert Duyckinck ten years later. The review, he went on to say, was in some respects accurate in terms of what it had to say about his style and taste, but it "paid little heed to what was really good in the thing": "Besides, he was rude & offensive & personal, in the manner of the thing, which he should not have been, in the case

2. Poe, review of *The Partisan*, in *Southern Literary Messenger*, January, 1836, rpr. in *Edgar Allan Poe: Essays and Reviews*, Library of America (New York: Literary Classics of the United States, 1984), 897. Cited hereafter as *Essays and Reviews*.

3. *Ibid.*, 901, 902.

of anybody,—still less in mine. My deportment had not justified it. He knew, or might have known, that I was none of that miserable gang about town, who beg in the literary highways. I had no clique, mingled with none, begged no praise from anybody, and made no conditions with the herd. He must have known what I was personally—might have known—& being just should not have been rude."[4]

As anyone familiar with Simms might also expect, he did not permit his personal resentment to hinder him from expressing his considerable admiration for Poe's talents, doing what he could to help Poe later on, and championing his cause. As for Poe, he later changed his tune, praised Simms's work, and the two Southern authors on the New York literary scene became friends.

Poe, as Simms wrote at various times, was a greatly gifted writer who lacked self-discipline in his personal life and could not always control his powerful emotions. On the surface it might seem incongruous that such a man should be, as a literary critic, the zealous advocate of cold-blooded craftsmanship, of iron control over the poem and the story. His best-known critical disquisition, "The Philosophy of Composition," described the writing of "The Raven" as an exercise in deliberate calculation, with everything in the poem carefully chosen in order to achieve a desired effect. Yet little knowledge of psychology is needed to grasp the obvious fact that the fixation upon authorial control, upon the necessity for employing calculation rather than emotion when composing a poem or story, the constant insistence that the writer must be absolute master of his material and shape everything in the work toward a predetermined end, are the expression of a dire personal need on his own part, and represent his effort to enforce such discipline upon his own very intense emotional life.

As everybody knows, T. S. Eliot wrote that "poetry is not a turning loose of emotion, but an escape from emotion; it is not the expression of personality, but an escape from personality. But,

---

4. William Gilmore Simms to Evert Augustus Duyckinck, March 15, 1845, in *The Letters of William Gilmore Simms*, collected and edited by Mary C. Simms Oliphant, Alfred Taylor Odell, and T. C. Duncan Eaves (6 vols; Columbia: University of South Carolina Press, 1952–1982), II (1952), 42–44. Cited hereafter as *Letters*.

of course, only those who have personality and emotions know what it means to want to escape from those things."[5] In recent years we have come to realize just how very personal, and how freighted with emotion, Eliot's poems were. His aesthetic, too, was a response to an agonizing personal need that required all the desperate self-restraint that Eliot could muster.

Simms was not the kind of man whose personal ambition often led him into attacks on other writers out of motives of personal jealousy. He wrote of Poe that "he seems too much the subject of his moods—not sufficiently so of principle."[6] One may assume that Poe's wanton attack on *The Partisan* and its author was prompted not only by the desire to create a reputation for himself as critic through the use of scalping tactics, but by considerable jealousy and envy as well. After all, here was a book by a Southern author who was clearly enjoying much success in New York. Within four years Simms had published a successful volume of poetry and four novels—while Poe had thus far attracted very little notice elsewhere for his own writings. Poe was the poorly paid assistant editor of a magazine; Simms was publishing his work in the most prestigious journals and his books were being brought out by the best houses.

Simms's naïve pride in his attainments, his success with work that was manifestly less than perfect, and the abundance of energy that enabled him to continue turning out book after book, must have exasperated Poe. He was piqued by Simms's pleasure at his own performance that the dedication indicated, by the satisfaction with which the South Carolina novelist accepted his fame; there was an openness about Simms that could and did vex persons jealous for their own reputation and lacking his energy and his determination. Later in his career he experienced something of the same vexation on the part of his young friend Henry Timrod, who, like Poe, knew he was a better craftsman than Simms and yet had thus far been unable to realize his own literary promise.

No doubt Simms was quite right when in 1846 he wrote to the by-now-beleaguered Poe urging him to cease embroiling himself

5. T. S. Eliot, "Tradition and the Individual Talent," *Selected Essays* (New York: Harcourt Brace and Co., 1932), 10–11.
6. Simms to Evert A. Duyckinck, March 15, 1845, in *Letters*, II, 43.

in the petty disputes of the New York literati and the journalistic name-calling he was engaged in, to control his personal habits, eschew the company of "men, whatever their talents, whom you cannot esteem as men," and make use of his own genuine gifts to rescue his fortunes. Poe had written a series of vignettes of New York literary figures for *Godey's Ladies Book,* some of which had caused considerable resentment, and the result had been accusations of misconduct, dishonesty, forgery, drunkenness, and the like. He had filed a lawsuit against one assailant, and won a judgment for libel, but only at the price of a public airing of charges and countercharges. Meanwhile his social reputation had fallen to a low ebb, and even his friends were disgusted with him. Poe's young wife had just died, he had almost no income; his fortunes seemed to be at rock bottom. Simms's advice was sound, but the distraught and unstable Poe was in no shape to act on it. Trapped as he was in a Grub Street–style existence, emotionally at the mercy of compulsions such as the more stable Simms could have only dimly understood, Poe was quite powerless to follow Simms's suggestion that he "return to that community—that moral province in society—of which, let me say to you, respectfully and regretfully,—you have been, according to all reports but too heedlessly and, perhaps, too scornfully indifferent."[7]

What Simms was telling Poe was that, as a Southern gentleman, he had no business flouting the canons of social respectability and getting involved in the literary and social lowlife of New York City. Writing in the *Southern Patriot* at about the same time, Simms declared that Poe was "a man, clearly, of sudden and uneven impulses of great nervous susceptibility, and one whose chief misfortune it is not to have been caught young and trained early. The efforts of his mind seem wholly spasmodic. He lacks literary industry, I take it, which, in the case of the literary man who must look to his daily wits for his daily bread, is something of a deficiency."[8] What he did have, however, was genius.

Poe and Simms were about as far apart in their personal habits and their attitude toward their literary work as it was possible to be. Simms craved an orderly social existence, sought and enjoyed

7. Simms to Edgar Allan Poe, July 30, 1846, in *Letters,* II, 76–77, 175.
8. Simms, "Literary Letter" to *Southern Patriot,* dated July 15, 1846, and published in the issue of July 20, 1846, quoted in *Letters,* II, 174n.

public status, was thoroughly responsible in business and financial affairs. Poe lived at the raw edge of personal and social chaos
throughout his adult life, and displayed almost no interest in politics or any kind of public status independent of his literary identity. At least from young manhood on he was in active rebellion
against the middle-class community of Richmond and its materialistic values; Simms by contrast wished to function as a citizen
within such a community, and to win distinction within it for his
literary attainments. Simms's personal ideal was that of the
Southern man of letters, very much a part of his society, in residence at his plantation. Poe liked to view himself as a Byronic
outcast, an Ishmael set apart from the common run of mankind
by virtue of the intensity of his artistic passion, and if he dreamed
at times of the wealth that went along with landed proprietorship,
his ever-present but never realized goal was to own and edit an
influential and successful literary magazine.

As writers the two were likewise in almost every respect dis-
similar. Simms worked rapidly and regularly, turning out a steady
flow of words in numerous genres. Poe could and did grind out a
supply of journalistic hackwork, but his fiction and poetry came
in small parcels and very irregularly. There were periods when he
went without writing anything at all. As a professional maga-
zinist he worked in the short forms—the lyric poem, the tale. His
writing was carefully tailored to size and shaped for maximum
emotional effect and shock value. In particular his poetry, heavily
cadenced, intricately rhymed, and designed for effects of sound at
least as much as of sense, often seems contrived and overwritten,
yet it is never devoid of passion. Simms, by contrast, was all too
willing to settle for the approximate word and meaning. Even his
best work betrays haste and carelessness. He worked in the long
forms—the book-length romance, the extended story, the multi-
part poem. His sense of literary style was to Poe's, one might say,
as Fenimore Cooper's was to Hawthorne's, or as the bowie knife
to the surgeon's scalpel.

No one would question the linking of Simms's work to his
time and place; to his contemporaries he *was* Southern literature.
In Poe's instance, however, the linkage is far less obvious and accepted. To be sure, Poe seems to have thought of himself as a
Southerner. He sometimes praised works of Southern literature

for being such, and several times he voiced the familiar complaint among Southern literary people that any writer who was publicly identified with the South found it extremely difficult to achieve recognition in New York and Boston. Like Simms and almost all the Southerners, he cared little for the Transcendentalists of Concord, and he disliked Boston for its habit of literary didacticism. There is no evidence of his ever dissenting from the Southern defense of Negro slavery. His writings shared certain characteristics with those of his Southern contemporaries, such as the concern for lyrical form rather than meter-making argument, a belief in beauty rather than truth as the proper stuff of poetry, and a taste for necrophilic lamentation over dead and buried female loveliness. His distaste for the poetry of ideas and his hostility to the didactic, indeed, were quite in keeping with Southern literary practice from colonial days on up to the Southern New Critics of the 1930s and 1940s. Yet as Robert D. Jacobs, who has written with most perception about Poe as a Southerner, has pointed out recently, a good case can also be made for Poe as an international artist, almost the only such in pre–Civil War America. Certainly his writing shares little with that of those writers of the American Renaissance who were his leading contemporaries. "Born in Boston and reared in Virginia," Jacobs has noted, "Edgar Poe has become a citizen of the world, a status he would have considered entirely appropriate."[9] Poe himself insisted that art was by its very nature international. His work is customarily set in faraway places, most often in Europe, and he wrote almost nothing in which a specifically Southern setting was important to his meaning. He found his greatest admirers in France, where he was honored by the Symbolists and has always been held in high repute. Baudelaire said that he wrote no fiction because Poe had already done the job for him. Rimbaud, Verlaine, Valéry praised his work. Mallarmé wrote a sonnet to honor his burial place. Whatever doubts his fellow countrymen may have held concerning his literary importance have not been shared by the French, for whom he was for generations the incarnation of the true artist.

9. Robert D. Jacobs, "Edgar Allan Poe," *The History of Southern Literature*, edited by Louis D. Rubin, Jr., Blyden Jackson, Rayburn Moore, Lewis P. Simpson, and Thomas Daniel Young (Baton Rouge: Louisiana State University Press, 1985), 135.

2.

English and American literary critics have never known exactly what to do with Edgar Poe. In his own lifetime his principal reputation was as a journalistic critic. His poetry continues to hold a powerful appeal for the young, and "The Raven" in particular has long enjoyed a popularity among the mass of readers such as no other American poem can command. Yet to sophisticated readers Poe's verse, with its singsong, overwrought, melodramatic stanzas and its reliance upon lurid, stagy technical effects at the expense of poetic meaning, has been suspect. Emerson called him "the jingle man." Aldous Huxley accounted for his high reputation among the French by proposing that an imperfect knowledge of the English language made them incapable of recognizing the vulgarity and contrivance that for an English or American reader are only too obvious.

It is Poe's fiction that has lasted best. Though overdone and given to sensational scenes, the short stories have a consistency of plot development and a narrative voice that sustain our interest and compel us to take what we are being told with seriousness. Poe is able to project into his first-person narrator a personality that is thoroughly plausible, and that forces the reader to view his situation with the importance he places upon it. "The thousand injuries of Fortunato I had borne as I best could; but when he ventured upon insult, I vowed revenge," the narrator of "The Cask of Amontillado" declares at the outset. "You, who know so well the nature of my soul, will not suppose, however, that I gave utterance to threat."[10] As readers we know no such thing, but in so asserting he negates our initial skepticism, so that whatever we may eventually come to think of him, there can be no question that he is a force to be reckoned with, and will not be deterred from stating his case.

Poe's first-person narrators are almost all fatalists; we recognize their obsessiveness almost immediately, and realize that in whatever they are setting out to tell us they will be involved so

10. Poe, "The Cask of Amontillado," *Collected Works of Edgar Allan Poe*, Vol. III, *Tales and Sketches, 1843–1849*, ed. Thomas Ollive Mabbott (Cambridge, Mass., and London: Belknap Press of Harvard University Press, 1978), 1256. Cited hereafter as *Tales and Sketches*, III.

compulsively that prior objections will not be tolerated: "True!—
nervous—very, very dreadfully nervous I had been and am, but
why *will* you say that I am mad? The disease had sharpened my
senses—not destroyed—not dulled them. Above all was the sense
of hearing acute. I heard all things in the heaven and the earth.
I heard many things in hell. How, then, am I mad? Hearken! and
observe how healthily—how calmly I can tell you the whole
story."[11] Such psychological description at the outset of "The Tell-
Tale Heart" is what Poe excels at; he is the master of the compulsive obsessive. His narrators inform us at once that they are
beyond the stage at which mere reason and common sense might
reach them. They have already anticipated the obvious objections, and *they* feel sure they have dismissed them. In the very
insistence upon their own reasonableness they reveal themselves
as caught up in irremediable compulsion.

In *Moby-Dick*, Herman Melville also depicts a man so thoroughly in the grip of an obsession that nothing may deter him
from his object. Captain Ahab realizes that he disguises his obsession to secure its pursuit, and recognizes the need to apply reason
as a means to indulge his madness. In Poe's fiction, however, there
is no Ishmael to interpret his various protagonists' obsessions by
the light of reason and normality, and no Starbuck to oppose himself to monomania or strive to convince his mad captain of his
madness. If in *Moby-Dick* the tragic outcome is theologically or
cosmologically foreordained, we can at least hope that it may yet
be avoided, and the growth of our helpless conviction that it *must*
happen makes possible the tragedy of its finally taking place. But
in Poe whatever happens has not only already taken place; it has
done so without hindrance. We are told what happened by the
madman who has made it happen. When he is done with his narrative we may lament what has occurred, and feel horror at the
revelation of the full enormity of the act of madness we have been
watching, but the possibility, even in retrospect, that it might yet
be prevented does not figure.

There can be no *tragedy* as such, because there is no opposition to the workings of fate, no hero caught in a moral dilemma
from which the struggle to escape only enforces his entrapment.

11. Poe, "The Tell-Tale Heart," *Tales and Sketches*, III, 792.

Tragedy, as Aristotle perceived it, must satisfy a moral sense; it must present a protagonist not eminently good or just, whose fall is brought on by error or frailty rather than by vice or depravity. In the fall of the erring tragic hero, there is affirmation of the workings of a moral universe.

In Poe, however, there is no such affirmation, and no moral sense is satisfied. The universe that Poe proposes possesses no discernible rational ordering, whether moral or otherwise; it is arbitrary, even capricious. That a protagonist succeeds or fails in his design usually signifies only that: individual success, individual failure; no more. Anything is possible because nothing is foreordained. The characters, not the universe they inhabit, are what embody the fatalism. Caught up in their obsession they are helpless, but human depravity and not tragic fate is what sends them along the route to destruction.

We don't know *why* the injuries and insults of Fortunato so outrage Montressor; no hint is given as to the motives behind Fortunato's behavior. All we know, or need to know, is that Montressor is out for revenge, and that Fortunato is to be the victim. When he walls up Fortunato alive in the Montressor catacombs, there is neither poetic justice nor inevitability at work, only anger and malevolence. The motto of the Montressors, we are informed, is *Nemo me impune lacessit,* "No one who injures me goes unpunished"—as thoroughly and primitively pagan a credo as might be imagined, the absolute negation of several thousand years of Christian teaching.

It is characteristic of Poe's fiction that the act of violence— murder, torture, whatever—usually achieves no known result beyond the commission of the act itself. It is not a deed involving purposiveness, so much as an expression of attitude. The violence is not only committed out of essentially arbitrary feelings of resentment, spleen, ill-will; it also constitutes *the expression of those feelings.*

It has not often been remarked that of all the leading American authors of his day, Poe seems by all odds the most urban in sensibility. His world is one of society—cities, crowds, tenements, mansions, estates, avenues, buildings. Though reared in the South, he did not often write fiction about nature and life in the outdoors. Few things of importance in Poe's fiction ever happen outside; even a seeming exception such as *The Narrative of Arthur Gordon Pym* is set largely in the confines of ships, in caves, and the like. When nature does impinge, it is in the form of immense, almost surrealistic cataclysms, maelstroms, dreary wastes with fantastic shapes and forms. The natural world is not so much re-created as bizarrely imagined. When, as sometimes does happen, the stories are set on rural estates, the action generally takes place inside, usually in rooms that are excessively decorated with tap-estries, furniture, portraits, armor, curtains, and ornaments. Even a venture into landscape gardening such as "Landor's Cottage," although set in a mountain vale, looks like an oil painting and is likened to a theatrical setting. The gardens, cottage, furniture, decorative materials have all been *planned*.

Poe's people are trapped within the walls of cities and build-ings. No escape into nature is ever possible. The American forest and frontier are missing from his art almost completely. The true wilderness for Poe is the city; it is man-made. Those who dwell in it are locked in solitude, behind shut doors and closed windows, while outside in the streets the anonymous masses of city dwellers stroll indifferently by.

In "The Man of the Crowd" the narrator observes from his window the comings and goings of swarms of Londoners, notes their appearance, the manner in which their dress is indicative of rank and occupation, until at length he spies an elderly man who seems to be the incarnation of "vast mental power, of caution, of penuriousness, of avarice, of coolness, of malice, of blood-thirstiness, of triumph, of merriment, of excessive terror, of in-tense—of extreme despair. I felt singularly aroused, startled, fas-cinated. 'How wild a history,' I said to myself, 'is written within that bosom!'"[12]

On an impulse he decides to follow him. All night long and through the ensuing day he keeps him in view, pursuing him through the streets without being observed. He notes that the old man cannot bear to be alone and therefore moves from crowd to

12. Poe, "The Man of the Crowd," *Collected Works of Edgar Allan Poe*, Vol. II, *Tales and Sketches, 1831–1842*, ed. Thomas Ollive Mabbott, with the assistance of Eleanor D. Kewer and Maureen C. Mabbott (Cambridge, Mass., and London: Belknap Press of Harvard University Press, 1978), 511. Cited hereafter as *Tales and Sketches*, II.

crowd, seeming to relax his anxiety only when among hordes of people, no matter how disreputable. Finally, as the second evening comes on, the narrator grows weary, and "stopping fully in front of the wanderer, gazed at him steadfastly in the face." But the old man takes no notice of him, and walks on. "'This old man,' I said at length, 'is the type and genius of deep crime. He refuses to be alone. *He is the man of the crowd.*'"[13] It is an extraordinary story—or rather, a sketch, since nothing happens and nothing is resolved. The conclusion would appear to be that there *is* no common human meaning to the city. If it is guilt or remorse that propels the old man through the streets in search of crowds, it must remain private and unexplained, for in the city there is no human to listen to him, no communion other than through arbitrary violence.

Here is the deracinated modern man, the face in the crowd, the dweller in the nineteenth-century metropolis that the Industrial Revolution has created. It is London, but it could be Paris, New York, Hamburg, Brussels. No other American author of Poe's day glimpsed anything resembling his vision of the disordered modern city, with its wandering crowds of nameless inhabitants, bereft of the traditional ties to land or institutions, their conduct and responses no longer regulated by religious or secular authority. Formidable in their very numbers, they are potentially menacing in their susceptibility to unscrupulous emotional appeal. These are not the senselessly violent but briefly tenured mobs of London during the Gordon riots, or the Parisian hordes of the Revolution in search of bread; those were made up of the poor, the dregs of society, and they rioted out of blind resentment against oppression. The faces that Poe saw in his vision of disorder are those of the various classes of the metropolis, franchised and employed, fixed within the routines of the new industrial society. They were here to stay, yet the traditional political, economic, religious, and social forms, restraints, and outlets could never suffice to encompass and regulate their needs. What would the fact of their mass existence, their needs and desires, mean for the society of the nineteenth century? Old expectations of community, hierarchy, social gradation, Christian subordination were

13. *Ibid.*, 515.

inadequate to their massive presence. New formulations—those of science, democracy, leveling, nationalism—seem no adequate replacement. In their collective anonymity they become not individual human beings living in a city, but The City, as a personified being, in itself. The metropolis assumes animate form; its potentiality for violence and its vast impersonal existence make it an omnipresent force in the consciousness of someone who, like Poe or Charles Baudelaire, comes to see it as if it were part of Dante's limbo of lost souls.[14]

What seems so startling is that it is Poe, the American, the Southerner, who first imaged this, and not from any firsthand adult acquaintance with the great industrial and financial cities of western Europe but out of his experience in the still relatively uncomplicated New World, where few of the more obvious disadvantages of the Industrial Revolution had yet manifested themselves. This is why Allen Tate could say of Poe that "in the history of the moral imagination in the nineteenth century, Poe occupies a special place. No other writer in England or the United States, or, so far as I know, in France, went so far as Poe in his vision of dehumanized man."[15] Walt Whitman, who is often said to have introduced the city into American literature as a subject, scarcely acknowledges the existence of what Poe recognized. Melville does little more than touch on it, as in "Bartleby the Scrivener." Emerson and Thoreau seem not to have inhabited the same universe as Poe. Hawthorne's vision, except perhaps in the authorial bewilderment of *The Blithedale Romance*, is too theological to see the dehumanization for what it was, although it seems clear that the formal confusion of that remarkable novel arises in part at least from his having glimpsed its presence. But Edgar Poe, with an inevitability that appears almost demonic in its intensity, was prepared to look "steadfastly in the face" of modern urban industrial society, in the dehumanizing form in which it presented itself to the literary imagination of the nineteenth century, untutored as that imagination still remained in

14. For an excellent discussion of this, see Wallace Fowlie, *Climate of Violence: The French Literary Tradition from Baudelaire to the Present* (New York: Macmillan, 1967), 13.

15. Allen Tate, "Our Cousin, Mr. Poe," *Essays of Four Decades* (Chicago: The Swallow Press, 1968), 395.

the knowledge of how to interpret it. No other author in the English language—except perhaps William Blake in his wilder moments—was ready yet to take that look. It was the French who responded to Poe's vision; they and, a little later on, the Russians were, by virtue of civic experience and ideological circumstance, prepared to pay heed to this Virginia author's notes from the underground.

3.

"Everything in Poe," Allen Tate declared, "is dead: the houses, the rooms, the furniture, to say nothing of nature and the human beings."[16] The remark is vivid, but not quite accurate. There is a great deal of life in Poe; in its manifestations it is even frantic. The vitality is almost entirely that of the beleaguered intellect. Consciousness has become so intense, and so devouring, that for nourishment it feeds vampire-like on the life of the emotions, so that the moment comes when, having been drained dry of all emotional resources, the body expires from sheer dessication. In that most rending of all Poe's tales, "The Fall of the House of Usher," the dying lady Madeline, escaped from the crypt where she had already been prematurely interred, falls upon her brother Roderick, and "in her violent and now final death agonies, bore him to the floor a corpse, and a victim to the terrors he had anticipated."[17] What has killed them both can only be the sheer collapse of the human organism from the drain made by the intellect upon its emotional resources. There is simply no more biological existence left for the mind to subsist upon any longer.

It can also work the other way, too. In one of the strangest of many strange stories, "The Facts in the Case of M. Valdemar," an aged man is mesmerized into a trance before his body has quite given out. Instead of dying, the mesmerized intellect continues to exist, forcing the body to stay alive, until at length it begs to be released from the trance that prevents it from giving way: "'For God's sake!—quick!—quick!—put me to sleep—or, quick!—waken me!—quick—*I say to you that I am dead!*'"

16. *Ibid.*, 398.
17. Poe, "The Fall of the House of Usher," *Tales and Sketches*, II, 316–17. Subsequent references will occur parenthetically in the text.

The narrator at first attempts to induce sleep; when that fails he seeks to bring awakedness. As he works away, the tongue of the man ejaculates the words "Dead! dead!," whereupon "his whole frame at once—within the space of a single minute, or even less, shrunk—crumbled—absolutely *rotted* away beneath my hands. Upon the bed, before that whole company, there lay a nearly liquid mass of loathsome—of detestable putridity." [18] Mesmerized, the intellect had arrested the forces of physical decay, kept flesh from decomposition. (This is the author, let it be recalled, who as critic scolded William Gilmore Simms for depicting the ugly and repulsive in fiction.)

It has long since become a truism to declare that in Poe the Cartesian duality of mind and body has run amuck, and that in his work each wars for independent existence. Not for Edgar Poe the optimistic wholeness of the Transcendentalists. What for Emerson was the intoxicating assurance of human oneness with nature— "I become a transparent eye-ball. I am nothing. I see all. The currents of the Universal Being circulate through me; I am part or particle of God" [19]—did not work in that way for Poe's urban muse. Instead, what Poe perceives in the horror stemming from the radical divorce of the intellect from the emotions. Any attempt to enforce their reunion through violence can only cause a symbiotic derangement. That is, the intellectual perceptions turn into states of feeling, while emotional urges are transformed into abstract patterning.

Poe's people almost all reflect and contain this confusion. The insistence upon rationality, upon cold logical reasoning, that some of them make goes beyond thought itself and into a passionate compulsion for intellectual acuity that transcends all human emotional requirements. Others allow the emotional states— grief, love, desire, fear—to become so dominant that these become ends in themselves, and the reigning emotional state is transformed into an intricately patterned, quasi-abstract entity, usually of pure pain, to be cultivated in and for itself, independently of the human circumstances that had prompted it. In

18. Poe, "The Facts in the Case of M. Valdemar," *Tales and Sketches*, III, 1242–43.

19. Ralph Waldo Emerson, *Nature* (San Francisco: Chandler Publishing Co., 1968), 13.

"Ligeia," for example, the devotion of Ligeia to her husband causes her to refuse to give in to physical death; her "dying" words are those of Glanvill: "'*Man doth not yield himself to the angels, nor unto death utterly, save only through the weakness of his feeble will.*'"[20] After the narrator remarries, and his second wife in turn is on her deathbed, the disembodied consciousness of Ligeia forces its identity upon the body of her successor. The physical entity of the Lady Rowena of Tremaine is turned into that of her predecessor; love has ceased to be an emotion and has become willpower.

It is no accident that Poe is the virtual inventor of the modern detective story. The emotional need to insist upon the primacy of logic and the reasoning intellect that prompted him to assert that the writing of "The Raven" was a coldly calculated exercise in technique for purposes of effect, and that led him to devote so much time and effort to devising and breaking secret codes and to exposing Maelzel's supposedly mechanical chess player, also produced C. Auguste Dupin, master sleuth of Paris. "Murders in the Rue Morgue," which created the cerebral-detective-and-obtuse-friend pairing that Conan Doyle and hundreds of others would later develop, exhibits one aspect of Poe's imagination at its most inventive.

Dupin and his friend the narrator live an isolated, cell-like existence within their Parisian apartment; only after dark do they emerge to walk the city streets. No structure, order, or rational meaning is to be found in the swarming existence of the vast metropolis; intrigue, evil, confusion, passion lie all around them as they stroll. Reading of an especially grotesque double murder that has horrified the public, Dupin is able, through the application of cold logical reasoning upon the available evidence, to deduce that the killer was no human being at all, but an ape, an ourang-outang. The murders are thus literally meaningless; there is no motive, no crime, no villain, but only helpless victims. Such is the true horror of Poe's cityscape.

The same cold intellect, the ability to look at the evidence without preconception or emotion, no matter how terrible and monstrous the circumstances, that enables C. Auguste Dupin to

20. Poe, "Ligeia," *Tales and Sketches*, II, 310.

solve such a crime, might just as readily be employed to commit one. In Poe's vision of the metropolis, there is no moral or ethical imperative that would act to deter such use of the intellect. During World War II, Winston Churchill once described what the world would be under Nazism in terms of its being made more sinister by the blue light of a perverted science, or words to that effect. It is as if the imagination of Poe was able to foresee just that condition.

The quality of excess—of emotion, of reason, of detail, technique, and expression—is central to the nature of Poe's writings. Over and beyond the needs of the story and poem, the excess calls attention to the *author*. When in "The Raven" we encounter stanza after stanza with lines such as "What this grim, ungainly, ghastly, gaunt and ominous bird of yore / Meant in croaking 'Nevermore,'" the ubiquitous technique, with its heavy-handed employment of consonance, alliteration, internal rhyme, and singsong rhythmic stress, does more than present the dramatic situation and the narrator's emotions. It also creates an atmosphere of overwrought sensibility, heaped-on effect. The craftsmanship of the poet becomes an aspect of the poem's meaning, which is that of a grief so overwhelming that its emblems are being helplessly manipulated by a poet whose intellectual cleverness can pattern but not affect or mitigate it. Perhaps a key word comes in the third stanza: "And the silken, sad, uncertain rustling of each purple curtain / *Thrilled* me—filled me with fantastic terrors never felt before" (italics added). For although the use of the word "thrill" to indicate apprehension and terror as well as more emotionally neutral excitement was common in the nineteenth century, there is an ambivalence to the verb, a suggestion that pleasure and enjoyment are being taken in terror and pain.

At times the Poe technique comes close to seeming tawdry, even cheap. The narrator's erudition is placed on public display, and too often it seems to be thin and superficial, the self-conscious effort to appear to be learned. Thus: "In looking around me for some subject by whose means I might test these particulars, I was brought to think of my friend, M. Ernest Valdemar, the well-known compiler of the 'Bibliotheca Forensica,' and author (under the *nom de plume* of Issachar Marx) of the Polish versions of

'Wallenstein' and 'Gargantua.'"[21] Or, "This was precisely what had formed the subject of my recollections. Chantilly was a *quondam* cobbler of the Rue Saint-Denis, who, becoming stage-mad, had attempted the *role* of Xerxes, in Crebillon's tragedy so called, and had been notoriously Pasquinaded for his pains."[22] Observe how very sophisticated and learned I am, Poe seems to be telling his reader—not without the suggestion of a wink. It is almost as if a somewhat seedy-looking pitchman were presenting a set of high-sounding professional credentials preparatory to selling a cancer cure. Poe's fondness for lurid, exotic European settings—catacombs, ancient castles, Venice, Germany, above all the city of Paris (where Poe had never been)—and the recurring use of quotations from classical and modern literary works in foreign languages are the mark of the ostentatiously erudite literary manipulator.

The device is not confined to fiction and poetry; it is employed in Poe's critical writings as well. There is an amusing moment, in one of Poe's reviews for *Burton's Gentleman's Magazine*, in which he examines the credentials of a work entitled *The Canons of Good Breeding; or, The Handbook of the Man of Fashion*, and announces that much of the material in the book has been lifted from anthologies and other works. The reader, he proposes, "will still pronounce it, without hesitation, the excessively-elaborated production of some partially-educated man, possessed with a rabid ambition for the reputation of a wit and *savant*," and who has drawn copiously on other books in order to do so. Poe proceeds to identify the books, among them Walpole, Bolingbroke, Chesterfield, Bacon, Burton, Burdon, Bulwer, D'Israeli, Seneca, Montaigne, Rochefoucauld, and so on. "We may be pardoned also," he continues archly, "for an allusion—which is enough—to such wealthy store-houses as the '*Lettres Edifiantes et Curieuses*,' the Literary Memoirs of Sallengre, the '*Melanges Literaires*' of Suard and Andre, and the '*Pieces Interessantes et peu Connuyes*' of La Place."[23] The appropriate maxim here is "Set a thief to catch

21. Poe, "The Facts in the Case of M. Valdemar," *Tales and Sketches*, III, 1234.
22. Poe, "Murders in the Rue Morgue," *Tales and Sketches*, II, 534.
23. Poe, review of *The Canons of Good Breeding; or, The Handbook of the Man of Fashion*, "by the author of the 'Laws of Etiquette,'" in *Essays and Reviews*, 456. Poe was hoisted upon his own petard here, for the "Suard and Andre" he cites was his misreading of the German "Suard und *Andere*" (and others).

a thief." Not only does Poe censure his author for doing what he so often does, but he names some of the books best adapted to such usage, and then caps the demonstration with a flagrant example of precisely the tactic that he is comically belaboring.

What all these elements—ostentatious erudition, excessively elaborated technique, virtuoso presence, delight in doubling and deliberate confusing of the "real" and the "imaginary," urgent insistence upon logic and cold-blooded analysis, together with the savage joy being taken in the evocation of emotionally suffused situations—constitute, it seems to me, is one of the most powerful, relentless, and omnipresent instances of obsessive *authorial personality* in literature. "Poe" is not only an author's name; it is a literary aesthetic *presence*, a performance. It is as if, on the dust jackets of his books, there were a legend reading *Edgar Poe Presents . . .*   The author is more than an artist; he is a mesmerist.

He is not, however, primarily a faker, a humbug. He is not merely tricking us or toying with us: *he is engaged in baring his soul.*

All authors project storytelling personalities, of course; rhetoric is a necessary element of any art based on the use of words. But where most good storytellers appear to us through and within their characters, settings, and plots, Poe *uses* those in order to project, as his ultimate objective, the personality in the act of doing the telling. The characters and situations, what is said and done, what happens, are placed in the service of the emotional needs of the storyteller, and it is this emotional condition that constitutes Poe's literary personality. The authorial despair, the sense of entrapment that permeate the narration of a masterpiece such as "The Fall of the House of Usher" are obvious. Not for nothing does Roderick Usher, who has seemed to the narrator-visitor to be losing his reason, turn to him and shout " '*Madman! I tell you that she now stands without the door!*' " (416). For the storyteller himself—not only the first-person narrator of the plot, but the authorial personality who is using that narrator as a device for telling what happens—seems in danger of giving in to unreason, so irrational and hopeless is the situation he has been imagining.

The same sense of irrationality and desperately controlled despair infuses stories such as "Murders in the Rue Morgue," which on the surface are about crime solving. The control is as important as the despair. Dupin's feat of detection constitutes an arbitrary application of logic and reason to solve one particular crime in a leaden time and place bereft of joy, hope, or expectation of meaning. The human situation posited by Poe in so much of his poetry and fiction is like that in Matthew Arnold's poem: a darkling plain, swept with confused alarms of struggle and flight, where ignorant armies clash by night—but without even the memory of a receding but once-sustaining religious faith. It is this psychological condition, and the dreamlike vagueness of technique required to communicate its unreason, that so attracted the attention of French Symbolist poets such as Baudelaire, who saw in Poe's work a striking articulation of the condition of nineteenth-century urban man.

4.

As the single antebellum Southern author whose work has importantly survived its occasion, Poe constitutes the sole important contribution of the Old South to the American Renaissance, that initial flowering of the young republic's literary imagination and the reaffirmation, on a new continent, of the Western world's cultural tradition. And what a sobering, even appalling reaffirmation his is! The tradition that spoke again through Poe was not that of the assertion of the freedom of the individual human being, or of man's oneness with and in the natural world, but of an appalled protest against dehumanization and the stifling of the human spirit in a mechanistic universe.

The Mississippi novelist Walker Percy, writing his essay "Notes for a Novel about the End of the World," describes the writer of fiction and poetry as "less like a prophet than he is like the canary that coal miners used to take down into the shaft to test the air. When the canary gets unhappy, utters plaintive cries, and collapses, it may be time for the miners to surface and think things over."[24] For all the achievements of the other leading authors of the antebellum United States such as Melville, Emerson, Whitman, Thoreau, and Hawthorne, it is in the vision of Poe, far

24. Walker Percy, *The Message in the Bottle* (New York: Farrar, Straus and Giroux, 1975), 101.

more than any of them, that one is made to perceive the human capacity for evil that was soon to result in the enormous blood-letting of the Civil War. While a greater poet than Poe, Walt Whitman, was celebrating a nation full of joy and promise, the future of whose individual states "I harbinge glad and sublime" ("Starting from Paumanok"), it was in Poe's work that we glimpse the capacity of Western man to create concentration camps. It was this that Stéphane Mallarmé recognized in the sonnet composed on the occasion of the erection of Poe's tombstone, which he depicted as a

> Calm block fallen here from some dark disaster
> May this granite at least mark forever the boundaries
> To black flights of blasphemy scattered in the future.
>
> ("The Tomb of Edgar Poe")

As noted earlier, it seems difficult to reconcile Poe's essentially urban cast of mind, his willingness to look so steadfastly in the face of the dehumanized man of the city, with his upbringing in Richmond, Virginia, in his day a small community in not-very-urbanized America. There were also, however, those five years, from age six to eleven, when he lived in or near London, almost always in schools where the Allans had left him to stay. The child Edgar must surely have absorbed impressions of a vast, unsympathetic metropolis. Risky though the business of attempting to characterize the nature of the artistic imagination from the circumstances of personal history may be, we must assume the presence of *something* in Poe's origins and experience that might offer an insight into why it was that this particular Southern author should have written as he did. We confront the obvious fact that of all the antebellum Southern authors it is Poe whose writings are *least* grounded in the particularities, settings, and issues of the place he grew up in, and equally *most* lastingly a part of world literature.

Now surely it is not the absence of the known setting as such, the failure to write about the everyday concerns and experiences of the antebellum Southern community, that accounts for his literary distinction. Hawthorne's Salem and Boston, Melville's New England whaling craft, Whitman's vision of Manhattan are absolutely central to the appeal of their work. Indeed, one would be hard put to come up with the names of many important authors whose writings do not seem to be steeped in the specificities of their time and place. The very nature of the literary work itself, based as it is upon the concrete image rather than abstract ideas, would render that unlikely. Yet except for one story, "The Premature Burial," neither Poe's fiction nor poetry draws importantly on the specific locales and institutions of the commonwealth of Virginia that he grew up in. ("The Ragged Mountains" is set in Charlottesville, but nothing is made of the fact.) So we must look elsewhere in Poe's work for material that might possess ties to its author's origins.

The events of Poe's life are well known. Born in Boston in 1809 to actor parents, his father a Baltimorean and his mother British by birth, he lived there only six months before the troupe in which his parents were employed moved to Charleston, South Carolina, and then to Richmond. His father either died or disappeared shortly before or following the move south; his mother died in Richmond in 1811, and the orphaned boy, lacking a month of being three years old, was taken into the house of a Scottish-born merchant, John Allan, and his Richmond-born wife, though he was never legally adopted. The Richmond in which Poe grew up was a small community whose business and commercial life was dominated by Scotch merchant families, such as the Allans, who were in the process of superseding the older colonial leadership, and who have maintained their social and financial hegemony in Richmond ever since. From 1815 until 1820 the Allans lived in England, where Poe was enrolled in good schools. After their return to Richmond, Poe attended school, made friends with various local youths of good family, became known for his prowess at swimming, and was a leader in a local military company. As a youth he fell in love with a young lady, Elmira Royster, and they were apparently engaged to be married when he left for the newly founded University of Virginia in Charlottesville in February of 1826.

Poe's often stormy relations with his "father," the tobacco merchant John Allan, have been the subject of much dispute and considerable romantic exaggeration. What does seem clear is that Allan, though he became very wealthy, was extremely tightfisted, and he wanted Poe to prepare himself for a business or professional career appropriate to his own notion of practicality and ambition for community standing; and equally that Poe was moody, temperamental, not very practical, and interested in becoming a poet, not a merchant, physician, or lawyer. Then as afterward it was considered quite proper in Richmond to maintain a gentlemanly interest in the arts, and even to write some occasional verse and publish it anonymously, but it was another and considerably less acceptable matter to desire to be a professional writer. To a man like Allan, hard-bitten, socially ambitious, and sufficiently coarse to have been involved in several extramarital affairs in which he fathered illegitimate children, what his "son" wished to become was almost as scandalous as seeking a career as a professional actor or actress.

For his part, Poe came early on to affect a Byronic contempt for mere practicality. When he enrolled at the university he proceeded to emulate the life-style of the young plantation gentry, which involved much drinking—a custom that has been said to survive even today at "Mr. Jefferson's University." The meager funds given him by Allan were scarcely sufficient to cover his basic entering expenses, and the result, Poe later claimed, was that he began gambling in order to earn money to pay his bills. He also used John Allan's reputation for wealth to run up large debts for clothing. Ultimately Poe succeeded in incurring debts amounting to several thousand dollars. Allan refused to pay even the legitimate obligations, and after a year's residence Poe was forced to leave Charlottesville in disgrace. As a student, however, he had done extremely well in his studies; his classmates later testified to his academic brilliance, in particular his skill in languages and at translating poetry.

Unable to resolve his differences with Allan or to find suitable employment, and in some danger of being arrested for debt, Poe left Richmond under an alias, hoping to discover better prospects as a poet in Boston. His engagement to Elmira Royster had long since been broken; the letters he wrote to her from the university had been kept from her, once her family learned that John Allan did not intend to make Poe his heir, and she married another, more suitable prospect.

In Boston, Poe published his first book, *Tamerlane and Other Poems* (1827), but found no poetic Eldorado there and so enlisted in the army under the name Edgar A. Perry. His regiment was soon transferred to Fort Moultrie, at Sullivan's Island near Charleston, and later to Fort Monroe, Virginia. He was promoted to regimental sergeant major, and seems to have been encouraged by his superiors to apply for a commission, through enrollment at the United States Military Academy at West Point, New York. Meanwhile his foster mother died, and there was a temporary truce with John Allan, who helped him get into West Point. In the interim Poe moved to Baltimore, where he published a second volume of poems. He had no real intention of becoming an army officer, however; his ambition was set upon being a poet, and once it became obvious that Allan was cutting him out of his will, he got himself court-martialed and dismissed from the academy—not, however, before securing subscriptions for a new book of poems from his fellow cadets. It 1831, *Poems* was published in New York, attracting little attention.

That year he moved back to Baltimore, began publishing some magazine fiction, and in 1833 submitted a group of stories including "MS. Found in a Bottle" to a competition sponsored by the Baltimore *Sunday Visiter*. He won the prize, and one of the judges, the novelist John Pendleton Kennedy, took an interest in him. A lawyer, politician, and man of affairs, Kennedy was everything that Poe was not. He recommended Poe to Thomas Willis White, the proprietor of the *Southern Literary Messenger*, a new literary magazine in Richmond, and in 1835, Poe became White's editorial assistant. Fired by White for drinking too much—before breakfast even, White said—he was soon rehired, and with him to Richmond in October of 1835 went his aunt, Mrs. Maria Poe Clemm, and her thirteen-year-old daughter Virginia, who became Poe's bride.

With Poe contributing fiction and poetry to the magazine and writing his sometimes tomahawking reviews, the *Messenger* prospered. Poe, however, soon began drinking to excess—apparently not very much drinking was needed to get him drunk, but he always managed to do whatever was necessary. It also became obvious to White that Poe considered his own literary taste and sensibilities much superior to his employer's, which was doubtless true enough—but White did not enjoy the role he was placed in. While he wanted the *Messenger* to increase its popularity, he did not especially covet the reputation it was acquiring as a combative, controversial critical organ, particularly when Poe's reviewing began to alienate some of the more highly regarded literary figures of the day and to incur the wrath of well-established, influential Northern periodicals. What White sought was cultural respectability, and he resented Poe's using the *Messenger* as a vehicle for advancing his personal reputation as a tomahawking critic. He also grew jealous of his young assistant's willingness to assume authority and to accept full credit for the magazine's success. Meanwhile the occasions when Poe was too "ill" to report for work increased, and in January, 1837, White discharged him. Poe and his entourage departed for New York City, leaving behind him the city he had grown up in and had considered his home, and a magazine whose circulation had increased from 500 to 3,500 copies (Poe claimed 5,000) and which, thereafter, swiftly receded into its former mediocrity.

Poe's subsequent not-quite-thirteen years of life were spent mostly in Philadelphia and New York City, where he worked on various magazines, did such hackwork as he could find, wrote the major portion of his best fiction and much of his best poetry, quarreled with all his employers, briefly owned a literary newspaper that soon failed, and acquired considerable fame and no little notoriety as a litterateur. With his fame came no financial rewards to speak of. His one continuing and never realized ambition was to be editor of a first-class literary magazine of the highest critical standards. In 1847, Virginia Clemm Poe died. After a period of utter prostration Poe eventually resumed his literary work, and became involved with several different women. He finally returned to Richmond to lecture, and there renewed his engagement to the now-widowed Elmira Royster Shelton. He then departed abruptly for the North by steamboat, arriving in Baltimore shortly before a municipal election. What happened can only be surmised; he is believed to have resumed drinking aboard ship, and upon arrival in Baltimore, where elections were notoriously corrupt, was possibly rounded up with a cortege of drunks and bums, kept intoxicated, and moved from one polling place to another to be "voted." Several days later he was discovered semiconscious, lying outside a polling place. He was taken to a hospital, where on October 7, 1849, he died.

The novelist Hervey Allen, in his detailed but overly romanticized biography of Poe, *Israfel* (1934), believes that Poe's heart had been failing, and that he required stimulants, which proved disastrous to his brain. Whether that is true or not, it is clear that he was under great nervous stress at the time and had shown signs of irrationality before he left Richmond. While he was dying in the hospital in Baltimore a physician later claimed that he replied, when told that he would soon be able to rejoin the company of his friends, that "the best thing his best friend could do would be to blow out his miserable brains with a pistol—that when he beheld his miserable degradation he was ready to sink into the earth."[25]

It was not until after his death that his full literary achievement began to be recognized. In his lifetime he was generally considered to be a somewhat unsavory hack writer given to sensational and tawdry effects. His literary reputation was as a critic. Only gradually did it begin to be evident, even to his numerous enemies, that here was no literary con man, but one of the giants of world literature.

5.

We have already noted some of Poe's affinities with the other Southern authors of his time—the concern for lyrical utterance rather than moral instruction in poetry, the morbid preoccupation with dead female beauty, the disapproval of New England transcendentalism as an insight into the nature of reality. Other traits in common might be added: an abiding formalism, an addiction to sometimes inflated rhetoric, and kind of arm's-length attitude toward direct autobiographical revelation in print, a skepticism about the perfectibility of man, and so on. Yet all such elements, even together with the fact that Poe certainly thought of himself as very much a Virginian and a Southerner, do not get around the obvious fact that Poe wrote almost *nothing* about the South, or about living there, or about Southern history and Southern society, or for that matter about any kind of history whatever. Southern writers were and still are supposed to have the historical instinct, whatever else may be lacking, and to scorn the impulse toward millennialism. But Poe used history only for purposes of

25. Quoted in Hervey Allen, *Israfel: The Life and Times of Edgar Allan Poe* (New York: Farrar and Rinehart, 1934), 675.

exotic setting, and before he died he wrote a prose narrative, *Eureka*, that depicts all life as devolving upon some future cataclysmic, redemptive event. Hervey Allen considered Poe to have been losing his reason by the time he wrote it; Allen Tate and Robert D. Jacobs, among others, have taken that work much more seriously.

The obliqueness of Poe's relationship as a writer to Virginia and the South is paralleled by a similar obliquity in his life. Although he was reared in Richmond, his status there was never secure. It was not a matter of being thought and treated as a parvenu, as was the case with William Gilmore Simms in Charleston. His dead parents' profession, the stage, was socially suspect, but the man and woman who raised him as their son, John and Frances Valentine Allan, held respectable places in Richmond business and social life. The Scottish-born Allan was not a member of the old planter aristocracy, but by the time of Poe's childhood the merchant and professional circles to which Allan belonged had all but captured control of the city's establishment. What seems clear, however, is that John Allan did not allow the young Poe to feel that he was secure in his situation with the family. Once Poe began to show signs of independence, Allan obviously took to reminding him of the fact that his status was less than legitimatized, and openly taunted Poe with the disreputable nature of his parents' profession. Beyond doubt, Poe himself was only too conscious that his schoolmates and their families were acquainted with the circumstances of his origin. His status in Richmond was at all times marginal, and he knew it all too well.

It is not surprising, therefore, that as a youth Poe grew more and more withdrawn, spent much of his time in isolation from others, reading and writing in his room—to the growing exasperation of Allan. The year at the University of Virginia, as we have noted, saw him make a wild attempt to pattern his conduct after the young men of the plantation gentry, drinking, gambling, running up bills for fine clothes, only to leave in social disgrace without making good his gambling and other debts. It was at this time, too, that, probably from John Allan himself, his fiancée's family learned that Poe was not going to come into any portion of Allan's considerable wealth.

What all these elements add up to is a young manhood of unhappiness and uncertainty, plagued with problems of status and identity. Certainly the aura of Byronism, the demonstrated disdain for the middle-class standards and values of mercantile Richmond, and the embracing of the role of the lonely, disenchanted artist, constituted a way of insulating himself from hurt. (One thinks of "Count No-Count" Faulkner in Oxford, Mississippi, a hundred years afterward.) And Poe had no need to invent the role of the disinherited poet; he was undergoing just that experience in his dealings with John Allan.

It must be remembered that there was definite financial logic on Allan's side. In setting out to be a professional author in the United States of the 1820s and 1830s, Poe was undertaking an all-but-hopeless task. Without any kind of independent income from a profession, he was staking his future welfare on the meager rewards of an author in a country without a sizable, established reading public, without well-paying literary reviews and magazines, and in the face of a publishing situation that, because of the lack of an international copyright agreement, permitted American publishers to pirate all the English writing they cared to without bothering to pay for it. It was thus virtually impossible for a writer, especially one of Poe's particular gifts, to earn a living by his pen alone. Neither by temperament nor by training was he equipped to combine his literary interests with political journalism. His opportunities as an editor were handicapped by his temperamental inability to disguise for very long his superior taste and sensibility; he quarreled repeatedly with his employers. As one who in society possessed insufficient self-discipline, he could not for long refrain from the occasional drink that was all that was needed to set him off.

Henry James wrote of Nathaniel Hawthorne that he had the imagination of disaster. So, certainly, did Edgar Poe; but in everyday life at least, Hawthorne was not the misanthropic, emotion-driven soul that Poe was. The insecurity, anxiety, and instability that characterized Poe's formative years helped to make him into one for whom, like Coleridge in England and Baudelaire in France, no truce with the workaday world around him could last for very long at a time. Unlike those European writers, he inhabited a practical, commercially minded society deficient in the cultural expectations and institutions that might otherwise have allowed him to achieve some kind of equilibrium, however uneven, within his community.

One cannot, finally, quarrel with the self-assessment that he offered in the poem, unpublished during his lifetime but now thought to be authentically his, entitled "Alone," which opens with the assertion that "From childhood's hour I have not been / As others were—I have not seen / As others saw" and that depicts him as having been in the grip of "The mystery that binds me still," concluding that he drew it, as part of his experience,

> From the sun that round me roll'd
> In its autumn tint of gold—
> From the lightning in the sky
> As it pass'd me flying by—
> From the thunder, and the storm—
> And the cloud that took the form
> (When the rest of Heaven was blue)
> Of a demon in my view.[26]

The demon, the "imp of the perverse" as he elsewhere termed it, that dominated his imagination was the product of a sensibility that was not merely disinherited but violently dissociated from its culture and community.

Earlier I suggested that Poe was really our first important urban writer, the first for whom the modern city became the locale that his imagination inhabited. His art, as we have seen, is predominantly that of interiors, of houses, apartments, rooms, city streets, castles, mansions, catacombs. There is no true recourse to nature. To have tried what Henry David Thoreau did at Walden Pond, abandoning the town for the woods so as to "live deliberately, to front only the essential facts of life,"[27] would have made no sense whatever to Poe. Reality for Poe, however bizarre and menacing it might often be, was to be found within society, not apart from it. Yet at the same time the actuality of urban society meant loneliness, isolation, the seeming absence of any kind of purposive social or moral ordering. To attempt to live alone within one's chambers was to confront the raven, with its non-reasoning, reflexive refrain; to go outside in the streets was to find only the face of the crowd.

Much like certain American and British authors of the twen-

---

26. Poe, "Alone," in *The Unabridged Edgar Allan Poe*, [ed. Tam Mossman] (Philadelphia: Running Press, 1983), 39.
27. Henry David Thoreau, *Walden* (New York: Thomas Y. Crowell, 1961), 118.

tieth century such as James Joyce and Thomas Wolfe, and Theodore Dreiser later in his own century, Poe responded to the insecurity and uncertain social identity of his childhood and youth by assuming the role of the Romantic artist set down among the Philistines, as we have seen, and by essaying that role in order to insulate himself against a disadvantaged reality and to elevate himself above it in his own mind. It is clear that Poe used the image of alienated, disinherited artist for purposes both of gaining sympathy and of permitting himself to feel socially respectable. In so doing, he was often none too scrupulous. We find him, for example, writing to John Pendleton Kennedy in Baltimore in 1834 that he had "looked forward to the inheritance of a large fortune, and, in the meantime, was in receipt of an annuity sufficient for my support," but that his adopted father's second marriage, along with certain follies of his own, had resulted in his having been disinherited. We can only agree with Robert D. Jacobs that the "kindest thing" to be said about the letter is that "Poe's imagination was running away with him," and that "if Poe really expected to inherit a large fortune from Allan he was sanguine to the point of idiocy; and Poe was never an idiot."[28]

Now since Poe's view of man in nature, as we have noted, permitted no vision of any kind of natural freedom or transcendental oneness with a world soul in the wilderness, the inevitable place for a disinherited artist was the world city, and equally it was the only place where someone intent upon pursuing a livelihood as a magazine journalist could possibly do so. Surely Poe can be said to have tried all the available literary centers in the new nation—Boston, New York, Philadelphia, Baltimore. And as his art so amply attests, obviously he cast longing eyes upon the great European cities, with their far more developed and complex, historically anchored cultural institutions.

Although lacking the talent to become a "transparent eye-ball," and unable to see the poet as keeper of God's sylvan temple, he seems to have moved swiftly into a supernal attitude toward the assumption of the poet's role. The artist possesses the capacity to see and hear what others are incapable of perceiving: the terror,

---

28. Robert D. Jacobs, "Poe in Richmond," *Southern Writers: Appraisals in Our Time*, ed. R. C. Simonini, Jr. (Charlottesville: University Press of Virginia, 1964), 34.

torment, and hopelessness that lie beyond and within all earthly reality. The poet's office is thus that of doomsayer. "I have no faith in human perfectibility," he wrote to James Russell Lowell (of all people). "I think that human exertion will have no appreciable effect upon humanity. Man is now only more active—not more happy—nor more wise, than he was 6,000 years ago."[29] Of that imperfectibility he had abundant evidence—in himself, in John Allan, in his relationships with "family," university, community, in Richmond, Virginia, and just about everything else connected with his experience.

6.

The critic Harry Levin, in his book *The Power of Blackness* (1958), as well as various psychoanalytic critics have developed interesting readings of some of Poe's work in terms of the impact of Poe's youthful experience of slavery upon his imagination. That there was a level of imaginative response in which the South's Peculiar Institution was of symbolic importance to Poe seems to me beyond question. But it had no place in the subject matter he chose to write about. None of the antebellum Southern authors of importance wrote fiction or poetry in which the rationale for chattel slavery came under direct, extensive scrutiny, in the way that Hawthorne examined Puritanism or Whitman looked at democracy and the individual sensibility. There is no Southern counterpart of *The Scarlet Letter*, in which the rival claims of individual emotional fulfillment and a totally theocratic social order are placed in opposition to each other. We may explain the absence of any Southern work like Melville's "Benito Cereno" as the product of community solidarity in the face of the growing political and economic sectional rivalry. What we cannot so readily explain is why *no* important work of the Southern literary imagination during the first half of the nineteenth century explores the situation of the individual in juxtaposition with society, or the rival claims of nature and society.

The appropriateness and relevance, even the inevitability of such themes for the writer in nineteenth-century America would seem obvious. It was precisely that for Cooper, Hawthorne,

29. Poe to James R. Lowell, July 2, 1844, in *The Letters of Edgar Allan Poe*, ed. John Ward Ostrom (2 vols.; Cambridge: Harvard University Press, 1948), I, 256.

Melville, Whitman ("I celebrate myself, / and sing myself, / and what I shall assume, you shall assume / for every atom of me as good belongs to you," as the opening stanza of "Song of Myself" has it). The confrontation of natural man with social man pre-occupied Emerson and Thoreau.

Its absence in Southern writing, on any important imaginative level, surely has something to do with the presence of slavery and the plantation system. For one thing, they were the only signifi-cant elements that were not common to both societies. Moreover, once the Civil War was fought and chattel slavery was abolished, almost every important Southern author thereafter began to grapple with the nature-versus-society theme. One thinks of *Huckleberry Finn*, "The Marshes of Glynn," *The Grandissimes*, the Uncle Remus stories, *In the Tennessee Mountains*.

If we assume, as seems justifiable, that the antebellum South-ern author's involvement in the Southern community was such as to direct his imagination away from the kind of dialectical ex-ploration of freedom in society and in nature, then it is only rea-sonable to expect that in one form or other the suppressed matter will crop up elsewhere in the writer's work—and that when it does it will bear at least an oblique relationship to whatever it is that has served to suppress it. In other words, if we take the spe-cific instance of Edgar Poe, what might we look for that stands in place of and that imaginatively replaces the emotions that might otherwise have been evoked through the depiction of slavery in Poe's fiction? Levin and others have proposed that the answer lies in Poe's obsession with blackness. This may well be true, but as Levin himself has so convincingly shown, there is every bit as much "blackness" in Melville and Hawthorne as in the work of the Southern-reared Poe. It seems to me that there ought to be something more specific than the motif of "blackness" in Poe's work, something that not only relates more directly to the slavery theme but that suggests its suppression as well. It is this that I want to look at.

7.

In "The Fall of the House of Usher" the narrator visits his old friend Roderick Usher, only to find that Usher's sister Madeline is gravely ill. Soon thereafter she dies, and the two men place her in a vault and fasten it securely. But in the days that follow, first Usher and then the narrator become increasingly disturbed because of certain sounds they hear. Ultimately the lady Madeline, who has been entombed while still alive, appears at the door of her brother's study and, upon entering, bears him to the floor a corpse while in her own death agony. The dead would not stay buried. As the narrator flees the house in terror, the hereditary mansion of the Ushers disappears beneath the surface of the tarn.

Lewis P. Simpson's interpretation of this remarkable story, in *The Brazen Face of History: Studies in the Literary Consciousness in America* (1980), builds upon its allegorical possibilities as a commentary on the imminent destruction of the Southern slaveholding aristocracy, linking it forthrightly to the collapse of the Jeffersonian dream of the virtuous agrarian republic. He describes it as "a ludicrously melodramatic yet darkly foreboding and compelling interpretation of the rationality represented by a slave-holding secular-spiritual elect who endorsed the Declaration of Independence." Poe's story, he says, dramatizes "how the faculties of intellect and feeling are enslaved to the inherent and unalienable will of the self, the all-possessive dominion of existence."[30]

The formulation is apt; as a teacher, I have for years suggested to my students that they consider what Poe's story might signify if the family seat of the Ushers, instead of being a decaying though still-intact mansion in some unidentifiable foreign place, were named *Monticello*. All of the immense learning and wisdom of the master of the house are insufficient to bring a halt to the imminent collapse of a structure set alongside a pestilential tarn, with "a barely perceptible fissure, which, extending from the roof of the building in front, made its way down the wall" (400).

The interpretation offers an interesting linguistic dimension to the narrator's statement:

To an anomalous species of terror I found him a bounden *slave* [italics added]. "I shall perish," said he, "I *must* perish in this deplorable folly. Thus, thus, and not otherwise, shall I be lost. I dread the events of the

30. Lewis P. Simpson, *The Brazen Face of History: Studies in the Literary Consciousness in America* (Baton Rouge: Louisiana State University Press, 1980), 101, 102.

future, not in themselves, but in their results. I shudder at the thought of any, even the most trivial, incident, which may operate under this intolerable agitation of soul. I have, indeed, no abhorrence of danger, except in its absolute effect—in terror. In this unnerved—in this pitiable condition—I feel that the period will sooner or later arrive when I must abandon life and reason altogether, in some struggle with the grim phantasm, FEAR." (403)

Jefferson's ringing assertion of the evils of slavery in his *Notes on the State of Virginia* may be remembered: "Indeed I tremble for my country when I reflect that God is just: that his justice cannot sleep forever: that considering numbers, nature and natural means only, a revolution of the wheel of fortune, an exchange of situation, is among possible events: that it may become probable by supernatural interference! The Almighty has no attribute which can take sides with us in such a contest."[31]

Almost four decades after he wrote the *Notes*, the Missouri controversy seemed to be fulfilling his prophecy. Writing to a correspondent soon after the sectional schism had been temporarily bridged by the drawing of a line westward to demarcate the boundaries of future slave and free states, Jefferson declared that "this momentous question, like a fire bell in the night, awakened and filled me with terror. I considered it at once as the knell of the Union. It is hushed, indeed, for the moment. But this is a reprieve, not a final sentence. A geographical line, coinciding with a marked principle, moral and political, once conceived and held up to the angry passions of men, will never be obliterated; and each new irritation will mark it deeper and deeper."[32]

Jefferson's striking image of the fire bell tolling in the night suggests the emotional undercurrents of the fear of servile uprising. Edgar Poe had not yet been born when the abortive Gabriel Prosser insurrection of 1800 had terrified the citizenry of Richmond, but the memory was still green during the years of his childhood in that city. Jefferson had urged Governor James Monroe not to execute the perpetrators, on the grounds that the same

31. Thomas Jefferson, *Notes on the State of Virginia* (New York: Harper and Row, 1964), 156.
32. Thomas Jefferson to John Holmes, April 22, 1820, in *Memoir, Correspondence and Miscellanies from the Papers of Thomas Jefferson*, ed. Thomas Jefferson Randolph (4 vols.; Charlottesville: H. G. Carr & Son, 1829), IV, 323–24.

qualities that led a slave to plan an insurrection would make such a person, if free, an ideal citizen. His recommendation, which was not followed, was to deport the leaders of the revolt to Africa. Thereafter the specter of a slave revolt was a part of the community consciousness in Richmond and elsewhere. As Hervey Allen writes in his biography of Poe, *Israfel*, "In the carefully fostered legend of the faithfulness and contentment of the slaves under the ancient regime in the South, it has been conveniently forgotten that one of the ever present fears under which a slave-holding community lived was the nightmare of a rebellion of the blacks. Nor was it an idle dream. There had been in Virginia already several alarming, though abortive, attempts on the part of the negroes which, however futile, had sufficed to raise the 'goose flesh' of the planters and the inhabitants of towns."[33]

Yet although there is little question that "The Fall of the House of Usher" can be read as an imaginative projection of the situation of a Southern liberal such as Thomas Jefferson, no one, so far as I know, has proposed that Poe consciously meant that story to be any kind of allegory of the collapse of Jeffersonian liberalism. No writer of his time was more conscious of what he was doing (or, at any rate, thought he was doing) in his fiction and poetry than Poe, yet on the face of things, it appears improbable that in this particular story Poe meditated political or social allegory.

So far as is known, Poe was not a dissenter from the Southern attitudes toward slavery and race, and he had no use for Abolitionists. Scholars now know that it was probably not Poe but Beverley Tucker who wrote the review of James Kirke Paulding's *Slavery in the United States* and the anonymous *The South Vindicated from Treason and Fanaticsim of the Northern Abolitionist* in the *Southern Literary Messenger* in 1836, which had been the principal evidence for his views on slavery. Even so, we have his review of James Russell Lowell's *A Fable for Critics*; angered by Lowell's treatment of him in the book, he declared that Lowell was "one of the most rabid of the Abolition fanatics; and no Southerner who does not wish to be insulted, and at the same time revolted by a bigotry the most obstinately blind and

33. Allen, *Israfel*, 100.

deaf, should ever touch a volume by this author." Lowell, he continued, was the type of man who, if he owned slaves, would mistreat them atrociously and want to murder any Abolitionist who might attempt to set them free.[34]

Poe was not inclined toward the Jeffersonian democratic view; he was politically a Whig, as indeed were a majority of Richmonders. The year when he was a student at the University of Virginia, 1826, was that during which Jefferson died. Although quite likely he met Jefferson during his stay in Charlottesville, for the third president took an active interest in the student body of the university he had founded, Poe's politics were much closer to those of an eminent fellow Richmonder, John Marshall.

That the fear of servile revolt must have played a role in the highly active imagination of an impressionistic youth growing up in Richmond is, to say the least, probable. As already noted, the Gabriel Prosser revolt was very much remembered, as were the violent events of the revolution in Santo Domingo. Stories of the horrors, real and imagined, of slave rebellions were almost certainly repeated among Poe's schoolmates and friends. As second-in-command of the Junior Morgan Riflemen, a Richmond military unit, Poe was among the volunteer militia that were issued arms from the city's closely guarded arsenal at the state penitentiary when the regiment of the State Guard that customarily stood watch in Richmond was away to help welcome the Marquis de Lafayette in 1824. As in other Southern communities, the principal function of the militia was to guard against slave revolts.

Poe's "father," John Allan, owned slaves as house servants. The young Poe is said to have gotten along well with them. Even so, one assumes that the black servants were not unaware of the high-strung youth's ambiguous social status. That Poe's relationship with the slaves was, as with almost everything else about his life, insecure seems evident from the letter he wrote to John Allan when he departed Richmond for Boston in 1827, in which he charged Allan with not only degrading him before friends and family but placing him in a subordinate relationship to the slaves as well.

34. Poe, review of *A Fable for Critics*, by James Russell Lowell, in *Essays and Reviews*, 815.

In 1831, when Poe settled in Baltimore following his time as a cadet at West Point, he was again living in a slaveholding community. The shock waves of the Nat Turner Insurrection in Southside Virginia that summer reached Baltimore very quickly. The homes of blacks were searched for weapons. There was a rumor that one of the conspirators had been captured in the city. It was in Baltimore that Thomas Gray published his widely read pamphlet giving the "confessions" of the leader of the revolt, with its lurid account of women and children hacked to death in their beds.

Indeed, what is unusual is not that Poe must surely have felt the impact of the fear of servile insurrection, but that, in the many situations involving terror and apprehension in his fiction, he never made use of the specific possibilities. Even in *The Narrative of Arthur Gordon Pym*, with all its many variations on violence and horror, including mutiny at sea, and in which the treacherous natives are black, he does not address it directly. Like every one of the other Southern authors of the day, he avoids any depiction of the less savory human dimensions of the Peculiar Institution.

The closest Poe does come to dealing with such matters is in a humorous sketch entitled "The System of Doctor Tarr and Professor Fether," which appeared in *Graham's Magazine* in 1845. What it does, I think, is to satirize Thomas Jefferson, Jeffersonian democracy, the social reformers of Boston and New England, and abolitionism. The story takes place while the narrator is on a journey through extreme Southern France. His route draws him near "a certain *Maison de Santé*, or private Mad House."[35] (The Maison Carrée, at Nîmes in Southern France, was well known as having been Jefferson's favorite building, which he used as a model for the Virginia State Capitol in Richmond.)

Having heard much of a famed "soothing system" whereby insanity was treated by indulging the patient in his derangement rather than through confinement and harsher methods, the narrator wishes to pay a visit to the asylum. As he makes his way there, the tone of the story momentarily changes from one of factual narration to apprehensiveness:

---

35. Poe, "The System of Doctor Tarr and Professor Fether," *Tales and Sketches*, III, 1002. Subsequent references will occur parenthetically in the text.

We entered a grass-grown by-path, which, in half an hour, nearly lost itself in a dense forest, clothing the base of a mountain. Through this dank and gloomy wood we rode some two miles, when the *Maison de Santé* came in to view. It was a fantastic *chateau*, much dilapidated, and scarcely tenantable through age and neglect. Its aspect inspired me with absolute dread, and, checking my horse, I half resolved to turn back. I soon, however, grew ashamed of my weakness and proceeded.

As we rode up to the gate-way, I perceived it slightly open, and the visage of a man peering through. In an instant afterward, this man came forth, accosted my companion by name, shook him cordially by the hand, and begged him to alight. It was Monsieur Maillard himself. He was a portly, fine-looking gentleman of the old school, with a polished manner, and a certain air of gravity, dignity, and authority which was very impressive. (1003)

The mood here is much like that of the opening paragraphs of "The Fall of the House of Usher," though less overwrought. Interestingly, the circumstances of terrain and approach are much like those that would have confronted a visitor to Monticello, which was located on a mountain several miles outside of Charlottesville. It is almost as if Monsieur Maillard were Jefferson himself, welcoming a visitor.

Once the narrator arrives at the Maison de Santé, however, the somber mood comes to an end. Monsieur Maillard is the superintendent, and he invites the narrator to come inside and dine. There are already a number of guests and members of the staff, mostly female, and they discuss certain lunatics who had been in residence until recently. Those present seem to be almost crazy in their own right. An orchestra is on hand, and the supply of food is lavish, though a bit bizarre. The superintendent explains that the famed "soothing system" is no longer in use; harsher treatment had become necessary, for the lunatics had been handled with so few restraints that they had seized an opportunity and thrown the keepers into jail.

What gradually becomes evident to the reader, if not to the somewhat obtuse narrator, is that the so-called guests and staff are the lunatics themselves, who have imprisoned their keepers. The latter are being held under what the superintendent calls his new medical treatment developed by the celebrated "Doctor Tarr" and "Professor Fether." Just as the dinner ends, the keepers break loose from their confinement and force their way into the dining hall: in Poe's description, "down among them pelé-melé, fighting, stamping, scratching, and howling, there rushed a perfect army of what I took to be Chimpanzees, Ourang-Outangs, or big black baboons of the Cape of Good Hope." These had indeed been tarred and feathered, then kept in confinement for more than a month, and fed on bread and water: "The latter had been pumped on them daily." Now they take over once again, and during the fighting the narrator receives "a terrible beating—after which I rolled under a sofa and lay still" (1021).

It turns out that the superintendent had himself become insane three years earlier, had been a patient in the asylum, and it was he who had masterminded the rebellion. Since his visit there, the narrator tells us, "the 'soothing system,' with important modifications, had been resumed at the *chateau*." Yet, he adds, "I cannot help agreeing with Monsieur Maillard, that his own 'treatment' was a very capital one of its kind" (1021–22).

The key to this wild story resides in one little detail, which is that as the imprisoned keepers break into the dining room, the members of the orchestra leap upon a table and "broke out, with one accord, into 'Yankee Doodle,' which they performed, if not exactly in tune, at least with an energy superhuman, during the whole of the uproar" (1020). The annotators of the Belknap Press edition of Poe's fiction, perplexed by this, comment in a footnote that "in Poe's day 'Yankee Doodle' was our most popular national air, but its selection by a French orchestra, even if made, was certainly extraordinary!" (1025n25). But that is precisely the point; the story is *not* about an insane asylum in France, but about life in the United States of America.

Poe offers us hint after hint as to what is involved. The narrator's tour is through "the extreme Southern provinces of France" (1002). The patients at the asylum, much like slaves in the American South, "while secretly watched, were left much apparent liberty, and . . . most of them were permitted to roam about the house and ground, in the ordinary apparel of persons in right mind" (1004). They had been "often aroused to a dangerous frenzy by injudicious persons who called to inspect the house" (1005)—*i.e.*, Abolitionists in the South. The narrator wonders what is going on, but "remembered having been informed, in Paris, that the southern provincialists were a peculiarly eccentric people, with a vast number of antiquated notions" (1008). The superintendent tells the narrator that "'we are not very prudish, to be sure, here in the South—do pretty much as we please—enjoy life, and all that sort of thing, you know—'" (1016).

The satire is not consistent in its references; at one moment Poe seems to be depicting the slavery system, at another the New England scene, and so on. One of the inmates-turned-keepers, Bouffon Le Grand (the "Godlike Daniel" Webster?), believes he has two heads: "'One of these he maintained to be the head of Cicero, the other he imagined a composite one, being Demosthenes from the forehead to the mouth, and Lord Brougham from the mouth to the chin'" (1013). (Brougham was the English statesman who led in the passage of the Reform Bill and in the abolition of slavery in English territories.) What Poe is mocking is the city of Boston, Abolitionists, Transcendentalists, Brook Farmers, and so on, as well as the various cults and causes associated with New England millennialism and reform, locating these, ironically, in the "extreme Southern province." I suspect that one Madame Joyeuse may be Margaret Fuller; anyone who is familiar with the New England intellectual scene during the 1830s and 1840s could probably identify a number of the figures being caricatured.

But the "crazies," as Poe has elsewhere referred to the leaders of the New England scene, can also be dangerous. A madman, Monseiur Maillard explains to the narrator, can create "'very great danger. . . . His cunning, too, is proverbial, and great. If he has a project in view, he conceals his design with a marvelous wisdom. . . . When a madman appears *thoroughly* sane, indeed, it is high time to put him into a straight jacket.'" The inmates, he says, had behaved remarkably well, which should have been a sign that trouble was brewing, until one day they overpowered the keepers and threw them into the cells:

> "You don't tell me so! I never heard of anything so absurd in my life!"
> "Fact—it all came to pass by means of a stupid fellow—a lunatic—who, by some means, had taken it into his head that he had invented a better system of government than any ever heard of before—of lunatic government, I mean. He wished to give his invention a trial, I suppose—and so he persuaded the rest of the patients to join him in a conspiracy for the overthrow of the reigning powers." (1018)

There Poe's target would seem to be the author of the Declaration of Independence. At other times Poe is obviously describing Transcendentalists. The emphasis upon the asylum's being located in the South would appear to be intended as a reversal of roles, with the "crazies" parroting the Southern slogans. It is also suggested that the best way to deal with meddling reformers and Abolitionists is through the prompt application of tar and feathers. There is the warning that should such reformers be permitted to gain control of the government and enact laws about the South's Peculiar Institution, the result would soon be a slave revolution that would place the white population in jeopardy. At the close, when the imprisoned keepers storm the dining hall, they are obviously meant to represent what would happen if a slave revolt occurred; a "perfect army of what I took to be Chimpanzees, Ourang-Outangs, or big black baboons of the Cape of Good Hope" would make quick work of their former masters.

It might be noted that the situation in "The System of Doctor Tarr and Professor Fether" resembles that depicted by Herman Melville in "Benito Cereno," in which escaped slaves overpower the crew of a ship and when a visitor comes aboard pretend that all is well and in order. But in Poe's tale it is handled comically, not tragically, and there is little or nothing of the terror and desperation portrayed in Melville's story—which postdates Poe's by more than a decade.

8.

We have remarked upon the similarity between Poe's account of his narrator's trip to the Maison de Santé in "The System of Doctor Tarr and Professor Fether" and the opening of "The Fall of the House of Usher." The two stories, however, seem otherwise to have no resemblances beyond the obvious one that in each tale a narrator visits a dilapidated mansion, discovers that things are considerably awry there, and barely escapes with his life when events precipitate themselves. Lewis Simpson and others have identified the situation of Roderick Usher as pertaining to the slaveholding South, though without claiming that the subject matter of the story is related to the Peculiar Institution on any literal level.

If we think of "The Fall of the House of Usher" in relationship to Poe's fiction as a whole, what is interesting is the use of the motif of being buried alive. As we have seen, the lady Madeline is placed in a vault. In the days that follow, the suspicion that she may have been entombed while still alive becomes more and more active, until at the climactic moment she appears outside her brother's study, her garments bloody from the struggle to free herself, and throws herself, dying, upon him. As he too dies the narrator flees, whereupon the hereditary mansion collapses.

The theme of burial while still living is present in Poe's work from the outset. The motif is not peculiar to Poe; it was a frequent theme in early nineteenth-century romantic fiction, no doubt for complex psychological reasons having to do with the state of medical knowledge, the growing awareness of the biological complexity of the physical body, and doubts about the certainty of an afterlife beyond the grave. Even so, Poe's fascination with the matter is obvious. One of the earliest prose pieces believed to be Poe's, "A Dream," published in the Philadelphia *Saturday Evening Post* for August 13, 1831, portrays a person who comes to "the burial ground of the monarch of Israel" and sees the monument begin to tremble. "Soon it was overturned, and from it issued the tenant of the grave. 'Twas a hideous, unearthly form, such as Dante, in his wildest flights of terrified fancy, ne'er conjured up. I could not move, for terror had tied up volition. It approached me. I saw the grave-worm twining itself amongst the matted locks which in part covered the rotten skull."[36] To be sure, this is not burial alive but the resurrection of the dead, but the motifs are closely connected.

One of the stories in the manuscript entitled "Tales of the Folio Club," which Poe wrote during the early 1830s, "Loss of Breath: A Tale Neither In Nor Out of 'Blackwood,'" involves a man who loses his breath and can't find it. Mistaken for a condemned criminal, he is hanged, deposited in a public vault, encounters another person in the same fix, and the two of them make themselves heard and are rescued. Two versions of the tale actually exist, one of them entitled "A Decided Loss."

Once attempted, the motif was used again and again by Poe. In "The Cask of Amontillado," Fortunato is bricked into the cata-

36. Poe, "A Dream," *Tales and Sketches*, II, 9.

combs and left to die. In *Arthur Gordon Pym* a man is smuggled aboard a ship and must stay inside a coffin-like box for six days and nights. In "Morella" a woman is buried, her daughter grows up to resemble her, and when she too dies it is discovered that the grave bears no trace of the mother. In "A Descent into the Maelstrom" a fisherman is sucked into the abyss of a whirlpool. In "The Pit and the Pendulum" a man is left in a dark cell, the walls of which he discovers are moving in upon him. In "The Tell-Tale Heart" a murdered man's body is buried beneath the flooring of a house, but his heart continues to beat. In "The Black Cat" a cat, walled in a tomb, reveals by its cries the presence of a murdered body. In "The Oblong Box" a distraught husband binds himself to a box containing the weighted corpse of his wife and in a shipwreck goes down to his death with it.

There are other variations on the theme in Poe's fiction, but the most detailed and full use of burial alive comes in "The Premature Burial," written at about the same time as "The System of Doctor Tarr and Professor Fether." The editors of the Belknap Press edition note that the impulse for the story was probably a well-known "life-preserving coffin" that was exhibited in New York City in 1843, and designed with safeguards against premature burial. From the evidence of the obsessive use of the motif throughout Poe's fiction, however, it seems clear that Poe needed no topical stimulation to address the theme.

"To be buried while alive is, beyond question, the most terrific of these extremes which has ever fallen to the lot of mere mortality," the narrator of "The Premature Burial" declares in a discussion of human calamities.[37] And again, "It may be asserted, without hesitation, that *no* event is so terribly well adapted to inspire the supremeness of bodily and of mental distress, as is burial before death" (961). Like many of Poe's stories, this one begins as if it were an essay, with the narrator discoursing on his chosen topic and citing supposed historical examples of burial alive, so as to appear to be giving a factual account. He discusses allegedly "well-known" cases, comments on the horror involved, then proposes to tell of his own experience. He is subject to inter-

37. Poe, "The Premature Burial," *Tales and Sketches*, III, 955. Subsequent references will occur parenthetically in the text.

vals of catalepsy, in which he may lie motionless for days at a time, apparently dead. His dread of such attacks causes him to have nightmares. In one instance he dreams he is in a "cataleptic trance of more than usual duration and profundity. Suddenly there came an icy hand on my forehead, and an impatient, gibbering voice whispered the word 'Arise!' within my ear" (964). He is shown a vision of the dead arising from the graves of all mankind. Clearly some who lie in death have been buried while still alive. The sight is pitiable beyond words.

The nightmares continue, and the narrator grows more and more fearful and distraught. He remodels the family vault to allow him to escape from it. He has the lid of his coffin fixed so as to open so that "the feeblest motion of the body would be sufficient to set it at liberty. Besides all this, there was suspended from the roof of the tomb, a large bell, the rope of which, it was designed, should extend through a hole in the coffin, and so be fastened to one of the hands of the corpse" (965–66).

The precautions are in vain, however, for a time comes when he finds himself slowly awakening from a trance. All is darkness. He tries to shriek, but can make no sound. He realizes he is in a coffin. Feeling for the bell rope, he cannot find it, and his nostrils inhale the strong odor of moist earth. He has been buried while away from home, he decides, and in a common coffin. In his agony he again seeks to cry aloud, and on his second attempt succeeds in doing so:

> "Hillo! Hillo, there!" said a gruff voice, in reply.
> "What the devil's the matter now?" said a second.
> "Get out o' that!" said a third.
> "What do you mean by yowling in that ere kind of style, like a cattymount?" said a fourth; and hereupon, I was seized and shaken without ceremony, for several minutes, by a junto of very rough-looking individuals. (968)

He finds himself awake, in a narrow berth aboard a small sloop. "The adventure occurred near Richmond, in Virginia. Accompanied by a friend, I had proceeded, upon a gunning expedition, some miles down the banks of James River" (968). Overtaken by a storm, they boarded a ship anchored in the stream, and had gone to sleep in the cabin. The berth was small and confined, and the awakening, the narrator says, was no nightmare but the result of his difficulty in regaining full consciousness after sleep. The voices he heard were those of the crew and some laborers come aboard to unload the cargo of garden mold. The episode, he tells us, was so horrible that thereafter he reformed his ways, ceased to brood upon death, read no more books on the subject, "no fustian about church-yards—no bugaboo tales—*such as this*. In short, I became a new man, and lived a man's life." The human imagination, he declares in concluding, is not meant to explore the horrors of the grave, the deathly, the spirit world, and sepulchral terrors in general: "They must sleep, or they will devour us—they must be suffered to slumber, or we perish" (969). This, of course, from the man whose career as a writer of fiction and poetry was rooted in just such exploration.

There are a number of things about "The Premature Burial" that are worth noting. For one thing, it is Poe's *only* story in which the locale is specifically ascribed to the Richmond neighborhood in which he grew to manhood. Moreover, the story is importantly autobiographical. Though not subject to cataleptic fits, Poe was obviously writing about his own obsession with the macabre. "There are certain themes," the story begins, "of which the interest is all-absorbing, but which are too entirely horrible for the purposes of legitimate fiction. These the mere romanticist must eschew, if he do not wish to offend, or disgust. They are with propriety handled, only when the severity and majesty of truth sanctify and sustain them" (954–55). As a writer addicted to just such grotesquerie, and as a man who obviously entertained such thoughts almost constantly, Poe is in effect discussing his own state of mind. The man for whom there was from childhood's hour "the cloud that took the form / (When the rest of Heaven was blue) / Of a demon in my view" is questioning the meaning of his penchant for horror and terror.

The poet Daniel Hoffman, whose book *Poe Poe Poe Poe Poe Poe Poe* (1972) is a deft examination of the intricate relationship between hoax and art in Poe's work, sees him as trying to tell us in "The Premature Burial" that he would very much like to rid himself of such speculations. By calling it a "bugaboo" tale, Poe

admits that he cannot shake himself free from the long shadow, the feeling of fatal and foetal enclosure.

If he cannot be free from it, though, he can figure out *how best to make use of it* in his ratiocinative-ecstatic-horrific tales. By means of whose telling he can all but control the terrors that shake him to the marrow of his soul.[38]

Hoffman very properly views the problem as one involving psychoanalytical elements, and he believes that, given the fact that there were no physicians available in America in Poe's day who could have helped him understand what was at issue, he had arrived at about as clear a perception, in this story, of his terrors as was possible to him. My own guess is that the dream reproduced in "The Premature Burial" must have gone well back into Poe's childhood, and that the fear of living entombment no doubt bore more than a casual relationship to the belief that his "father," John Allan, was intent upon suppressing his masculinity and his individuality. What I find interesting in terms of Poe as a Southern writer, however, is the particular form that the obsession assumed.

In *The Narrative of Arthur Gordon Pym* there is an episode in which certain black-skinned warriors manage by means of a landslide to entomb some white-skinned mariners within a rocky fissure. Poe has his narrator depose as follows:

I firmly believe that no incident ever occurring in the course of human events is more adapted to inspire the supremeness of mental and bodily distress than a case like our own, of living inhumation. The blackness of darkness which envelops the victim, the terrific oppression of lungs, the stifling fumes from the damp earth, unite with the ghastly considerations that we are beyond the remotest confines of hope, and that such is the allotted portion of the dead, to carry to the human heart a degree of appalling awe and horror not to be tolerated—never to be conceived.[39]

In that passage the blackness, the smell of damp earth, the hopelessness and terror are directly linked to the *fear of blacks*—in other words, to slave insurrection. It is as if the young Edgar Poe, lying in his bed in the darkness of John Allan's house in Richmond, imagined that he was in imminent danger of death; at any

38. Daniel Hoffman, *Poe Poe Poe Poe Poe Poe Poe* (Garden City, N.Y.: Doubleday and Co., 1972), 221.

39. Poe, *The Narrative of Arthur Gordon Pym of Nantucket*, in *Collected Writings of Edgar Allan Poe*, Vol. I, *The Imaginary Voyages*, ed. Burton R. Pollin (Boston: Twayne Publishers, 1981), 182.

moment the Allans' supposedly docile house servants might rise in revolt with the thousands of other slaves in Richmond and slaughter the family.

We have seen how, in "The Premature Burial," one of the narrator's nightmares involved, in the darkness of a trance, awakening to find that "suddenly there came an icy hand on my forehead." One of Poe's youthful companions, John McKenzie, once spoke of Poe's "timidity in regard to being alone at night." He had heard Poe say, when grown, that "the most horrible thing he could imagine as a boy was to feel an ice-cold hand laid upon his face in a pitch-black room when alone at night; or to awake in semi-darkness and see an evil face gazing close into his own; and that these fancies had so haunted him that he would often keep his head under the bed-covering until nearly suffocated."[40]

In the Richmond of Poe's boyhood, and in almost every other city or town of consequence, the signal for spreading the alarm was the ringing of a bell. Usually this meant that there was a fire. On Capitol Square in Richmond, first a wooden and after 1824 a brick bell-tower "was for generations the tocsin of Richmond— pealing for joyful events, tolling for funerals, and warning of fires and other alarms." We may assume that alarm rang out when word of the Gabriel Prosser insurrection came in 1800, just over a decade before Poe's birth. In the words of Mary Newton Stanard in her history of Richmond, although Gabriel's "plot failed, the dread undercurrent that it bore witness to caused uneasiness long afterward. Two years later night watches were appointed for each ward, and to any that lay awake shuddering at thought of dangers that might be lurking in the dark streets, their chant: 'Oyez, oyez, twelve o'clock and all's well' (or one, two or three o'clock, and so on), brought a comfortable sense of security."[41]

Poe described such a fire bell vividly and all too alliteratively in his poem "The Bells":

> *What* a tale of terror, now, their turbulency tells!
> In the startled ear of Night
> How they shriek out their affright!
> Too much horrified to speak,

40. Quoted in *Tales and Sketches*, III, 953.
41. Mary Newton Stanard, *Richmond: Its People and Its History* (Philadelphia and London: J. B. Lippincott, 1923), 67, 168.

> They can only shriek, shriek,
>   Out of tune,
> In a clamorous appealing to the mercy of the fire—
> In a mad expostulation with the deaf and frantic fire
>
> . . . .
>
>   Oh, the bells, bells, bells!
>   What a tale their terror tells
>   Of despair![42]

Jefferson's vivid image of the slavery controversy as a fire bell tolling in the night is appropriate here. We recall that as lieutenant of
the Junior Morgan Riflemen, Poe was involved in drawing rifles
from the city armory to defend Richmond when the State Guard
was away from town. It was servile revolt, not fire, that such
armed guards were meant to suppress if needed. It is not difficult
to imagine the young second-in-command, having petitioned for
his youthful associates to be permitted to retain their rifles at
home, lying in the dark in bed, hearing the bell in the tower ringing the alarm for a fire, and wondering what would happen if a far
more sinister alarm were to sound next.

In "The Premature Burial," it should be noted, not only does
the narrator plan to have a large bell suspended above his coffin
with a cord leading inside, to be pulled in the event of burial alive,
but the culminating burial episode takes place following "a gunning expedition, some miles down the banks of James River."
Thus both these motifs, as well as that of the icy hand in darkness, are among the conspicuous details used by Poe in this story
that, alone of all his works, is importantly set in part in the Virginia of his younger days.

Admittedly a fear of the dark, or of evil spirits, is scarcely restricted to the experience of youthful antebellum Southerners.
Yet the frequency with which episodes involving burial alive, suffocation underground, and dead persons emerging from graves appear in Poe's fiction, and the numerous motifs that link such episodes to Poe's youthful days in slaveholding Richmond, seem to
me to indicate a connection between the two that should not be
casually dismissed.

It is interesting that the same connection is to be found in a
post–Civil War story by Thomas Nelson Page. All the stories in

42. Poe, "The Bells," in *The Unabridged Poe*, 1177.

Page's first and most important book, *In Ole Virginia* (1887), have to do with slavery, but except for one they are all eulogistic, for Page, a member of one of the most distinguished of Virginia families, was a wholehearted defender of the *ancien régime* in the Old Dominion. Even so, writing when it was no longer obligatory for a writer to insist at all times upon the docility and faithfulness of the slaves of antebellum years, Page felt free to develop certain motifs that were formerly taboo.

Ghost stories were extremely popular at the time, and Page wrote one entitled "'No Haid Pawn,'" in which the presence of runaway slaves in rural Virginia is linked directly to the fear of darkness, ghosts, and burial alive. "We were brought up to believe in ghosts," he writes. Although parents laughed at such superstition, "the old mammies and uncles who were our companions and comrades" informed young people differently. The pond at a deserted plantation had supposedly been the scene of an outbreak of typhus at one time. That it had spread elsewhere "did not prevent the colored population from recounting year after year the horrors of the pestilence of No Haid Pawn as a peculiar visitation, nor from relating with blood-curdling details, the burial of scores, in a thicket just beside the pond, of the stricken 'befo' dee *daid*, honey, *befo' dee daid!*'"[43]

Page goes on to link the appearance of an apparition at the deserted plantation house with a runaway slave and the threat of Abolitionist incitement to rebellion: "No idea can be given at this date of the excitement occasioned in a quiet neighborhood by the discovery of the mere presence of such characters as Abolitionists. It was as if the foundations of the whole social fabric were undermined. It was the sudden darkening of a shadow that always hung in the horizon. The slaves were in a large majority, and had they risen, though the final issue could not be doubted, the lives of every white on the plantation must have paid the forfeit."[44] The story, which contrasts so strangely with others in Page's collection, goes on to develop an explanation for the supposed ghost: it was a runaway slave, hiding out in the deserted

43. Thomas Nelson Page, "'No Haid Pawn,'" *In Ole Virginia, or Marse Chan and Other Stories*, Southern Literary Classics Series (Chapel Hill: University of North Carolina Press, 1969), 164, 168.

44. *Ibid.*, 173–74.

house, who was being cared for by the local slaves. The runaway had disappeared after it was discovered that he had been involved in secret meetings with Abolitionist agents. He would otherwise have surely been executed or at the least deported. What was appalling to the narrator when young was the realization that the local blacks were looking after the runaway.

I know of no other story by a nineteenth-century Southern writer that so vividly depicts the abiding fear of servile revolt. The need to work out a plausible ghost story would appear to have touched off elements in Page's imagination that severely undercut his otherwise consistent depiction of antebellum Virginia as a Golden Age. His description of the anxiety and dread he had felt as a child, its link with the stories told him by the blacks, and the horror over the notion of people being buried alive make an interesting correlation with Poe.

As we have already seen, the fear of slave rebellion was very much a part of the antebellum Southern scene. Travelers to the region from the North and elsewhere, such as Frederick Law Olmsted, repeatedly cited the presence of militia units and arsenals throughout the South for protection against uprisings. The elaborate slave laws were clearly designed to minimize all situations that might permit blacks to foment plans for insurrection. Fanny Kemble, the English actress who married a Georgia planter and briefly resided on a plantation, insisted that the Southern ladies with whom she talked all admitted to living in terror of blacks. As Mary Boykin Chesnut noted in her wartime journals, the usual response to such apprehension was to insist passionately upon the devotion and trust between one's own slaves and oneself.

As the historian Clement Eaton writes, "the stringent slave codes, the patrol system, the efforts to get rid of the free Negro, the prevalence of alarming rumors, the flimsy evidence of the existence of plots which was credited, all indicate a certain current of uneasiness in Southern society, a feeling that stern precautions should be taken against possible slave revolt." Hinton Rowan Helper, the North Carolinian whose book *The Impending Crisis* (1857) fulminated against the political and economic thralldom in which the non-slaveholding white Southern majority was held by the planter leadership, demanded rhetorically of the slaveholder, "Do you aspire to become the victim of white non-slaveholding vengeance by day, and of barbarous massacre by the negroes by night? Would you be instrumental in bringing upon yourselves, your wives, and your children a fate too horrible to contemplate? shall history cease to cite, as an instance of un-exampled cruelty, the Massacre of St. Bartholomew, because the world—the South—shall have furnished a more direful scene of atrocity and carnage?"[45] Such was the milieu in which the youthful Edgar Poe grew to maturity.

9.

To understand what slavery and slave insurrections meant for Edgar Poe's art, it is necessary, I think, to dismiss the notion of conscious intention or one-for-one allegorical relationships, and begin with the assumption that what is involved is a complex emotional and psychological response to the experience of grow-ing up in Richmond as the "foster son" of a dour Scots merchant, as a member of a slaveholding household in which his status and identity were sometimes painfully oblique.

It would scarcely do to claim that Poe's fiction and poetry are what they are *because* the author was an orphan child in a South-ern city in which slavery was practiced. Literature doesn't usually work so neatly and obviously as that. What can be said is that, in a poetic sensibility predisposed to ultrasensitive emotional shad-ings, the youthful experience manifested itself in an obsessive use of certain kinds of imagery and dramatic situations, having to do with a fear of darkness, blackness, burial alive, icy hands, suffoca-tion, and helpless terror.

It was Poe's Richmond experience that helped to propel his imagination inward, in the direction of the exploration of the in-terior landscape of the mind, rather than outward, toward nature and the situation of the individual in reaction to the external community. Reared in a community in which the expectation of

45. Clement Eaton, *The Freedom-of-Thought Struggle in the Old South* (Rev. and Enl. ed.; New York: Harper and Row, 1964), 116; Hinton Rowan Helper, *The Impending Crisis of the South: How to Meet It* (New York: Burdick Bros., 1857), 128.

gentlemanly rank and public role was assumed, yet simultaneously encountering a pervasive undercutting of the status and assurance upon which that expectation was based, Poe chose the
pose of Byronic poet as a way of transcending the situation in
which he found himself. Although he later modified the role, he
never abandoned it thereafter.

Inevitably that choice moved him toward the experience of the
world city. What he discovered there was foreign to the social assumptions that were his Southern inheritance, and he was tem-
peramentally unable to enter wholeheartedly into the commercial, competitive middle-class life of metropolitan journalism in
Philadelphia and New York. The result was a profound alienation
from democratic American society. Emotionally, imaginatively
he inhabited a realm that was "out of place, out of time"—the
bizarre, solipsistic landscape of his own inner consciousness,
which at various times he chose to designate as London, Paris,
Venice, Rome, Bohemia, or whatever.

Denied by heritage, temperament, and circumstance the great
themes of rebirth in the wilderness of the new continent and the
clash between the private individual and the social community
that were so richly available to the other major literary talents of
the American Renaissance, Poe was left with but one subject: the
separateness and loneliness of the alienated sensibility. He turned
his imagination inward, allowing it to project itself in fantastic
shapes and extraordinary forms, upon which he strove to enforce
an ordering and patterning that must at times have seemed as
abstract and arbitrary as the boundaries of his imagining.

Yet again and again that imagining returned to certain subjects, certain themes and motifs, bestowed upon his sensibility
through the memories of his childhood and youth. Inevitably they
led his musings to a particular place. "During the whole of a dark,
dull, and soundless day in the autumn of the year, when the
clouds hung oppressively low in the heavens, I had been passing
alone, on horseback, through a singularly dreary tract of country;
and at length found myself, as the shades of the evening drew on,
within view of the melancholy House of Usher" (397). In that
place were to be found ruined grandeur, burial while still alive,
terror of blackness, suffocation, the failure and defeat of reason
and rationality, hopelessness, loss. Whatever the compulsive

repetition that drew him there, his imagination fastened upon its symbols as if it were his home.

The extent to which Poe ever attempted to sort out in his mind what his attitude toward Richmond, the South, and its social and political views was, is not known. Undoubtedly he affected the pose of disinherited aristocrat during his years in the North, and it seems clear that he was no Jacksonian Democrat and that his politics, such as they were, were Whig. If we attempt to guess at his attitude toward slavery, all that we really have to go on for sure are his strictures on James Russell Lowell as an Abolitionist. But that review was written for the *Southern Literary Messenger*, and was a product of his anger at Lowell's treatment of him in *A Fable for Critics*, and Poe was not above using any available weapon to further his ends. Knowing that a Richmond audience would have little use for any author, however meritorious his work, who opposed the Peculiar Institution, Poe doubtless used that knowledge to gain reader sympathy for his quarrel with Lowell, which was personal and literary. Moreover, as we have seen, he added the comment that if Lowell were himself a slave-owner he would be the kind who wished to murder all Abolitionists, which would indicate that Poe had no special love for extreme proslavery advocates, either.

My own assumption is that Poe was profoundly apolitical; he was simply uninterested in sectional politics. It was literature, both as a profession and a way of viewing the world, that was his dominant, almost his sole concern. When, to repeat, he wrote that "From childhood's hour I have not been / As others were—I have not seen / As others saw," he was only saying what was obvious.

His attitude toward Richmond, I suspect, was one of mingled contempt and nostalgia. It had been the only place where he had ever known any security, and where he had enjoyed friendship and lived anything that resembled a "normal" existence. Yet he had also, both as a child and later, experienced deep-rooted unhappiness there. It was there that his mother had died, and during the months of her final illness he must have known a terrible insecurity, which a sensitive not-quite-three-year-old could never have totally overcome, however it might be buried in his psyche. Until his mother's death his life had been as a child of an actress; there is even some speculation that he might have appeared onstage on several occasions. It would have been only the theatrical custom of the day if he and his brother and sister had been introduced to the audience on the occasion of the benefit performance for Elizabeth Poe shortly before she died. Less than three weeks after her death the theater in which she had performed was the scene of a disastrous fire, in which numerous prominent citizens died, and the city was thereafter plunged into mourning for weeks. Something of what had happened must have reached his ears. Surely he learned, too, of the social disrepute that in early nineteenth-century America was attached to actors and actresses. Several of those who knew him when he was a boy have reported that some of his schoolmates and their families looked down upon him because of his parents' profession, and that on at least one occasion he is said to have been denied a position of leadership because of it.

Richmond was the community in which a John Allan could win wealth and distinction, and in which a flinty tobacco merchant commanded the respect that an ambitious young poet, and later a talented young magazine editor, could not hope to receive. The cultural life of Richmond in Poe's day, such as it was, was thin and principally social in nature, administered by merchants and lawyers with a mild taste for the arts. When Poe returned to the city to work for Thomas Willis White as editorial assistant for the *Messenger* in 1835–1836, his career there brought him little distinction in the eyes of the local citizenry. He drank to excess, his wife was only thirteen years old, he was freakish, bohemian. Almost certainly there was gossip—about his origins, his relations with the recently deceased John Allan, his disgrace at the University of Virginia, and now his child bride, his drunkenness. The friends of his youth who had attended school with him were now prospering as lawyers, doctors, merchants; he was living in a boardinghouse and working for the minuscule wages paid by White. One wonders to what extent his drinking was in part a way of drowning his resentment and frustration. *These* soulless, unimaginative, money-grubbing people dared to consider themselves superior in rectitude and attainment to him! Dared to make insinuations about his dead mother and father, who had been talented actors! Dared to gossip about his relations with his thirteen-year-old bride!

Burial while alive, death from suffocation, menacing fears of blackness and terror—what these speak to is the situation of a talented, overly emotional youth who wished desperately to transcend the frustrations of his own time and place. "In Heaven a spirit doth dwell / Whose heart-strings are a lute—; / None sing so wild—so well / As the angel Israfel—." If only he might dwell elsewhere, in a place where poetry was possible: "Where Love is a grown god— / Where Houri glances are— / —Stay! turn thy eyes afar!— / Imbued with all the beauty / Which we worship in yon star." But the appalling barriers and nightmare distortions of his life, the situation of a young man of hypersensitive imagination and rending inner contradictions, unsure of his status and identity, dubious of his future prospects (as well he might be), held in contempt by his practical-minded foster father and in disdain by others because of his parentage, allow him to occupy no such blessed realm:

> If I could dwell where Israfel
> Hath dwelt, and he where I,
> He might not sing one half as well—
> One half as passionately,
> And a stormier note than this would swell
> From my lyre within the sky.[46]

It seems obvious that Poe was alienated from Southern society to a far greater extent than William Gilmore Simms or any of his other contemporaries. But I do not think that such alienation was simply a matter of having quarreled with John Allan and having failed to make a place for himself in Richmond, so that he was obliged to live out his days in the cities of the Northeast. Rather, it was a condition of the soul, one might say, and it began very early in his life. When Poe departed from Richmond for Boston in 1827 under the alias of Henri Le Rennet, it was only the geographical, physical confirmation of a spiritual distancing that had been long in developing and by the mid-1820s was irreversible. (It is interesting that early in "The Premature Burial," the only one of Poe's stories importantly located in Virginia, near Richmond, there is a character named M. Rennell.)

Yet it seems quite clear that the Richmond experience figured

---

46. Poe, "Israfel," in *The Unabridged Poe*, 68–69.

profoundly in Poe's imagination—which is hardly surprising, since it was where the greatest part of his childhood and youth was spent. When, in *Absalom, Absalom!*, William Faulkner declares of Quentin Compson that "his very body was an empty hall echoing with sonorous defeated names; he was not being, an entity, he was a commonwealth,"[47] he could as well have been writing about Edgar Poe.

There is something exquisitely pathetic about William Gilmore Simms urging Poe to "return to that community—that moral province in society" to which he was "too heedlessly and, perhaps, too scornfully indifferent."[48] Be a Southern gentleman, the South Carolinian was telling him, by which he meant an attitude toward himself, his community, his place in society. But Poe had long since departed from such attitudes, and could never have regained them. He knew things, thought thoughts such as Simms could not have known existed.

As a former Southerner, what did Poe think about slaves and slavery? We do not know. Far more important than what he thought, I believe, was what he felt. My own hunch is that what they meant to him was FEAR. He might jest about it in "The System of Doctor Tarr and Professor Fether," but it was no lighthearted humor that was involved. Whatever his thoughts about the rightness or wrongness of the Peculiar Institution, what haunted his imagination were blackness, suffocation, the menace of revolt, the dread of vengeance.

Did he, as a youth in Richmond, witness slave auctions, see coffles of blacks led off to the Deep South? He could scarcely have failed to do so. What was his relationship, given his oblique position in the Allan household, with the family servants? When in his presence might they have been sufficiently bold to say things, reveal attitudes that they would not have otherwise dared reveal? What might they have told him about his mother? Might they not, as we have seen Thomas Nelson Page indicate, have told him horror stories, given him details of the suffering and agonies of the great theater fire that took place so close after his mother's death? There is simply no telling, although it needs no stretching of the

47. William Faulkner, *Absalom, Absalom!* (New York: Random House, 1936), 12.
48. Simms to Poe, July 30, 1846, in *Letters*, II, 176.

imagination to see the younger Edgar Poe eavesdropping raptly, down in the cellar of the Allan residence, as the slaves conversed and told stories.

For anyone who would allegorize Poe's fiction or search for items of autobiography, the prospect is bewildering. We have no real idea as to just how conscious he was of the presence of such allusions in his work. We know, for example, that Arthur Gordon Pym sounds much like Edgar Allan Poe, and that he attends a school in which Poe was enrolled. We recognize, in "William Wilson," the Manor House School at Stoke Newington that Poe attended in England, and the headmaster of that school. Poe's mother was known to have as her closest friends a brother and sister, James Campbell Usher and Agnes Pye Usher, who were said to have been extremely neurotic. And so on. One sometimes has the sense that Poe frequently went to considerable pains to work allusions to his own life into his writings.

But beyond the conscious, intended references, there are motifs, incidents, relationships that must surely have forced their way into the ways he thought and felt, and which come from the deepest levels of his experience. We have seen how, in "The Premature Burial," he wrestles with the hold that they had on his imagination. What is the source, for example, of his fascination with ourang-outangs? The horrible killings in "Murders in the Rue Morgue" are by an ape; in "The System of Doctor Tarr and Professer Fether" the imprisoned keepers of the Maison de Santé who break out of their cells, having previously been tarred and feathered, resemble "Chimpanzees, Ourang-Outangs, or big black baboons of the Cape of Good Hope." What have they to do with the black slaves of his boyhood years in the South?

10.

In what was probably Edgar Poe's last short-story, "Hop-Frog," a certain dwarf, crippled, a professional jester, adept at arranging novel pageants and outlandish characters, is summoned by the king, who forces him to drink wine. "Hop-Frog was not fond of wine; for it excited the poor cripple almost to madness; and madness is no comfortable feeling."[49] But the king orders him to

49. Poe, "Hop-Frog," *Tales and Sketches*, III, 1347. Subsequent references will occur parenthetically in the text.

drink, and when Trippetta, the girl he loves and who loves him, "very little less dwarfish than himself (although of exquisite proportions, and a marvelous dancer)," attempts to intercede, the king thrusts her away and dashes the wine in her face (1346). Whereupon Hop-Frog drinks more wine and arranges a delightful entertainment. He persuades the king and his seven councillors to engage in a masquerade which he calls the "Eight Chained Ourang-Outangs":

The king and his ministers were first encased in tight-fitting stockinet shirts and drawers. They were then saturated with tar. At this stage of the process, some one of the party suggested feathers; but the suggestion was at once overruled by the dwarf, who soon convinced the eight, by ocular demonstration, that the hair of such a brute as the ourang-outang was much more efficiently represented by *flax*. A thick coating of this latter was accordingly plastered upon the coating of tar. A long chain was now procured. First, it was passed about the waist of the king, *and tied*; then about another of the party, and also tied; then about all successively, in the same manner. (1350–51)

The great hall in which the masquerade party takes place is illuminated by a huge chandelier, with burning wax candles, suspended by a chain from the ceiling. At Hop-Frog's suggestion the chandelier is removed from the chain to prevent wax from dripping onto the guests in the crowded room. At midnight the chained masqueraders come into the room. There is tremendous excitement and even panic; a rush is made for the doors, but they have been locked: "While the tumult was at its height, and each masquerader attentive to his own safety—(for, in fact, there was much *real* danger from the pressure of the excited crowd)—the chain by which the chandelier ordinarily hung, and which had been drawn up on its removal, might have been seen very gradually to descend, until its hooked extremity came within three feet of the floor." The dwarf loops the connecting chains of the eight "ourang-outangs" over the hook. Then "the chandelier-chain was drawn so far upward as to take the hook out of reach, and, as an inevitable consequence, to drag the ourang-outangs together in close connection, and face to face" (1352). The dwarf scrambles over the heads of the crowd, procures a flambeau, returns to the center of the room, and utters a shrill whistle. The ourang-outangs are hauled thirty feet into the air, with the dwarf, mounted above

them, holding onto the chain. "'Ah, ha!' said at length the infuriated jester. 'Ah, ha! I begin to see who these people *are*, now!'" He
holds the flambeau to the flaxen coat of the king, which bursts
into "a sheet of vivid flame. In less than half a minute the whole
eight ourang-outangs were blazing fiercely, amid the shrieks of
the multitude who gazed at them from below, horror-stricken,
and without the power to render them the slightest assistance."
The dwarf climbs higher up the chandelier chain to avoid the
flames and delivers a speech:

"I now see *distinctly*," he said, "what manner of people these maskers
are. They are a great king and his seven privy-councillors—a king who
does not scruple to strike a defenceless girl, and his seven councillors
who abet him in the outrage. As for myself, I am simply Hop-Frog, the
jester—and *this is my last jest*."

Owing to the high combustibility of both the flax and the tar to which
it adhered, the dwarf had scarcely made an end of his brief speech before
the work of vengeance was complete. The eight corpses swung in their
chains, a fetid, hardened, blackened, hideous, and indistinguishable
mass. The cripple hurled his torch at them, clambered leisurely to the
ceiling, and disappeared through the skylight.

It is supposed that Trippetta, stationed on the roof of the saloon, had
been the accomplice of her friend in his fiery revenge, and that, together,
they effected their escape to their own country; for neither was seen
again. (1354)

On October 11, 1811, Elizabeth Arnold Poe, a member of Placide's
Company of players, appeared as the Countess Wintersen in *The
Stranger*, at the brick theater on Broad Street Hill in Richmond. It
was her last performance. On November 29 the Richmond *Enquirer* published this notice:

TO THE HUMAN HEART

On this night, *Mrs. Poe*, lingering on the bed of disease and surrounded
by her children, asks your assistance and *asks it perhaps for the last
time*. The Generosity of a Richmond Audience can need no other appeal.
For particulars see the Bills of the Day.[50]

She died eight days later. Less than three weeks after Elizabeth
Poe's death, many of Richmond's most distinguished citizens

---

50. Richmond *Enquirer*, November 29, 1811, quoted in Martin Staples
Shockley, *The Richmond Stage, 1784–1812* (Charlottesville: University Press of
Virginia, 1977), 349.

crowded into the same playhouse to see a performance. The afterpiece was under way, a melodrama entitled "Raymond and Agnes, or, the Bleeding Nun." Following the first act, in which a large chandelier was suspended from the ceiling, there was a change of scenery. A stagehand was told to lift the lamp out of view. The stagehand remonstrated, for one of the two oil wicks was still burning, but he was ordered to proceed. The theater propertyman, recognizing the danger, instructed a carpenter to lower the lamp and blow out the flame at once.

When the carpenter attempted to do so, the cords of the trolley became entangled, and the chandelier began oscillating. A workman moved to free the lines, jerking them, until the lamp swerved from its perpendicular position and swung against the lower part of one of the front scenes. In no time the canvas scene was on fire, and flames rose six or seven feet to the ceiling. There were cries of "Fire!" and assurances, "Don't be alarmed." An actor stepped to the front of the stage. "The house is on fire!" he called out.

Within minutes the whole roof of the theater was a sheet of flame. The audience crowded toward the exits; 598 of them had to pass through a single door, which opened inward. Men, women, children fell against each other as a narrow, curved stairway to the exit caved in. "The volume of smoke, which could not at first escape through the roof, was bent downwards; black, dense, almost saturated with oily vapours. Many were suffocated by it, who might have strength enough to leap the windows."[51]

Thomas Ritchie, editor of the Richmond *Enquirer*, was in the audience, and described the scene:

The fire flew with a rapidity, almost beyond example. Within 10 minutes after it caught the whole house was wrapped in flames. —The colored people in the gallery most of them escaped through the stairs cut off from the rest of the house—some have no doubt fallen victims. The pit and boxes had but one common avenue—through which the whole crowd escaped, save only those who leaped through the windows.

But the scene which ensued—it is impossible to paint. Women with dishevelled [sic] hair; fathers & mothers shrieking out for their children, husbands for their wives, brothers for their sisters, filled the whole area

51. Thomas Ritchie, "Narrative," Richmond *Enquirer*, December 31, 1811, quoted in Shockley, *The Richmond Stage*, 366.

on the outside of the building. A few who had escaped, plunged again into the flames to save some dear object of their regard—and they perished. The Governor perhaps shared this melancholy fate. Others were frantic, and would have rushed to destruction, but for the hand of a friend. The bells tolled. Almost the whole town rushed to the fatal spot.[52]

Despite heroic efforts by a muscular slave blacksmith and a local doctor, who together extricated a dozen women, seventy-two persons died, including Governor George W. Smith and numerous other well-known Richmond citizens.

Memories of the horrors of the Richmond theater fire lasted for many years. The disaster was considered by many to have been a sign from heaven to sinful people who frequented theaters and witnessed their immoral performances. As a Baltimore newspaper declared, "Is not the Playhouse the very exchange of harlots? The Players, generally speaking, who are they? Loose, debauched people."[53]

It was decided that the appropriate memorial for those who died in the theater fire would be to erect a church on the site. Among those contributing to the building fund was John Allan. On May 4, 1814, the Monumental Episcopal Church was opened. Its communicants included John Allan, his wife, and their foster son. The family pew was No. 80, just across the nave from that of Chief Justice John Marshall, and directly below the pulpit. There, on the site of the theater Elizabeth Arnold Poe had appeared in for her final role as a member of Placide's Company, the young Edgar Allan Poe was taught to sing hymns.

For anyone familiar with the details of Poe's relationship with the citizenry of Richmond, Virginia, "Hop-Frog" offers interesting reverberations. I am not suggesting that the story is a flat-out allegory of Poe and the young Virginia Clemm amid what he surely must have considered the philistinism and cruel snobbery of the community of his rearing and first editorial employment. If any allegorization was involved (and I think it quite possible) in this bizarre little tale, its target was very likely broader than that,

---

52. Thomas Ritchie, "Overwhelming Calamity," Richmond *Enquirer*, December 27, 1811, quoted in Shockley, *The Richmond Stage*, 361–62.

53. Quoted in Virginius Dabney, *Richmond: The Story of a City* (Garden City, N.Y.: Doubleday and Co., 1976), 92.

having to do with the American social and cultural establishment as a whole.

Yet the imaginative details of the story draw quite strikingly on images and motifs that one associates with Poe's Richmond. In their commentary on "Hop-Frog" the editors of the *Collected Works* speculate that the manner of chaining apes described in the story may well have been borrowed by the author from an incident in the 138th chapter of Froissart. Edgar Poe's imagination did not need Froissart's *Chronicles* for a description of black men chained together. The business of the chandelier chain being lowered, the association with trapped victims burned black, seem close to the events of the Richmond theater fire, the lurid details of which Poe must certainly have heard again and again from his childhood friends and from the Allan family servants. And surely the youthful Poe had greater emotional reason than most to identify himself with the scene of that catastrophe, and the theatrical company during whose performance it took place.

The victims of the fire included many of the leading citizens of Richmond, the city's social and commercial elite; they had come there to take part in a cultural event offered by the very company of actors of which Poe's mother had been so recently part. "On this night, *Mrs. Poe,* lingering on the bed of disease and surrounded by her children, asks your assistance and *asks it perhaps for the last time.*"

It is almost as if, somewhere within the imagination of her son, what happened at the brick theater on Broad Street Hill less than three weeks after Elizabeth Arnold Poe's death were transformed into a punishment for the community's indifference to the plight of the Poe family, as well as for the later conduct of genteel Richmond toward a needy young poet-editor and his child bride. "As for myself, I am simply Hop-Frog, the jester—and *this is my last jest.*"

Among the victims of the theater fire, too, were black people: "At this stage of the process, some one of the party suggested feathers; but the suggestion was at once overruled by the dwarf, who soon convinced the eight [the king and his seven councillors], by ocular demonstration, that the hair of such a brute as the ourang-outang was much more efficiently represented by *flax.*" The full title of Poe's last story, it should be kept in mind, is "Hop-Frog; or, the Eight Chained Ourang-Outangs."

"The eight corpses swung in their chains, a fetid, hardened, blackened, hideous, and indistinguishable mass."

V. THE POET LAUREATE OF THE CONFEDERACY

If Edgar Poe was by all odds the most accomplished and important of all the writers of the antebellum South, the only Southern author whose writings are read today for reasons other than scholarly interest (not that there is anything disgraceful about that), then it must follow that it was his oblique relationship to the contemporary Southern scene that had something to do with it. Like it or not, the genius of a Poe seems to have been required to overcome the barriers that prevented the region's authors from successfully grounding the literary imagination in the meaningful details of community experience. I have tried to suggest reasons why it happened this way.

The *only* other Southern poet whose best work can stand up to much objective literary scrutiny nowadays was William Gilmore Simms's younger Charleston contemporary, Henry Timrod. As I hope to show, some eight or ten of Timrod's lyrics remain very much worth reading today, more than a century after their composition. All of them are concerned with the War Between the States, and were written after the Southern states declared their independence and sought to sustain it on the battlefield.

The American Civil War was not notably productive of lasting poetry. Of the many thousands of verses, mostly hortatory and patriotic, produced during the four years of sectional conflict, only some few poems by Walt Whitman, by Herman Melville, and in the South by Timrod, have survived their occasion. Timrod has been called the "Poet-Laureate of the Confederacy," and I think it is an accurate designation, although not in quite the way that those who called him that meant it. That he was assuredly the most gifted of the Southern war poets is beyond question, even though his work has suffered from the handicap of having been written on behalf of the losing side. When in one poem he refers to "the true martyrs of the fight, / Which strikes for freedom and for right," the likelihood that a modern reader, whether Northern or Southern in historical allegiance, can read the lines without perceiving an irony quite unintended by the author is not very good. In the same way, when a reader encounters such lines as "There, where some rotting ships and crumbling quays / Shall one day mark the Port which ruled the Western seas"[1] and understands that the poet was referring not to Charleston or Mobile but to New York Harbor, he can scarcely fail to entertain certain reflections that are very different from what Timrod had in mind.

What distinguishes Timrod's best poetry from that of Simms, Paul Hamilton Hayne, and others, however, is that he was far more interested in language than they were. A figure such as "meadows beaten into bloody clay," from his 1861 sonnet "I Know Not Why," was simply beyond the reach of his contemporaries. Yet for the most part this is true only of Timrod's *war* poetry, and not all of that. It is *not* true of the poetry he wrote before 1861, nor is it true of the poems written *after* 1861 that do not concern themselves with war and the Confederate cause. And the fact that it isn't, and that certain war poems are not merely better than but seem to be altogether in a different league from any of his other verse, is very significant. What I want to try to show is why.

Henry Timrod was born in Charleston, South Carolina, in 1828 and died in 1867, just over two years after the Confederate surrender. Never of robust health, he suffered acutely from poverty during the last years of his life, and was often close to starvation. During the war he saw only limited military duty, and when as a war correspondent he went out to join the Confederate army in the summer of 1862, it was just in time to experience the retreat from Shiloh, under conditions he proved pathetically unable to endure. He spent the remainder of the war as a newspaper editor

---

1. Timrod, "The Cotton Boll," *The Collected Poems of Henry Timrod: A Variorum Edition*, ed. Edd Winfield Parks and Aileen Wells Parks (Athens: University of Georgia Press, 1965), 99. Subsequent references will occur parenthetically in the text.

in Charleston and Columbia, and afterward did such work as he could find, which was not very much. His friends knew he was in desperate need of money, but they had little enough to give him. His death came of tuberculosis on October 7, 1867.

Timrod was writing poetry regularly from the late 1840s onward. His only book published during his lifetime, *Poems* (1859), contains poems about nature, love, and philosophical topics, and the influence of Wordsworth and later of Tennyson is predominant. The inherited vocabulary of the poetry of English Romanticism keeps him at an artificial distance from his experience. Lacking the capacity to immerse himself in Wordsworth's Egotistical Sublime, he is unable to give his work the meditative depth that such verse requires. One such poem, a sonnet, begins

> Poet! if on a lasting fame be bent
> Thy unperturbing hopes, thou wilt not roam
> Too far from thine own happy heart and home;
> Cling to the lowly earth, and be content![2]

The advice given to the ambitious poet to cling to the earth is just what he cannot himself follow. The stilted diction and obligatory high-mindedness of the poetic Ideality of his day force him to elevate his subject above the dross of the supposedly vulgar particulars of his middle-class experience, and the result is usually a bloodless abstraction. Unable to deal directly with the actualities of his own time and place or to investigate his personal relationship to the land or to the life around him, he is compelled to be lofty-souled and Poetic. The result is a cloying self-consciousness that weakens his every assertion.

From all accounts, Henry Timrod was a very unworldly soul to begin with, not very adept at the more practical aspects of daily life. In this respect he was in contrast to his father, William Henry Timrod, a bookbinder of German descent. The elder Timrod's shop was something of a mecca for literary-minded men in Charleston, who liked to gather there and discuss books and writers while he worked away. A local publisher who employed him to bind some of his books was impressed with the way that leading citizens of class-conscious Charleston made a habit of stopping in for a talk:

2. Timrod, "Sonnet: Poet! If On a Lasting Fame," *Collected Poems*, 18.

"There was no cessation of his work when these distinguished gentlemen came to see him. With his coat off, his sleeves rolled, and his apron on, he continued his occupation without apology. He had that true dignity, and independence, which scorned to make apologies or ask indulgences from men, who seemed to be so much higher on the social scale."[3] William Henry Timrod was a graceful minor poet in his own right, and several of his poems that have survived are of considerable merit. During the war against the Seminole Indians in 1836 he captained a company of German fusiliers, but while in Florida he contracted a disease, probably tuberculosis, from which he died in 1838 when his son was ten years old.

Henry Timrod's mother enrolled him at Christopher Coates's school, where one of his classmates was the future poet Paul Hamilton Hayne, and thereafter the two were intimate friends. The Haynes were a wealthy and distinguished Charleston family. Hayne's father, a naval captain, died when his son was young, and for a time Hayne was raised by his uncle, Robert Young Hayne, who as a United States senator had engaged in the famous Webster-Hayne debate over Nullification and the protective tariff. Timrod's circumstances were considerably less advantaged. His father left him little money. Like William Gilmore Simms, Timrod and his family were not of the Charleston social establishment.

Probably through the generosity of a family friend, Timrod spent a year at the University of Georgia, then returned to Charleston and briefly read law at the office of the distinguished attorney James Louis Petigru. The spirit of jurisprudence was not in him, however. On one occasion Petigru became so exasperated at his forgetfulness that he declared, "Harry, you are a fool!" Deserting the law for belles-lettres, Timrod in the years that followed managed a modest living as a tutor to the children of the Low-country gentry on various plantations and as a teacher in rural schools. On weekends he hurried back to the city, where he was not above making up for lost time insofar as partying was concerned.

When *Russell's Magazine* was established in Charleston in 1857, with Hayne as editor, Timrod began contributing not only

3. James McCarter to Paul Hamilton Hayne, December 2, 1867, in Jay B. Hubbell (ed.), *The Last Years of Henry Timrod* (Durham: Duke University Press, 1941), 175.

new poetry but several perceptive critical essays having to do with the nature of poetry and the dangers of literary nationalism. Except for certain essays and reviews by Poe, no other critical writing by an antebellum Southern author possesses the cogency and subtlety of Timrod's. Clearly he thought in professional terms about his art, and he had little patience with the amateur litterateurs of Charleston and the South:

There is scarcely a city of any size in the South which has not its clique of amateur critics, poets and philosophers, the regular business of whom it is to demonstrate truisms, settle questions which nobody else would think of discussing, to confirm themselves in opinions which have been picked up from the rubbish of seventy years agone, and above all to persuade each other that together they constitute a society not much inferior to that in which figured Burke and Johnson, Goldsmith and Sir Joshua. All of these being oracles, they are unwilling to acknowledge the claims of a professional writer, lest in doing so they should disparage their own authority.[4]

In contrast to Hayne, who was both gifted at and assiduous in the cultivation of useful literary friendships, Timrod had little talent for promoting himself. At times he verged on the misanthropic. On at least one recorded occasion he seems to have been unable to suppress his impatience with the older and ebullient Simms, who was given to expressing his opinions rather pontifically, and whose opinion of the merits of his own verse tended to be extremely laudatory. In William P. Trent's words, "Timrod was critical by nature and Simms was vulnerable in many places. Timrod knew that he could write real poetry, while Simms could not, and it probably vexed him to hear the older man airing his often crude views on poetical subjects in his positive Johnsonian manner." Although the distinction Trent makes between "real" and presumably "unreal" poetry is debatable, it is also quite possible that, like Poe before him, Timrod was envious of Simms's success, attained as it was through hard work and a commitment to his vocation such as Timrod could never muster. Exactly what transpired between Simms and Timrod is not known, but it was sufficiently unpleasant to prompt Hayne, when writing to ask

4. Timrod, "Literature in the South," *Russell's Magazine*, V (August, 1859), 385–95, rpr. in *The Essays of Henry Timrod*, ed. Edd Winfield Parks (Athens: University of Georgia Press, 1942), 100.

Simms to review Timrod's *Poems*, to stress that "after what has occurred, *he* can urge *no possible* claim upon your notice, but, nevertheless, I wish you *would* notice him." As might be expected, Simms forgave the younger man, and when after the war Timrod was in desperate straits he did his best to help him. Some tension between the two remained until the end, however. Simms seems to have suspected that at least some of Timrod's difficulties were due to weakness of resolve, and to have suggested as much to Timrod's wife and sister. "I am very much afraid that Mr. Simms talks thus of me elsewhere than in my home," Timrod wrote to Hayne in June of 1867. "Save me from such a friend."[5] On that occasion at least, if we are to believe Timrod's wife (not an unimpeachable source), Simms was unable to recognize just how serious his friend's health was. Four months later Timrod was dead.

2.

Unlike his friends Simms and Hayne, Timrod was not in favor of the secession of South Carolina from the Union. Yet however much he opposed his native state's action following Abraham Lincoln's election to the presidency in 1860, the formation of the Confederate States of America and the resulting war gave him, for the first time, the public situation and the subject matter that he required as a poet.

Immediately preceding "Ethnogenesis," Timrod's first war poem, in the variorum edition is a short poem entitled "Why Silent." It would seem to be a reaction to the failure of his *Poems* to attract much critical notice. The poem expresses a general dissatisfaction with his own published verse. For "a little praise," he declares, "I have paid too dear"—he has published his poems and thereby trivialized what he had to say:

> For, I know not why, when I tell my thought,
>   It seems as though I fling it away;
> And the charm wherewith a fancy is fraught,
>   When secret, died with the fleeting lay
>   Into which it was wrought.

5. William P. Trent, *William Gilmore Simms* (Boston and New York: Houghton, Mifflin and Co., 1892), 233–34, 233; Timrod to Hayne, June 4, [1867], in Hubbell (ed.), *Last Years of Henry Timrod*, 84.

What he calls his "butterfly-dreams" seldom take flight "from their chrysalis"; his best poems remain unwritten even "While the world, in its worldliness, does not miss / What a poet sings." The only recourse that would seem open to him is not to write poems; the poem itself is in the form of an answer to the question propounded at the outset: "Why am I silent from year to year? / Needs must I sing on these blue March days?"[6]

On December 20, 1860, South Carolina enacted its secession ordinance. The other states of the Deep South followed, and on February 8, 1861, a provisional Confederate government was established in Montgomery, Alabama. The formation of the new nation aroused Henry Timrod's enthusiasm, and on February 23 the Charleston *Daily Courier* published an "Ode on Occasion of the Meeting of the Southern Congress / By Henry Timrod." It was widely circulated and republished, and a year later Timrod revised it somewhat under the title "Ethnogenesis."

What immediately strikes the reader about it is the change of poetic voice, set forth in the opening stanza:

> Hath not the morning dawned with added light?
> And shall not evening call another star
> Out of the infinite reaches of the night,
> To mark this day in heaven? At last, *we* are
> A nation among nations; and the world
> Shall soon behold in many a distant port
>   Another flag unfurled!
> Now, come what may, whose favor need *we* court?
> And, under God, whose thunder need *we* fear?[7]

Essaying the Pindaric ode, Timrod immediately asserts his oneness with his community. He is now a public poet, and he links his own personal hopes with the political objectives of his fellow Southerners. The sun and the elements are portrayed as joining in the new nation's cause, for the Confederacy's identity is that of an agricultural nation: "Thank God who placed us here / Beneath so kind a sky." The sun, the ocean breezes, dew, and rain wage

---

6. Timrod, "Why Silent," *Collected Poems*, 91–92.

7. Timrod, "Ethnogenesis," *ibid.*, 92, italics added. Subsequent references will occur parenthetically in the text.

"noiseless battle for us" (92), and the months of the unfolding year produce grain, while

> many an ample field
> Grows white beneath their steps, till now, behold
> Its endless sheets unfold
> THE SNOW OF SOUTHERN SUMMERS! (93)

There is personification in Timrod's imagery, but there is no abstraction involved; the elements and the seasons are seen as enlisted in behalf of the new nation because they bring about the growth of its cotton and grain. It is the cotton crop, Timrod declares, that will protect the Confederacy, for its economic might is such as to make the South invulnerable to attack:

> beneath those fleeces soft and warm
> Our happy land shall sleep
> In a repose as deep
> As if we lay entrenched behind
> Whole leagues of Russian ice and Arctic storm! (93)

As noted earlier in this book, Timrod's poetic vision of the Confederate South's future hopes in "Ethnogenesis" seems surprisingly materialistic. Not only does the new nation's protection rest upon the economic value of cotton to the world economy, but the depiction of the South's virtues, as opposed to those of the North, contains its own kind of capitalistic satisfaction. The North is the place of "Fair schemes that leave the neighboring poor / To starve and shiver at the schemer's door, / While in the world's most liberal ranks enrolled, / He turns some vast philanthropy to gold" (94). The South, by contrast, exhibits a "scorn of sordid gain," but also offers "Faith, justice, reverence, charitable wealth, / And for the poor and humble, laws which give, / Not the mean right to buy the right to live, / But life, and home, and health!" (94). Clearly Timrod's Good Life is one in which, if money is not to be worshipped for its own sake, it is ethically desirable even so to provide full employment, a comfortable home, and to possess "charitable wealth."

The close of the poem, as remarked in an earlier chapter, makes the case for Southern virtue along lines that a John D. Rockefeller or an Andrew Carnegie could have happily endorsed:

> For, to give labor to the poor,
>   The whole sad planet o'er,
> And save from want and crime the humblest door,
> Is one among the many ends for which
>   God makes us great and rich! (95)

For a poet who until then had during fifteen years of writing
and publishing verse composed nothing whatever of a practical,
utilitarian nature, the transition is astounding. It is as if, in iden-
tifying himself with the community's political hopes, he also, and
for the first time, puts away the notion of the poet as being outside of and above the concerns of the everyday world, and wholeheartedly espouses the community's values. By doing so, however, he gains poetic access to the language in which those values
are customarily couched, and relies notably less upon elevated
abstractions. We begin to encounter phrases such as "a distant
port," "on our errands run," "every stick and stone shall help us,"
"our stiffened sinews," "wealth, and power, and peace," "codes
built upon a broken pledge," "some vast philanthropy," "give
labor to the poor," "the cold, untempered ocean"—Timrod can
now draw upon a vocabulary and an idiom that will allow him to
document his experience in the language, however intensified, in
which as a middle-class American he normally thinks.

In "The Cotton Boll," composed late in 1861, "THE SNOW OF
SOUTHERN SUMMERS" becomes the central metaphor for the Confederacy's existence. "While I recline / At ease beneath / This im-
memorial pine, / Small sphere!" he begins, addressing the principal product of his country's economy, and adds, "(By dusky
fingers brought this morning here / And shown with boastful
smiles)," thereby linking it with the South's Peculiar Institution.
The "soft white fibres," he declares, "with their gossamer bands, /
Unite, like love, the sea-divided lands." Thus the cotton which is
exported across the ocean to the spinning mills of England and
France dissolves distances, and joins the agricultural South with
the great world beyond its coasts,

> Breaks down the narrow walls that hem us round,
> And turns some city lane
> Into the restless main,
> With all his capes and isles!

The westward expanse of the new nation, stretching from oceanside to "the crimson hills and purple lawns / Of sunset, among plains which roll their streams / Against the Evening Star" is now identifiable as part of a single agricultural, cotton-growing community:

> The endless field is white;
> And the whole landscape glows,
> For many a shining league away,
> With such accumulated light
> As Polar lands would flash beneath a tropic sky!

It is as if he stood "in some great temple of the Sun" and viewed

> pastures rich and fields all green
> With all the common gifts of God,
> For temperate airs and torrid sheen
> Weave Edens of the sod;
> Through lands which look one sea of billowy gold
> Broad rivers wind their devious ways.

Great mountains "lift their plumed peaks cloud-crowned"; and he sees an "unhewn forest . . . / In whose dark shades a future navy sleeps!"

Again Timrod unites the aesthetic appeal of nature and the land with the appreciation of its material uses; the vision of agricultural plenty, the timber for building a merchant marine and navy, the rivers and bays on which commerce may move, is fused with the sunlight, the winds, the clouds, the temperate climate that make the crops and forests grow. Such is the poet's country:

> Bear witness with me in my song of praise,
> And tell the world that, since the world began,
> No fairer land hath fired a poet's lays,
> Or given a home to man!

The vision of the opulent Southland, he continues, has already been widely sung, by no less a singer than

> The Poet of "The Woodlands," unto whom
> Alike are known
> The flute's low breathing and the trumpet's tone,
> And the soft west wind's sigh—

by, that is, William Gilmore Simms. But where, he asks, is the
poet "who shall utter all the debt . . . / The world doth owe thee
at this day, / And which it never can repay / Yet scarcely deigns to
own!" Where is the poet who can go beyond celebration of the
Southern countryside and cities to memorialize the lofty social
and economic mission of the new nation, and

> fitly sing
> That mighty commerce which, confined
> To the mean channels of no selfish mart,
> Goes out to every shore
> Of this broad earth, and throngs the sea with ships
> That bear no thunders.

His country's true role, he declares, "gladdening rich and poor,"
will bring prosperity to "Parisian domes" and "English homes";
so long as the sun shall continue to ripen the agricultural produce
of the South, no foe will prevail against it. Thus it may even,
through the beauty it provides,

> As the years increase—
> Still working through its humbler reach
> With that large wisdom which the ages teach—
> Revive the half-dead dream of universal peace!

In "Ethnogenesis," Timrod had expressed his country's determination to maintain its independence in battle. By the time he
wrote "The Cotton Boll," Fort Sumter had been fired upon and
the Confederate army had routed the Union army at Manassas
Junction in July of 1861. It was clear that the South would indeed
have to win its right to nationhood on the battlefield, and, moreover, the struggle would be lengthy and arduous. Timrod believed
in the need to persevere and chose to express it with an extended
Miltonic simile, in later years much admired, in which he likened
the situation of the embattled South to miners in Cornwall who
worked away under the ocean floor, and who,

> when a storm rolls overhead,
> Hear the dull booming of the world of brine
> Above them, and a mighty muffled roar
> Of wind and waters, yet toil calmly on,
> And split the rock, and pile the massive ore.

Like them, he declares, "I, as calmly, weave my woof / Of song, chanting the days to come," despite the gathering of armies and the savage fighting. Yet for all his confidence in the outcome, he "may not sing too gladly." What will be is in God's hands; and the poem closes with a plea to God to help the South

> to roll the crimson flood
> Back on its course, and while our banners wing
> Northward, strike with us! till the Goth shall cling
> To his own blasted altar-stones, and crave Mercy.

The final lines, in which the fate of once-proud New York Harbor is described as that of decay and ruin, "where some rotting ships and crumbling quays / Shall one day mark the Port which ruled the Western seas," are quite appropriate for a poem that celebrates the South's staple product. They sum up the argument of the poem very accurately, for those "soft white fibres" which "Unite, like love, the sea-divided lands" and break down "the narrow walls that hem us round" will, if the South can win its independence, no longer be carried to New York City and from there shipped to Europe and elsewhere. The protective tariff designed to protect Northeastern manufactures against overseas competition will no longer apply; free trade will permit the South to sell its cash crop to the highest bidder, and purchase what manufactured items it needs in the open world marketplace. New York City, in short, will henceforth not continue to grow rich off the South's agriculture.

Poems such as "The Cotton Boll" and "Ethnogenesis," as we have seen, pose formidable difficulties for the reader of a century afterward, written as they are from the standpoint of what proved to be the losing side, and with no concessions whatever to what must inevitably pose a severe moral problem for the twentieth-century reader, whether Northern or Southern. For we are all too conscious that the labor that the South would have offered "to the poor, / The whole sad planet o'er" and the "mighty commerce which, confined / To the mean channels of no selfish mart, / Goes out to every shore" would have been founded upon human slavery.

Thus the vigor of Timrod's language and the vividness of his imagery in these two poems are qualified by a sense of what to us is special pleading, and that leads us to withhold our full assent. Sectional patriotism cannot overcome a hundred and more years of subsequent American history, the more so because closer to our own time we have seen a second effort to remove the racial injustice that the earlier conflict did not eradicate. This is not the poet's fault; it is, however, an inescapable limitation.

I have noted that the argument which Timrod adopts for his poem gives him access to a vocabulary much more closely related to his everyday middle-class circumstance than was true for his prewar poetry. There is more to it than that, however. For what is interesting is the extent to which the imagery of "The Cotton Boll" is not only practical, but repeatedly intermixes terms that are appropriate to the language of commerce, commodity, and power. A "*golden* chime" rings down. There is "whatever *golden* mystery," and "one sea of billowy *gold*"—three specific references to the precious metal. He speaks of "*accumulated* light," "simple *influence*," "pastures *rich* and fields all *green*," "*gifts* of God," "peaks cloud-*crowned*," an "*unhewn forest*" where "a *future navy* sleeps." There are "*powers* that *bind* a people's heart." "The world doth *owe*" the South a "*debt*" which it "never can *repay*" and "scarcely deigns to *own*." The South's "*mighty commerce*" is confined to "the *mean channels* of no *selfish mart*." Its strands are "gladdening *rich and poor*," and they "*gild* Parisian domes." The years "*increase*." The men of Cornwall who "*labor* in that *mine*" will "*toil*" on and "*pile the massive ore*." He tells his country that "in *offices* like these" its mission lies. He knows that the end "must *crown* us." The imagic convergence is fascinating. "The Cotton Boll" is a poem not only about Southern nationalism but about *money and power*. As a poet, Timrod is thoroughly aware of the economic considerations that underlie the movement for Confederate independence.

One has the sense that, in this poem and to a somewhat lesser extent in "Ethnogenesis," the poet seems to assume that it is his role to link community ideals to the potential economic opportunity. He develops an economically based conceit—the appropriateness of the cotton boll as symbol of Southern agricultural life—into an aesthetic and idealistic argument for nationhood, which, however, he views in language and images that are, no doubt unconsciously but not the less surely, drawn from the vocabulary of financial profit. The language of everyday life, he appears to believe, *is* the language of moneymaking.

Whatever the ingredients of the imagery, the result is a poetics that offers a firmness of figure and concreteness of reference, places the poem and the poet in much closer contact with the everyday world that the poet inhabits, and provides his poetic imagination with a much more direct access to his community's political, economic, and social life and institutions than had been true in any of his earlier verse.

3.

Both of Timrod's Pindaric odes express confidence in the Confederacy's future. The South will gain its independence because it is economically potent, because it is fighting for freedom, because God is on its side in its struggle against selfish Yankee materialism and hypocritical Puritan fanaticism, and because it is honorable, just, charitable, high-minded, and valiant in its own defense. At the same time, however, Timrod did feel obliged to acknowledge that victory and independence were by no means assured; his newfound stance as public poet did not restrict his utterance to what by right ought to be. Both "Ethnogenesis" and "The Cotton Boll" express, as subject matter and in their underlying imagery, apprehension as well as hope. In "Ethnogenesis" he declares that "To doubt the end were want of trust in God." If God "has decreed / That we must pass a redder sea / Than that which rang to Miriam's holy glee," the Almighty will nonetheless provide "A Moses with his rod" to part the waters. "But let our fears—if fears we have—be still," he urges, and offers a prophecy of victory (94). In "The Cotton Boll" he concedes that the outcome is not certain,

> In that we sometimes hear
> Upon the Northern winds, the voice of woe
> Not wholly drowned in triumph, though I know
> The end must crown us, and a few brief years
> Drown all our tears (95)

and he invokes God's help for his country's cause.

By intention these are public poems, shaped to express the community's hopes and convictions, and if he cannot ignore the need to voice his apprehension along with the celebration and high hope, nevertheless the occasion and the genre demand a positive, optimistic stance. Privately Timrod was not so sanguine. Thus at about the same time that he published "The Cotton Boll," he wrote a sonnet in which he expressed his doubts about the future. "I Know Not Why" is a remarkable poem, one of his two or three best. It develops no public, rhetorical voice. Ostensibly it does no more than express his personal, private thoughts. Indeed, it begins with a denial of any relevance to specific events, public or private:

> I know not why, but all this weary day,
> *Suggested by no definite grief or pain,*
> Sad fancies have been flitting through my brain.[8]

Yet, as he proceeds to describe those fancies, each turns out to pertain to the situation of the South at war. "Now it has been a vessel losing way, / Rounding a stormy headland," he declares, an obvious allusion to the Southern ship of state and, whether or not consciously intended, a commentary on the ship motif of "Ethnogenesis"—"in many a distant port / Another flag unfurled"—and of "The Cotton Boll"—"a future navy sleeps," "a mighty commerce which . . . throngs the sea with ships / That bear no thunders," as well as an ironic allusion to his forecast in the latter poem that "rotting ships and crumbling quays" will ultimately "mark the Port which ruled the Western seas."

Next he describes "a gray / Dull waste of clouds above a wintry main." The contrast is all too striking between this and the ardent likening of the South, in "Ethnogenesis," to the "vast gulf which laves our Southern strand," pouring "its genial streams" into the "cold untempered ocean," so that

> far off Arctic shores
> May sometimes catch upon the softened breeze
> Strange tropic warmth and hints of summer seas! (95)

In a prewar poem, "A Rhapsody of a Southern Winter Night," Timrod had used almost the exact same image as in the sonnet:

> The feeble tide of peevishness went down,
> And left a flat dull waste of dreary pain
> Which seemed to clog the blood in every vein. (46)

---

8. Timrod, "Sonnet: I Know Not Why," *Collected Poems*, 100, italics added.

In that poem he was describing a feeling of personal hopelessness
and futility. The image, which was to reappear again in later wartime poems, undoubtedly signified an especially desolate mood
for Timrod.

Following the reference to the "wintry main" is an image of
military defeat: "And then a banner drooping in the rain, / And
meadows beaten into bloody clay." Composed at a time when the
victory at Manassas Junction was still fresh in everyone's mind,
and when the Union armies had won no important engagements
of any kind from the Confederacy, Timrod's lines nonetheless exhibit an attitude toward the future very different from that in his
public poetry. The sestet that closes the sonnet moves from apprehensiveness into stark foreboding:

> Strolling at random with this shadowy woe
> At heart, I chanced to wander hither. Lo!
> A league of desolate marsh-land, with its lush,
> Hot grasses in a noisome, tide-left bed,
> And faint, warm airs, that rustle in the hush
> Like whispers round the body of the dead! (100)

The cotton of "Ethnogenesis" was supposed to have made possible the repose of "our happy land" in a sound sleep that came of
knowing that it was entrenched "behind / Whole leagues" of
Arctic ice and storm. But here the expanse is anything but re-
assuring. The "Strange tropic warmth" has become fetid, rank
marsh-land, with the tide having gone out and left a bed of warm
mud, while the "breezes of the ocean" that in "Ethnogenesis" had
run errands for the new nation are seen now as present at a fu-
neral. The implied metaphor is that the high tide of hope is running out for the speaker, and what remains is a situation that is
merely physical and biological, a kind of death-in-life.

The Low-country salt marshes that provide the setting for
Timrod's figure here were certainly familiar to him from long experience, and the desolation that they convey, the sense of biological entrapment, serves to link the poet's private apprehen-
sions and fears of oblivion with the public fear of defeat and
destruction for the new nation. The image used to express such
dismay clearly goes deep into the poet's conscious and uncon-
scious identity; in the view of the ship losing way rounding
a headland, the drooping banner, the bloody meadows, there is
an unmistakable suggestion of thwarted masculinity, while the

marsh-land with its lush, hot grasses and tide-left bed communicates a dread of cloying sexual stultification, a suffocation of the spirit.

What is amazing is the way in which the coming of secession and war has transformed Timrod's mode of poetry. Nothing could be further removed from the poetic abstraction, unanchored Ideality, and affected self-consciousness of his prewar verse than a poem such as "I Know Not Why," with its precise diction, fusion of emotion and image, and vernacular firmness of diction. Except for the transitional "hither. Lo!" at the close of the second line of the sestet, there is almost no recourse to the stilted Poetic diction of the English Romantic heritage. Instead, Timrod grounds his personal sensibility and the language used to express it in the specific experience of the community, and comments on the relationship of the community identity to his private sensibility. The one is identified with the other.

In this poem by Henry Timrod, therefore, as in no other Southern poetry of the time, *the deepest social and political concerns of the community are addressed as an aspect of the private, personal experience of the poet.*

4.

The advent of secession and civil war had the result of giving a talented Southern poet the imaginative access to his own social and political experience as fit subject for literature. Amid the ultimate conditions of survival or surrender, it was no longer inevitable that an exploration of community identity come up against the social and moral dimensions of slavery. The Southern community was now engaged in a desperate military struggle for the right to exist, and however the Peculiar Institution might have been involved in the causes of sectional war, it was the military conflict itself that was at the center of the community's identity. Whether one favored or disapproved of slavery, believed in states' rights or did not, supported or was hostile to the free trade and the tariff, favored upper-class rule or believed in egalitarian democracy, such matters were only ancillary to the more basic and primary community relationship: the defense of the homeland against military invasion. What this meant was that the moral or social factors that might have been at work to encourage the antebellum Southern author to wish to look elsewhere than at the moral and social underpinnings of his community were now overshadowed by the visceral, elementary identification with the besieged South. The Southern writer—or, in any event one Southern writer—was placed in touch with some of the most deeply felt emotional and intellectual themes of the nineteenth century: freedom, nationhood, independence.

In the two odes, Timrod had made implicit reference to slavery. These were in intention and execution public poems, crafted to express a public mood, expressions of the poet's eagerness to identify himself with the community and to articulate its hopes. Had he been impelled to do so in the prewar years, it would have been necessary for him to defend the Peculiar Institution. In "Ethnogenesis" he had been moved to do just that, in terms not of its right or wrong as such but of supposed Southern and Northern attitudes toward religion, commerce, and social responsibility. In "The Cotton Boll," written a year later, he had dealt with the economic implications of the South's cotton growing, while omitting any comment on the social foundations of that activity. But in the sonnet "I Know Not Why," crafted without any conscious intention of speaking either *for* or *of* the community, the war and the apprehension of disaster constitute his subject, and the poem is "public" only—and profoundly—because the poet's inmost emotional concerns are at the same time those of his embattled community.

Just how enthusiastic Henry Timrod actually was about slavery I do not know. The reference to it in "Ethnogenesis" came only in the revised version, and the single reference to slavery as such in his essay on Southern literature seems almost in the nature of an afterthought intended to make it clear to the excessively politicized readership of *Russell's Magazine* that in censuring Southern literary chauvinism, he was not thereby attacking Southern community values. Timrod was no James Louis Petigru, so solidly established in the community's esteem that he could publicly decline to recognize South Carolina's withdrawal from the Union; and even Petigru, while opposing secession, was no foe to chattel slavery. In any event, I assume that Timrod was not a dissenter from the racial assumptions on which he had been weaned.

Yet at the same time it does seem quite obvious that a talented but hitherto minor poet's sudden emergence as an important

Southern literary voice occurs when for the first time in the history of the South the social defense of chattel slavery was superseded as the dominant political concern of the community by the military defense of one's homeland from invasion. And this fact of itself, it seems to me, serves to subvert the notion that the existence of slavery in the Old South was not an important reason for the failure of its writers to make any major contribution (except for the writings of Poe) to the distinguished flowering of the national literature that we call the American Renaissance.

During the three years of bitter fighting that took place after the writing of "The Cotton Boll" and "I Know Not Why," Timrod composed other war poems. Several of these, such as "Carolina" and "A Cry to Arms," though understandably popular among Timrod's fellow citizenry during the war and afterward, seem today only so much patriotic rhetoric. The poet who composed them was intent upon rallying the martial ardor of his community, and no searching out of private meaning for public attitude takes place. But in other, more meditative poems, Timrod built upon the strength of language and vividness of community identification that made a poem such as "I Know Not Why" so remarkable an expression of that identity.

The poem entitled "Charleston," composed in late 1862 as Timrod's native city readied its defenses for an onslaught by the armored gunboats of the Union navy, is a mixture of some of his most effective verse and certain reflexive lapses into the stilted diction of rhetorical Ideality. The very first stanza exhibits both modes at work in successive lines:

> Calm as that second summer that precedes
> The first fall of the snow,
> In the broad sunlight of heroic deeds
> The city bides the foe.[9]

The poem proceeds to describe the defenses of the city in images of compelling vividness. The "bolted thunders" of the coastal artillery are ready. Fort Sumter, "like a battlemented cloud," faces oceanward:

> No Calpe frowns from lofty cliff or scar
> To guard the holy strand,

---

9. Timrod, "Charleston," *Collected Poems*, 115–16.

> But Moultrie holds in leash her dogs of war
>   Above the level sand.
>
> And down the dunes a thousand guns lie couched,
>   Unseen, beside the flood
> Like tigers in some Orient jungle crouched
>   That wait and watch for blood.

Here Timrod's language is at its most sensuous and evocative. Unfortunately, two stanzas later, in describing how the populace awaits the attack, Timrod continues with his animal imagery, this time with considerably less plausibility:

> And maidens, with such eyes as would grow dim
>   Over a bleeding hound,
> Seem each one to have caught the strength of him
>   Whose sword she sadly bound.

(It seems to have been a concomitant for Timrod, when writing about Southern Womanhood, to lapse into strained, too-affective figures of speech. It would have been poetically more felicitous, at the very least, not to have specified the particular brand of dog being wept over.)

Having depicted his city, "girt without and garrisoned at home," looking out "from roof, and spire, and dome, / Across her tranquil bay," he describes the harbor crowded with ships that have carried weapons of "Saxon iron and steel" through the blockade for her defense, and brought "summer to her courts." But the time is winter, not summer, and he offers a look at the ocean, where the blockading Union warships are stationed:

> But still, along yon dim Atlantic line,
>   The only hostile smoke
> Creeps like a harmless mist above the brine,
>   From some frail, floating oak.

Here is the same wintry sea that we have encountered in the sonnet "I Know Not Why" and elsewhere, with the note of apprehension that accompanies it. This poem will not close with the rhetorical assertion of confidence in Southern martial might that exhortatory poems such as "Carolina" and "A Cry to Arms" offer. Instead, Timrod continues to develop his seasonal metaphor, and with it the figure of the city as a woman who is under the land's protection. Spring will be a time of testing:

> Shall the spring dawn, and she still clad in smiles,
>   And with an unscathed brow,
> Rest in the strong arms of her palm-crowned isles,
>   As fair and free as now?

The imagery is neither random nor arbitrary. The city is a woman, threatened with assault. From the beginning of the poem the metaphor of summer–Indian summer–winter–spring has been sustained, and the sea islands, with their "thousand guns" hidden from sight and waiting, like tigers in a jungle, to repel the invading fleet, have been portrayed as the city's protectors. As for the outcome, the poem concludes, that must await what will happen:

> We know not. In the temple of the Fates
>   God has inscribed her doom;
> And, all untroubled in her faith, she waits
>   The triumph or the tomb.

What makes Timrod's best war poetry superior in kind to the now-forgotten verses of all his Southern contemporaries is just this ability to go beyond the patriotic assertion of loyalty and defiance into a deeper evocation of the historical occasion. Despite occasional flourishes such as "the broad sunlight of heroic deeds" and resolute Southern maidens becoming misty-eyed over bleeding hounds, he is intent upon exploring all the human meanings of his subject, for his identification with the beleaguered seaport city is such that the public circumstance is his own personal situation as well. His friend Paul Hayne, in a similar poem entitled "Charleston at the Close of 1863," will admit to no doubts about the future, and thinks only of voicing the city's resolve:

> She is guarded by Love and enhaloed by Fame,
>   And never, stern foe, shall your footsteps be pressed
> Where her dead martyrs rest!

Timrod by contrast leaves the issue undecided, as indeed it was, and closes his poem with the word "tomb" as echoing rhyme to "doom."[10]

10. A number of years ago I wrote an essay, "Henry Timrod and the Dying of the Light," published in *Mississippi Quarterly*, XI (Summer, 1958), 101–11, developing a reading of "Charleston" as a prediction of Confederate disaster, and placing particular emphasis upon the fact that the poem ended with the rhyme

It is in this sense, rather than as author of rhetorical exhortations to victory, that Timrod can appropriately be termed the "Poet-Laureate of the Confederacy." For what his best poems do is to re-create the complexity of the community's experience as an aspect of his own identity, encompassing doubt as well as hope, apprehension as well as resolve. Less than perfect though his best wartime poems may be—and none of them is flawless, each contains instances of awkwardness and momentary imprecision—at their best they offer a portrait of a public and private historical confrontation that can be very revelatory and at times quite profound.

As the war wore on, and the Union armies in the west drove deeper and deeper into the besieged Confederacy, Timrod's verse grew less and less celebratory, and the private sensibility ever more wary. In "Ethnogenesis" and "The Cotton Boll" he had casually claimed the partnership of nature for the cotton South's cause: "the very sun / Takes part with us; and on our errands run / All breezes of the ocean; dew and rain / Do noiseless battle for us." But in the poem entitled "Spring," written in the spring of 1863 as the warring armies prepared for another year of bloody conflict, what he produces is a commentary on the age-old theme of the indifference of nature to human needs and concerns. The opening lines hint at the congruence of vernal rebirth and a heightened sense of mortality: "Spring, with that nameless pathos in the air / Which dwells in all things fair." A lengthy depiction of the soon-to-awaken earth follows:

> As yet the turf is dark, although you know
> That, not a span below,
> A thousand germs are groping through the gloom,
> And soon will burst the tomb.

Everywhere there is anticipation, as if crowds were awaiting the commencement of a May Day pageant,

---

"doom . . . tomb." In their excellent variorum edition of Timrod's poems, Edd Winfield Parks and Aileen Wells Parks questioned my reading, describing it as "a somewhat tortured analysis of the poem" (194). I am inclined to agree with them; at times during my reading, my youthful enthusiasm carried my judgment along with it. But that the poem's underlying attitude is on the apprehensive side of things is, I think, undeniable. And it *does* end with the word "tomb," echoing the rhyme "doom."

> and you scarce would start,
> If from a beech's heart
> A blue-eyed Dryad, stepping forth, should say,
> "Behold me! I am May!"

Nothing might seem further removed from war and slaughter: "Who in the west-wind's aromatic breath / Could hear the call of Death!" But the war is not to be denied:

> Yet not more surely shall the Spring awake
> The voice of wood and brake
> Than she shall rouse, for all her tranquil charms,
> A million men to arms.

> There shall be deeper hues upon her plains
> Than all her sunlit rains,
> And every gladdening influence around,
> Can summon from the ground.

Having remarked the contrast between human purposes and the natural world, the poem concludes rather less persuasively with a bizarre portrayal of a now-partisan Spring kneeling on the ground, "Lifting her bloody daisies up to God" and calling upon the hills "To fall and crush the tyrants and the slaves / Who turn her meads to graves."[11]

Later that summer he composed what is perhaps the most powerful of all his wartime poems. With an unintended appropriateness "The Unknown Dead" was published in the *Southern Illustrated News* on July 4, 1863, the day when Vicksburg surrendered to General Grant in the West while, in Pennsylvania, Lee's army prepared to return to Virginia following its repulse at Gettysburg. This remarkable poem opens with the speaker gazing out of his window:

> The rain is plashing on my sill,
> But all the winds of heaven are still;
> And so it falls with that dull sound
> Which thrills us in the church-yard ground
> When the first spadeful drops like lead
> Upon the coffin of the dead.
> Beyond my streaming window-pane,
> I cannot see the neighboring vane,

11. Timrod, "Spring," *Collected Poems*, 122–24.

> Yet from its old familiar tower
> The bell comes, muffled, through the shower.

None of Timrod's Southern contemporaries was capable of this descriptive use of commonplace sensory detail to re-create a shared experience. Gravely, subdued, the poem proceeds in short, measured couplets, with a precise, almost fated inevitability of rhyme and meter. The language is unadorned and understated. Words such as "dull," "lead," "coffin," "dead," "muffled" convey the sense of somber foreboding. What is being re-created is a state of mind, a private despair. The falling rain, the graveyard allusion, the bell establish the feeling of gloom. Everything is in images; there is not a real abstraction or a generalization in the first five couplets. The poem firmly develops a personal emotion before it moves toward its public reference, and then only as an after-thought, an unintended association of ideas:

> What strange and unsuspected link
> Of feeling touched, has made me think—
> While with a vacant soul and eye
> I watch that gray and stony sky—
> Of nameless graves on battle-plains
> Washed by a single winter's rains.

Again there is the image of joyless wintry expanse noted in previous poems. What he hears, feels, and sees there in his room as he gazes out into the rain reminds him of the war and the sol-diers who lie in fresh graves. He proceeds to develop a contrast between famous and high-ranking generals who "dying, see / Their flags in front of victory" and the thousands of little-known and unchronicled troops who have fallen. (Stonewall Jackson had died after being wounded during the victory at Chancellorsville not long before the poem was written.) It is not the famous chieftains who "Claim from their monumental beds / The bitterest tears a nation sheds," he says, but "the true martyrs of the fight" who lie in graves that are "By all save some fond few forgot," and about whose deaths "No grateful page shall farther tell / Than that so many bravely fell." Of the suffering that their deaths have brought to their families, he declares,

> we can only dimly guess
> What worlds of all this world's distress,

> What utter woe, despair, and dearth,
> Their fate has brought to many a hearth.

It is these men whose deaths come to his mind as he watches the
falling rain and hears the muffled sound of the church bell: the
common soldiers who, as a later Southern poet would put it, fell,
"rank upon rank, hurried beyond decision," and who now lie in
recently dug graves, mourned by those who survive them in
households throughout the South.

"The Unknown Dead" closes with eight rhymed lines in
which Timrod joins the thought of the fallen soldiers with the
rain he has been watching, even while he steps back from private
and public involvement alike to view the situation in terms of the
distance between the external natural world and the concerns of
human beings. The rain ought always to fall upon these graves, he
thinks, and the sky above remain forever somber in tribute to
their loss:

> Just such a sky as this should weep
> Above them, always, where they sleep:
> Yet, haply, at this very hour,
> Their graves are like a lover's bower;
> And nature's self, with eyes unwet,
> Oblivious of the crimson debt
> To which she owes her April grace,
> Laughs gaily o'er their burial place.

Except for certain lines midway through the poem in which, discussing the military situation, he moves reflexively into patriotic
rhetoric—the dead are "a myriad unknown heroes," the army in
whose ranks they served "strikes for freedom and for right," and
theirs is a "patriot zeal and pride"—Timrod's elegy for the slain
Confederates is composed in a language both dignified and re-
strained, understated yet in no way mechanical or monotonous,
simple and evocative in the clear precision of its diction and
thought.[12]

5.

As has been pointed out several times before, no other Southern
war poetry can come close to the emotional evocativeness and

---

12. Timrod, "The Unknown Dead," *ibid.*, 126–27.

controlled eloquence of Timrod's best work. The fusion of personal feeling and community responsibility results in poems that get at the latent emotions beneath the rhetorical exhortation. The poetry goes beyond patriotic declaration into a meaning that is at once personal and public. Nothing in Timrod's pre-secession verse really prepares us for this sudden maturation as a poet. It is as if the advent of secession and the war had jarred him loose from his preoccupation with his own personality, the obsessive self-consciousness of his role as sensitive spokesman for aesthetic Ideality, into an abrupt confrontation with his identity as a member of the civil community. He responds with poems that explore that discovery in a language that is able to a significant extent to throw off the elevated abstraction of the imported poetic vocabulary of the English Romantics and ground itself in a middle-class, more nearly vernacular American actuality.

As the war wore on, his best verse becomes measurably less given to rhetorical statement and more involved with the personal experience of war, struggle, and survival until, although never entirely free of stock responses, it attains an almost classical severity of statement. Paradoxically, it is precisely this heightened personal response that gives his poems their strength as an expression of the public circumstance, because he was thereby able to articulate more deeply the Southern people's common ordeal of defeat, grief, and loss as hopes for Confederate victory and Southern independence dwindled away.

And it *was* a personal ordeal for him. In the late months of the war Timrod, now married and a father, found it extremely difficult even to keep his family provided with the bare necessities. He held down an arduous, poorly paying job as a newspaper editor, while his already-poor health deteriorated. Once the war was lost, even that job was unavailable. In precarious condition, he did whatever work he could find, which was sporadic and ill-paid. His infant son died, plunging him into deep grief. Without work, without funds, he was in despair. Friends such as William Gilmore Simms sought to help him, but they too had been able to salvage little or nothing from the common devastation. Simms was driving himself beyond even his strength, grinding out fiction for third-rate, poorly paying publications in order to provide for his family. Paul Hayne took what little was left of his family's wealth, set himself up in a cheap cottage near Augusta, Georgia, and lived an exile's life, able to keep food on the table but with little more than that. Timrod had not even that much to sustain him. All he could do was to sell off such family possessions as were marketable. "We have eaten two silver pitchers, one or two dozen forks, several sofas, innumerable chairs and a bedstead," he wrote to Hayne in early 1866. "I not only don't write verse now," he declared in the same letter, "but I feel personally indifferent to the fate of what I have written. I would consign ever[y] line I ever wrote to eternal oblivion for one-hundred dollars in hand."[13]

Timrod died on October 7, 1867, at the age of thirty-eight. His loyal friend Hayne worked very hard to arrange for an edition of his verse, and in 1873, *The Poems of Henry Timrod* was published in Boston by E. J. Hale and Son. Literary hostilities between the sections had begun to abate by then, and the volume received favorable notices. However, it was not until publication of the memorial edition of Timrod's poetry, arranged for in Charleston and published by Houghton, Mifflin in Boston in 1899, that his reputation as the South's war poet was fully established. Those who accorded him the questionable title of Poet Laureate of the Confederacy had in mind chiefly poems such as "Ethnogenesis," "The Cotton Boll," "Carolina," and such. The greater achievement of the less celebratory war poetry generally goes unremarked.

Timrod's work has received very little critical analysis, and only a few of the general textbook anthologies of American literature still include selections from his verse. This is regrettable, for his best war poems deserve a place, however modest, in the permanent American literary record, alongside those of Whitman and Melville.

It is with Melville's war poetry rather than Whitman's that Timrod's verse has the greater affinity. The conditions under which he wrote obviously precluded the extended ironic examination of the meaning of the civil conflict that Melville was able to undertake, but the two men were about the only American poets able in their best work to step back from the partisan tumult and public exhortation and portray what was happening.

13. Timrod to Hayne, March 30, 1866, in Hubbell (ed.), *Last Years of Henry Timrod*, 60, 61.

In July of 1865, Timrod wrote to Hayne that "I begin to see (darkly) behind that *divine* political economy which has ended in the extinction of slavery and the preservation of the union." I daresay that he would have agreed with Melville's Supplement to *Battle-Pieces* (1866): "Let us pray that the terrible historical tragedy of our time may not have been enacted without instructing our whole beloved country through terror and pity; and may fulfillment verify in the end those expectations which kindle the bards of Progress and Humanity."[14]

Timrod wrote his best war poetry in the shadow of defeat and, in his own instance, imminent oblivion, for surely he more than suspected that the hemorrhages of his lungs that he began experiencing during the war were no encouraging augury for personal survival. Whatever the high hopes expressed so enthusiastically in the two secession odes, the author of the sonnet "I Know Not Why" had never been convinced of the assurance of Confederate military success. His experiences as a correspondent in the debacle of the retreat from Shiloh disabused him of any lingering hope that Southern victory would come without a desperate and protracted struggle. As a newspaper writer in Columbia and Charleston toward the end of the war, he wrote editorials that breathed defiance and urged the Southern community to sustain its resolve. But except for one poem, "Carmen Triumphale," composed in the late spring of 1863 when things were momentarily looking better for the Confederacy, the note that sounds repeatedly in his poetry during the last several years of the war is that of grief, loss, and the apprehension of disaster.

The death of Timrod in 1867, and of Simms three years later, in effect wrote an end to the literary record of the Old South. Poe was dead, as were William Alexander Caruthers and Philip Pendleton Cooke. John Pendleton Kennedy wrote no more fiction. Paul Hayne, it is true, lived on until 1886, but his poetry has not survived the change in literary tastes that brought an end to the mid-nineteenth-century poetry of Ideality. The Virginia novelist

14. Timrod to Hayne, July 10, 1865, quoted in Hubbell (ed.), *Last Years of Henry Timrod*, 47; Herman Melville, "Supplement to *Battle-Pieces*," in *Selected Poems of Herman Melville: A Reader's Edition* ed. Robert Penn Warren (New York: Random House, 1970), 199.

John Esten Cooke continued to produce fiction, but his best work was long since past him. Thus the principal literary memorials of the antebellum South remain Poe's writings, Simms's historical romances, Kennedy's *Swallow Barn*, and Timrod's war poetry. These, and the vigorous subliterary sketches of the Southwestern humorists, are what have endured.

Several years after the end of the war Hayne, on a visit to Charleston, stopped in at Russell's Book Store, where barely a decade earlier there had appeared to be developing the closest approach to a genuinely professional literary situation that the antebellum South ever knew. It was there that *Russell's Magazine* had been planned and edited, setting out with high hopes, only to fall victim to the political obsession of the Old South, which as the 1850s drew to an end reached manic proportions. In *Russell's*, under Hayne's editorship, were published the critical essays of Timrod, which argued so cogently and, as it proved, fruitlessly for a fully rendered literature, free of chauvinism and attuned to the developing literary and cultural modes of the mid-nineteenth century.

When Hayne called, "Lord" John Russell, now old and dispirited, was still there. "The superb collection of beautifully-bound books," Hayne wrote, "had disappeared, and I glanced over a 'beggarly account of empty, or half-empty shelves.' . . . Truly, to both of us, it was a place of ghosts. The gay, the learned wont to assemble there had disappeared, and along the dreary spaces I seemed to hear the rustling of the dead."[15]

There were ruins in the center of the city of Charleston, and weeds grew in its downtown streets. The waterfront along the Cooper River, where the merchant marine of several continents had called to load the seemingly endless bales of cotton that had so inspired the confidence and the bravado of the slaveholding South and provided Timrod with the metaphor for his Confederate odes, was now a morass of burnt-out and decayed docks. The once-prosperous banks and insurance companies were either defunct or else beginning to resume operations on a scale far below that of their prewar affluence. The white people of the once-lordly

15. [Paul Hamilton Hayne,] Ante-Bellum Charleston. Third Paper," *Southern Bivouac*, n.s., I (November, 1885), 335.

city-state were slowly and grudgingly making their adaptation to greatly changed circumstances, but the blight of invasion, defeat, and occupation was still everywhere observable. The community had sustained a staggering blow, physically, commercially, morally. For years afterward, it existed in a state of semi-shock. To those surviving Charlestonians who may have purchased and read copies of the edition of Timrod's verse that Hayne edited in 1873, lines such as these from "Ethnogenesis" must have seemed pathetic indeed:

> Could we climb
> Some mighty Alp, and view the coming time,
> The rapturous sight would fill
> Our eyes with happy tears!

6.

Timrod's poetry—what he wrote, what he failed to write—is the great Might Have Been in the literary history of the Old South. He had the richest poetic gift of all his Southern contemporaries, the literary intelligence that made language a way of discovery. He very much needed the critical and creative stimulus of a professional literary situation—and in the middle 1850s this is what appeared to be developing in Charleston. He had friends and associates who, like him, viewed literature not as an avocation for gentlemen but as a technique for apprehending life. And had it not been for the intensifying political crisis, he might very well have developed into a major American poet.

Yet here we have a paradox. For it was precisely the outcome of that political crisis, eventuating as it did in secession and civil war, that enabled him to write all of his best poetry. (That the political situation, and not a developing technical maturity within Timrod himself, was responsible is evident from the fact that the verse he wrote during the war years that did *not* have the public situation for its subject matter represents no great change from his pre-1861 verse.) Secession and the war gave Timrod his subject matter, through allowing him to ground his personal sensibility in the public, community experience. So when I say that had it not been for the sectional politics of the 1850s he might have written better poetry, it might seem to be a contradiction.

What I believe, however, is that the professional literary situa-

tion that was developing in Charleston in the 1850s was incipiently such as to give its participants membership in an intellectual community, linked to yet in certain crucial respects set
apart from the political and social community. The possibilities
for a literary identity inherent in that community were of sufficient intensity to have enabled its members to sense a genuine
dialectic between its values and attitudes and those of the general
community. This is what was beginning to happen—until the developing sectional crisis and the coming of secession killed it off.

It was just this kind of cultural dialectic that accounted for the
artistic achievement of the American Renaissance of the 1840s
and 1850s in the Northeast. The writers who were involved could,
indeed must, view the commercial, political, and social world of
the urbanizing mid-century United States from the perspective of
a different and sometimes opposing set of values and allegiances,
and yet they were also part and parcel of that world as well. The
result was a body of literature that, in depicting human experience in the forms they saw it, could get beneath the surfaces and
dramatize the root issues. "'Who's over me?'" Captain Ahab demands, as noted earlier. "'Truth has no confines.'"[16] But it was
whales that the *Pequod* was after, to be rendered and the sperm
oil sold on the Boston market.

There might have been, for Henry Timrod, the equivalent of
occasions such as that in the Berkshires in 1850 when, with
Hawthorne, Holmes, Evert Duyckinck, Puffer Mathews, and
James T. Fields for company, Herman Melville climbed Monument Mountain and watched the thunderstorm. By this I mean
that the incipient vision of a talented poet, able to view his experience through language that explored its meaning rather than
merely ratifying it, might have been both nurtured and challenged
into new discovery, if the *Russell's* group had been permitted to
realize its potentiality.

The necessary ingredients were there, I think. We can see them
at work in Timrod's vigorous reply to the publication in *Russell's
Magazine* of William John Grayson's essay attacking the poetry of
nineteenth-century Romanticism. The appearance of Grayson's

16. Herman Melville, *Moby-Dick, or The White Whale* (New York and Toronto:
New American Library, 1961), 167.

piece touched off in Timrod a response in which he worked out a theory of poetry far in advance of the critical assumptions of his contemporaries. In his essay on "Literature in the South" he challenged shallow sectionalism in literature, at a time when anything even hinting of implied criticism of the Southern community was in danger of being proclaimed treasonous.

Timrod's move to identify himself with secession and the new Southern nation, once it came into being, is revealing in this respect. For as we have seen, his abrupt transformation into a public poet resulted, in the two secession odes, in a poetry laced with the imagery and even the outright thematic assertion of materialistic achievement. It is as if, in accepting the ideology of secession that had come to dominate the politics of the community, Timrod envisioned himself as embracing an explicitly materialistic and commercial set of values. The task of the author of "Ethnogenesis" was to justify those values by pointing out the moral and social benefits they would thereby confer upon others:

> the distant peoples we shall bless,
> And the hushed murmurs of a world's distress:
>   For, to give labor to the poor,
>   The whole sad planet o'er,
>   And save from want and crime the humblest door,
>   Is one among the many ends for which
>   God makes us great and rich!

The only conclusion to be drawn from such a passage, in such a poem, is that the poet must have been convinced that whatever else might lie behind the rationale for secession and the defense of slavery, the desire for power and wealth was not least among the objectives. One assumes that privately Timrod must have been of two minds about the whole business.

That in neither his wartime verse nor his earlier work did he venture the slightest criticism of the values and institutions of his community is scarcely surprising. Yet what, after all, was the implicit meaning of the poem entitled "Why Silent," written just prior to his conversion to secession? The world, he declares, "in its worldliness, does not miss / What a poet sings." The South, the nation, and the world were too busy getting and spending to worry about the kind of truth that poets were concerned with (and

Timrod, in his essay on "What Is Poetry?," explicitly cited his conviction that, Edgar Poe to the contrary, truth and not beauty was the poet's concern). But with the advent of secession and the formation of the Confederacy, the prospect of separate nationhood would seem to have overcome, for the time being, the poet's objections to the community's materialistic ethos. Just as his much-admired Wordsworth might complain that the world was too much with him and his fellow Britons, or call upon the memory of the poet Milton to redeem the "stagnant fen" of present-day indolence and materialism, yet when his country was threatened by Napoleonic invasion write poems extolling English nationality, so for Timrod nationhood and war spoke more strongly to his emotions than did the need to rebuke materialism.

The alacrity with which Timrod became the Poet Laureate of the Confederacy seems to me to indicate not only his patriotic fervor but also his eagerness to *be a public poet*. It is as if he had finally discovered a mode whereby he might deal, in his poetry, with some of the foremost concerns and issues of his community. Until South Carolina seceded and the Confederacy was formed, such a role was denied him, for to attempt it would have been to criticize the values and institutions of the community. Not only would that have been taboo in the political climate of the day, but as a member of the Southern community he had no desire whatever to censure that community at a time when it was under political, economic, and moral attack.

What I do suspect, however, is that *if* the *Russell's* group had been able to continue to exist and to flourish, the conditions whereby that kind of censure might be delivered were becoming implicit in the dynamics of the group. *If* the obsessive preoccupation with politics and the defense of slavery had not made it impossible for the association of professional men of letters to gain a foothold, then what Lewis Simpson has described as the "third realm," a "clerisy" whose traditional role in Western society was the defense of humane letters against materialistic forces, might well have emerged. The vigor and boldness of Timrod's war poems, written as they were when at last it *had* become possible to write a public poetry, constitute strong evidence that the impulse was there.

To say that, however, is to talk about a South, and a Southern literary situation, that never was —or, rather, that would not come into being for another seventy-five years. War, defeat, and subjugation welded the Southern community into a cohesive unit that for generations would constitute a force impervious to any kind of genuine critical dialectic. Not until well into the twentieth century would the political, economic, and social condition of the Southern community be such that a barrier would no longer exist to exploration of the social and moral underpinnings of the society. Henry Timrod's war poetry remains an illustration of what was possible when, because of the fierce passions, loyalties, and perils of war, a Southern poet did manage to assert a public identification in his verse without having to suppress or importantly restrict the assertion of his private identity as well. What finally mattered to him, as poet and as citizen, was *survival*. And that is what his best poems are about.

7.

On June 18, 1866, the Charleston *News and Courier* published the text of a new poem by Henry Timrod, written to be sung on the occasion of decorating the graves of the Confederate dead at Magnolia Cemetery. Charleston, as we have seen, was in shambles. Although General Sherman had for military reasons abandoned his plan of sowing salt in the streets of the city that had been the hotbed of rebellion and treason, as he viewed it, there was devastation everywhere. Trade was at a standstill. Men, women, and children went hungry. Not only was most of the material wealth of the citizenry gone, but the community's very lifeblood had been drained; one in every ten of the city's adult white males had perished in the war, and as many again bore crippling wounds. The high hopes and ambitions of only five years earlier were utterly depleted. Where there had been eagerness, defiance, arrogance, now there was only exhaustion. Federal troops garrisoned the city. Even by so much as venturing to hold a public ceremony to place flowers upon the graves of the Confederate dead, the citizenry were making a gesture that was certain to be viewed with suspicion by their conquerors.

The poem that Timrod composed for the occasion contained nothing of defiance. There was no note of rancor in the words that were sung at the cemetery. As published in the *News and Courier* as first written, and again in revised form on July 23 of that year, it offered no topical allusions whatever, no specific references even that might identify it with the time and place. Only the subtitle, "Sung on the occasion of decorating the graves of the Confederate dead, at Magnolia Cemetery, Charleston, S. C., 1866," linked the poem to the recently concluded war. Otherwise, it could as appropriately have been sung by English voices at the battlefield of Saratoga, or by French voices at Borodino, or Scots at Culloden—anywhere that the dead soldiers of a lost war were interred.

In his verses the poet aimed at the utmost simplicity of utterance. Only 3 of the poem's 119 words contain as many as three syllables. In the bare statement of defeat and loss, the anguish, frustration, and humiliation of the South's thwarted will are put aside, and grief and pride alone find expression. There was no need for the poem to claim a significance for the specific occasion, to assert its lasting importance with patriotic rhetoric, or to argue that the cause the soldiers died for, though lost for now, might ultimately live. Nor is there any consolatory motif of *dulce et decorum*. The poem did not have to claim these things because they were assumed, held in common by poet and audience.

The Magnolia Cemetery ode, then, is a flawless example of a ceremonial public poem, in which the speaker and those addressed share so thoroughly the same emotions, assumptions, and loyalties that no rhetorical persuasion is in order. The role of the poet, rather, is to express, in language, what the occasion itself signifies. His individual personality requires no separate assertion, either; it can locate itself totally within the public emotion. If ever a work of literature was thoroughly and profoundly grounded in the social and moral experience of a community, this one was. All the complex elements that had served to prevent the Southern author's art from expressing the fundamental concerns of the community were inoperative. Loss and mourning require no explanation, no subtle balancing of political, moral, and ethical considerations, no evasion. The poem is as complete a union of individual and community as could occur. Timrod, who had opposed secession, and Gilmore Simms, who had favored it, might with equal assent recite or sing it. Were they still alive, so might James Henry Hammond, who had sought so passionately to bring on the war, and James Louis Petigru, who had refused to have anything whatever to do with disunion. Only the shared grief and pride mattered now.

So Henry Timrod's ode is an appropriate conclusion to what was best and worth commemorating about an era, a community, and a body of writings in which there was much to deplore, much to excuse, much to pardon, in which good people and bad sought out or were caught up in circumstances that proved to be beyond rational solution, and that exacted, from all who were involved, a high price for being human:

ODE

SUNG ON THE OCCASION OF DECORATING THE GRAVES OF
THE CONFEDERATE DEAD, AT MAGNOLIA CEMETERY,
CHARLESTON, S. C., 1866

> Sleep sweetly in your humble graves,
>   Sleep, martyrs of a fallen cause!
> Though yet no marble column craves
>   The pilgrim here to pause.
>
> In seeds of laurels in the earth,
>   The garlands of your fame are sown;
> And, somewhere, waiting for its birth,
>   The shaft is in the stone.
>
> Meanwhile, your sisters for the years
>   Which hold in trust your storied tombs,
> Bring all they now can give you—tears,
>   And these memorial blooms.
>
> Small tributes, but your shades will smile
>   As proudly on these wreaths today,
> As when some cannon-moulded pile
>   Shall overlook this bay.
>
> Stoop, angels, hither from the skies!
>   There is no holier spot of ground,
> Than where defeated valor lies
>   By mourning beauty crowned.[17]

17. Timrod, "Ode," *Collected Poems*, 129–30.

INDEX

Numbers in boldface refer to primary discussions of Cooper, Poe, Simms, and Timrod